"John Peckham provides a deeply moving and profoundly theological case for prayer to a consistently good and trustworthy God. He makes sense of the conundrum of unanswered prayer, describing the parameters that impact the hearing and answering of our prayers. Peckham's clear case for a God who is not distant or immovable but affected by our words and actions demonstrates that humans are genuine partners with God in accomplishing his will. Every Christian, indeed everyone contemplating a conversation with God, will be enlightened by this important work."

—**Ingrid Faro**, Northern Seminary

"In this outstanding discussion of petitionary prayer, Peckham reassures us that prayer really does make a difference. Peckham shows how cosmic conflict is central to a biblical theology of prayer. God has created a world in which we are invited to strive, with him, against the powers of darkness. Tough questions about unanswered prayer are not ignored, even as the overall picture of God that emerges is reassuring. Readers will learn much from Peckham's rich theological treatment of prayer. And more than that, they will be inspired to pray!"

—**Kevin Kinghorn**, Asbury Theological Seminary

"The disciples asked Jesus to teach them how to pray, and he did. Even more now than then, the world needs prayer, and Peckham has not only cogently offered us the biblical antecedents and exemplars for this primal human speech but also thoughtfully argued the theological and philosophical bases for prayer. From discussing simple prayers on our own behalf to prayers for catastrophic events to what might be termed 'warfare prayer' on a cosmic spiritual level, Peckham runs the gamut of possible philosophical arguments for and against the necessity of prayer—especially why a good, omniscient, and all-powerful God needs our prayers to act in any dimension at all."

—**Esther E. Acolatse**, Garrett-Evangelical Theological Seminary

"Lucidly written and normed by Scripture, this book explains why we pray if God is all-powerful, all-knowing, and all-loving. *Why We Pray* addresses Western concerns about how prayer can influence such a God as well as what to do with unanswered prayers and the problem of divine hiddenness. I found myself both challenged and encouraged by this stimulating engagement with prayer. Most of all, I found myself wanting to pray more, which is a testament to the theological task and to this work specifically."

—**Christa L. McKirland**, Carey Baptist College; executive director, Logia International

T0311012

"It is not every book of serious theology that leaves one eager to pray, but this one does—not by admonition but by fundamentally shifting our view of God and how he works in the world. It eases long-lasting puzzles (and the perplexity they cause) by putting more pieces of the providential jigsaw on the table. It even defuses the disturbing implications of the doctrine of predestination along the way. The only disappointment of this book is that it doesn't come with a free pair of kneepads!"

—**Michael Lloyd**, Wycliffe Hall Oxford

"In *Why We Pray* Peckham tackles a series of fundamental questions that I and many others have about the nature of prayer and our disappointments with it. He approaches these puzzles with a pastoral sensitivity that is both theologically astute and scripturally infused. In this book you will not find easy answers, trite sayings, or pointless advice. Instead, expect a thoughtful, mature Christian wrestling with profound mysteries and discovering more and more reasons to pray."

—**David B. Capes**, director, Lanier Theological Library

Why We Pray

Why We Pray

Understanding Prayer
in the Context of Cosmic Conflict

JOHN C. PECKHAM

Ɓ
Baker Academic
a division of Baker Publishing Group
Grand Rapids, Michigan

Published by Baker Academic
a division of Baker Publishing Group
Grand Rapids, Michigan
BakerAcademic.com

Printed in the United States of America

Library of Congress Cataloging-in-Publication Data
Names: Peckham, John C., 1981– author.
Title: Why we pray : understanding prayer in the context of cosmic conflict / John C. Peckham.
Description: Grand Rapids, Michigan : Baker Academic, a division of Baker Publishing Group,
    [2024] | Includes bibliographical references and index.
Identifiers: LCCN 2023046613 | ISBN 9781540966285 (paperback) | ISBN 9781540967817 | ISBN
    9781493446230 (ebook) | ISBN 9781493446247 (pdf)
Subjects: LCSH: Prayer—Christianity. | Good and evil—Religious aspects—Christianity.
Classification: LCC BV210.3 .P43 2024 | DDC 248.3/2—dc23/eng/20231128
LC record available at https://lccn.loc.gov/2023046613

Baker Publishing Group publications use paper produced from sustainable forestry practices and postconsumer waste whenever possible.

24   25   26   27   28   29   30   7   6   5   4   3

To my parents,
Ernest and Karen,
with profound gratitude
for their many prayers

Contents

Acknowledgments

I am grateful to many people for their invaluable help and support relative to this book. First, I would like to extend my deepest gratitude to Jim Kinney at Baker Academic for his great support and guidance of this project. Melisa Blok also deserves special thanks for her excellent work shepherding this book through the editing process. I am also indebted to the entire Baker Academic team, with whom it is always a joy and a privilege to work.

I would like to also express my profound gratitude to my colleagues in the Theology and Christian Philosophy department of the seminary at Andrews University. It has been a great honor to work with such wonderful colleagues and friends. Thanks are also due to those who took the time to read parts or the entirety of this work, providing helpful feedback and encouragement. To these and all others who have contributed to this project, I extend my heartfelt appreciation.

I am most grateful to my family. My parents, Ernest and Karen, deserve immeasurable thanks for their tireless and unwavering support. To my son, Joel, I continue to be profoundly grateful for you and the immense joy you bring to my life. I am incredibly blessed to have you as my son. Finally, no words can adequately convey the love, gratitude, and admiration I have for my amazing wife, Brenda—my best friend and the most wonderful wife and mother. I am forever grateful for you and to you.

1

Does Petitionary Prayer Make a Difference?

Two Problems of Petitionary Prayer

The fierce storm raged. Waves crashed over the boat, threatening to sink it. Everyone in the boat was terrified—except Jesus. While his disciples feared for their lives, he slept peacefully. The disciples woke him, saying, "Teacher, do you not care that we are perishing?" (Mark 4:38). Then Jesus "rebuked the wind and said to the sea, 'Be silent! Be still!'"[1] Immediately, "the wind ceased, and there was a dead calm" (4:39). Like the flip of a switch, terror and chaos turned to calm and peace. Amazing.

We often encounter storms in our lives, some more massive than others. Sometimes, all we can bring ourselves to do is moan in tears. In such circumstances, Christians typically cry out to God, praying that God will bring deliverance.[2] Such prayers that plead with God for deliverance or some other

---

1. Unless otherwise noted, all biblical quotations are from the NRSVue.

2. Prayer might be minimally defined as communication with God, which Scripture often speaks of as calling on the name of the Lord. J. Gary Millar explains, "The idea of calling on the name of Yahweh is intrinsically related to God's commitment to rescue his people and deliver on his promises" (Millar, *Calling on the Name of the Lord*, 25). See also P. Miller, *They Cried to the Lord*, 32–48; Seitz, "Prayer in the Old Testament," 6.

kind of divine action (for oneself or for others) are *petitionary* prayers—prayers that request or "petition" that God do something.[3]

Perhaps you have wondered, Where is God in the storm? Does God care about our problems? If so, why does God sometimes seem to be hidden or silent in the midst of storms in our lives? Where is God when it seems our prayers are unanswered? And, if God loves us and desires only our good, why would we need to ask him to bring deliverance (or otherwise act) in the first place? This book focuses on these and related questions about petitionary prayer in the context of Christian faith.[4]

When he calmed the storm, Jesus quickly responded to his disciples' questioning pleas. In many other cases, however, God's response to prayer seems to be delayed or entirely absent. Questions regarding God's apparent silence in response to pleas and petitions frequently appear in Scripture. For instance, in the midst of distress, God's people cry out,

> Where is the one who brought [us] up out of the sea
>   with the shepherds of his flock? . . .
> Where are your zeal and your might?
>   Your great pity and your compassion are withheld from me.
>   (Isa. 63:11, 15)

Likewise, in Malachi, the people "cover the LORD's altar with tears, with weeping and groaning because he no longer regards the offering or accepts it with favor," and they ask, "How have we wearied him?" and "Where is the God of justice?" (Mal. 2:13, 17).[5] Elsewhere, people ask God,

> Why, O LORD, do you stand far off?
> Why do you hide yourself in times of trouble? (Ps. 10:1; cf. 30:7)

> How long, LORD, have I called for help,
> And You do not hear? . . .
> Why are You silent when the wicked swallow up
> Those more righteous than they? (Hab. 1:2, 13 NASB)

3. "Petition means that we ask God for something that we desire to happen" (Fisher, *Prayer in the New Testament*, 71). Millar adds, "It is no accident that all the words in the Bible for 'prayer' mean the same thing—they mean to ask." Millar, *Calling on the Name of the Lord*, 238.

4. This focus on petitionary prayer should not be taken to imply that petitionary prayer is more important than other aspects of prayer, such as confession/repentance, thanksgiving, and lament. Yet, as Bloesch points out, "there is present in all these the element of petitionary prayer . . . because all these forms of prayer spring from human need and seek an answer to human need." Bloesch, *Struggle of Prayer*, 69.

5. In this case, they have been "faithless" (Mal. 2:14–16).

In the midst of profound agony, Job wrestles with this problem of seemingly unanswered prayer, saying to God, "I cry to you, and you do not answer me; I stand, and you merely look at me. You have turned cruel to me" (Job 30:20–21). Likewise, much later, the apostle Paul prays to God to relieve some malady he calls a "thorn . . . in the flesh, a messenger of Satan to torment me. . . . Three times I appealed to the Lord about this, that it would leave me, but he said to me, 'My grace is sufficient for you, for power is made perfect in weakness'" (2 Cor. 12:7–9).

And, shortly before the crucifixion, Jesus himself "fell on His face and prayed, saying, 'My Father, if it is possible, let this cup pass from Me; yet not as I will, but as You will'" (Matt. 26:39 NASB; cf. 26:42). Yet, despite Christ's prayer, the cup of suffering and dying *did not pass*. Christ suffered immensely and finally died on the cross after crying out, "My God, my God, why have you forsaken me?" (27:46).

Why do prayers sometimes seem to go unanswered, as if God is hidden? If God hears our prayers, why does it sometimes seem as if prayers make no difference? And, if God loves us, why would prayer make any difference in the first place?

These questions sum up two closely related problems regarding petitionary prayer: (1) the problem of *seemingly* unanswered prayer and (2) the classical problem of petitionary prayer, which asks, If God is entirely good, all-knowing, and all-powerful, how could offering petitionary prayers make any difference?[6] Would not God act in the most preferable way, regardless of whether anyone asks him to do so?[7]

This book focuses on these two problems of petitionary prayer, exploring how a cosmic conflict understanding might help address these questions. It outlines a fresh way of thinking about and approaching petitionary prayer by way of careful theological reflection on selected passages of Scripture, with practical implications for how we might pray and live in ways that advance God's kingdom of unselfish love.

Prayer is integral to Christian faith and practice, and the way we pray reflects our deeply held theological beliefs and values and has massive implications for how we live our faith. This is conveyed in the traditional Christian phrase "*lex orandi, lex credendi, lex vivendi*," which expresses that the way one prays (*lex orandi*) is integrally connected to one's regulating beliefs (*lex credendi*) and way of life (*lex vivendi*). Our understanding of petitionary prayer, then, is inseparable from our understanding of the God to whom

6. See, e.g., Origen's discussion in *Prayer*, 6–7 (pp. 30–36).
7. See Eleonore Stump's seminal article, "Petitionary Prayer."

we pray. Accordingly, this book will also shed significant light on the nature and character of the God to whom Christians pray and the often mysterious workings of divine providence and suggest practical implications for prayerful living.

In what follows, I make no attempt to answer every question but instead seek to outline an approach that might make sense of some of the most troubling questions about petitionary prayer, focusing on how petitionary prayer could make any difference in the first place and how we might understand the fact that many prayers are seemingly unanswered.

The Persistent Widow and the Problem of Petitionary Prayer

Jesus once told a parable about a persistent widow and an unjust judge—"a parable about their need to pray always and not to lose heart" (Luke 18:1). Although the judge "neither feared God nor had respect for people," the widow "kept coming to him" and requesting "justice" (18:2–3). The judge refused for a while but eventually thought, "Though I have no fear of God and no respect for anyone, yet because this widow keeps bothering me, I will grant her justice, so that she may not wear me out by continually coming" (18:4–5). Regarding this, Jesus asked, "Will not God grant justice to his chosen ones who cry to him day and night? Will he delay long in helping them? I tell you, he will quickly grant justice to them. And yet, when the Son of Man comes, will he find faith on earth?" (18:7–8).

At first, one might assume that the judge represents God and wonder why the widow would need to *persistently* petition the judge to bring justice. If God is perfectly good and just, God would already prefer to bring about justice (in the right way, at the right time, and for the right reasons), whether or not he is petitioned. Further, if God is all-knowing and all-powerful, no request could either provide information to God about injustices that need to be righted or grant God additional power to bring justice. That is, an all-knowing (omniscient), perfectly good (omnibenevolent), and all-powerful (omnipotent) God would know all *preferable* goods that he could bring about, prefer to bring about such goods, and be capable of doing so.[8] How, then, could petitionary prayers impact whether God brings about justice or any other good thing? This is one form of the classical problem of petitionary prayer, the problem of how petitionary prayer is consistent with

---

8. I deliberately refer to what is "preferable" (in light of all other factors) rather than what is the "best possible good" because there may not be a "best possible" course. See Adams, "Must God Create the Best?"; cf. Reibsamen, "Divine Goodness," 136–37.

God's omniscience, omnibenevolence, and omnipotence. Closely related to this is the problem of seemingly unanswered prayer—the problem of why some prayers for good things seem to go unanswered, especially when it comes to matters of life and death. To both of these problems we will return shortly.

First, however, let us revisit the assumption that this judge represents God. Jesus himself calls him "the *unjust* judge" (Luke 18:6). Yet Scripture consistently teaches that God is perfectly good and just. Indeed, God's "work is perfect, and all his ways are just. A faithful God, without deceit, just and upright is he" (Deut. 32:4; cf. Rev. 15:3; 19:1–2). God "is righteous; he does no wrong" (Zeph. 3:5; cf. Dan. 9:14). Further, "righteousness and justice are the foundation of [God's] throne," and "steadfast love and faithfulness go before [him]" (Ps. 89:14; cf. 85:10). He "is just in all his ways and kind in all his doings" (145:17), for he "is upright" and "there is no unrighteousness in him" (92:15). Accordingly, "God cannot be tempted by evil" (James 1:13; cf. Hab. 1:13), for "God is light and in him there is no darkness at all" (1 John 1:5).

According to these (and many other) biblical passages, God is perfectly good and just. If so, then the unjust judge cannot represent God. The unjust judge eventually responds to the widow's persistent requests for justice only "so that she may not wear me out by continually coming" (Luke 18:5). Conversely, the God of Scripture is compassionate and always already active for the good of all concerned, motivated by his infinite, unselfish love. The unjust judge does not represent God, then, but is contrasted to God—if even an unjust judge will respond to such persistence, how much more will the good and loving God respond to his children's requests (cf. Matt. 7:7–11)?[9]

Yet the questions remain: Why would it matter whether we bring our requests to God in the first place? Why would humans "need to pray always and not to lose heart" (Luke 18:1)? Given God's perfect goodness, knowledge, and power, how could fervent, persistent prayer make any difference?

Two Problems of Petitionary Prayer: Seemingly Unanswered Prayer and the Influence Aim

Many have given up on God because their prayer for a loved one to be healed or for some terrible evil to be stopped was seemingly unanswered. Their prayers seemed to fall on deaf ears. I recall being puzzled as a young child when I heard people pleading with God to heal a loved one from a terminal

9. See, further, chap. 5.

illness, praying, "Lord, if it is your will, please heal my loved one." I distinctly remember thinking, "*If* it is your will? Why would it not be God's will to heal a loved one? Doesn't God want only what is good for us? Why would God not will to heal someone from a horrible illness? Why would we even need to ask God to do something so obviously good?" I did not have labels for these questions then, but I was wrestling with the classical problem of petitionary prayer.

Does Petitionary Prayer Influence Divine Action?

Some resolve this problem by denying that prayers influence God's action, while maintaining that prayer nevertheless accomplishes some good outcomes by impacting those praying. In Søren Kierkegaard's words, "Prayer does not change God, but it changes the one who offers it."[10] Petitionary prayer, in this view, should be aimed not at influencing what God brings about but at affecting those praying (e.g., bringing human desires more in line with God's will).[11]

Such a view rightly emphasizes that prayer often brings about positive effects by affecting those praying. Prayer is often deeply therapeutic: "Offering petitionary prayers might lead to peace of mind, or gratitude, or a welcome sense of dependence upon God."[12] As Paul teaches, "Let your requests be made known to God. And the peace of God, which surpasses all understanding, will guard your hearts and your minds in Christ Jesus" (Phil. 4:6–7; cf. 1 Pet. 5:7). Further, petitionary prayer might motivate those praying to act to bring about the goods for which they pray. In short, Scott A. Davison explains, petitionary prayer often "changes the person who prays, unites people in a common cause, and communicates important values to others, to name just a few examples."[13]

---

10. Kierkegaard, *Purity of Heart*, 51; cf. Calvin, *Institutes*, III.20.3; Luther, *Large Catechism*, part 3, on the Lord's Prayer. Thomas Aquinas, conversely, argues, "We pray not that we may change the Divine disposition, but that we may impetrate that which God has disposed to be fulfilled by our prayers" (*Summa Theologiae* 2a.2ae.83.2). Here, prayer is more than merely therapeutic—prayer functions as a secondary cause relative to what God brings about, but it doesn't influence God's action in a way that might change whether God brings about some outcome. See, further, Woznicki, "Is Prayer Redundant?"; Woznicki, "What Are We Doing When We Pray?"

11. I use the term "influence" in the sense of (counterfactually) affecting what God brings about, which does not entail influence on what God ideally desires.

12. Davison, *God and Prayer*, 3. Augustine writes, "The Lord our God requires us to ask not that thereby our wish may be intimated to Him, for to Him it cannot be unknown, but in order that by prayer there may be exercised in us by supplications that desire by which we may receive what He prepares to bestow." Augustine, *Confessions and Letters* 130.8.17 (p. 464).

13. Davison, *Petitionary Prayer*, 7.

This is undoubtedly true. Prayer might focus one's attention on God and bring those praying into greater alignment with God's will and otherwise into closer relationship with God (a great good) and might bring numerous other therapeutic benefits (cf. Phil. 4:6–7). However, the additional claim that prayer does *not* influence God's action stands in stark contrast to the way Christians typically pray—today and throughout Christian tradition—and seems to be out of step with many biblical passages that instruct believers to offer petitionary prayers and indicate that (at least in some cases) such petitionary prayer actually makes a difference relative to God's action.[14]

As Karl Barth puts it, many Christians believe that "God answers. God is not deaf, but listens; more than that, he acts. God does not act in the same way whether we pray or not. Prayer exerts an influence upon God's action."[15] Likewise, Davison writes, "One of the primary purposes of petitionary prayer, according to those who practice it, is to influence God's action in the world."[16]

Further, Scripture repeatedly teaches that God is "moved by prayer" (e.g., 2 Sam. 24:25 NASB95; cf. 21:14) and "relents" in response to human repentance and entreaty (e.g., Exod. 32:14; Joel 2:13–14; Jon. 3:9–10). In one striking example, Elijah prays for a child to come back to life, crying out, "O LORD my God, let this child's life come into him again." And "the LORD listened to the voice of Elijah; the life of the child came into him again, and he revived" (1 Kings 17:21–22).

Throughout Scripture, God frequently invites humans to offer petitionary prayers and indicates that such prayers make a difference with respect to divine action. For instance, when Solomon's temple is dedicated, God declares, "If my people who are called by my name humble themselves, pray, seek my face, and turn from their wicked ways, then I will hear from heaven and will forgive their sin and heal their land" (2 Chron. 7:14). Elsewhere, God promises his covenant people, "When you call upon me and come and pray to me, I will hear you" (Jer. 29:12; cf. 33:3).

Psalm 34:17 adds, "When the righteous cry for help, the LORD hears and rescues them from all their troubles" (cf. Ps. 145:18). Again, "Truly God has listened; he has heard the words of my prayer" (66:19). From bondage, the Israelites "cried out" to God, who "heard their groaning" and delivered them (Exod. 2:23–24). Later, Hannah fervently "prayed to the LORD and wept

---

14. Regarding theories that deny the view that petitionary prayer might influence divine action, David Crump asks "whether such theories can cohere with the exegetical evidence" and concludes that the answer is no and that such "appears to be a classical example of eisegesis." Crump, *Knocking on Heaven's Door*, 219–20.

15. Barth, *Prayer*, 13.

16. Davison, *Petitionary Prayer*, 7.

bitterly" for a son, and God "granted" her "petition" (1 Sam. 1:10, 27). Still later, Hezekiah prayed for healing, and God replied, "I have heard your prayer, I have seen your tears; indeed, I will heal you. . . . I will add fifteen years to your life. I will deliver you and this city" (2 Kings 20:5–6; cf. Josh. 10:12–14; 2 Chron. 30:27; Amos 7:2–9). Even later, Daniel prayed for his people in exile (Dan. 9), and God heard and responded.

Like Samuel long before, John the Baptist was an answer to prayer. "Elizabeth was barren" and "getting on in years" (Luke 1:7). But, one day, an angel appeared to her husband, Zechariah, saying, "Do not be afraid, Zechariah, for your prayer has been heard. Your wife Elizabeth will bear you a son, and you will name him John" (1:13).

Jesus himself frequently instructs his followers to offer petitionary prayer. The Lord's Prayer itself consists of a series of petitions (Matt. 6:9–13; see chap. 3), and Jesus teaches that prayer influences God's action: "Ask, and it will be given to you; search, and you will find; knock, and the door will be opened for you. For everyone who asks receives, and everyone who searches finds, and for everyone who knocks, the door will be opened." He continues, saying, "Your Father in heaven" will "give good things to those who ask him!" (7:7–8, 11; cf. Luke 11:1–13). Regarding this passage, Daniel Simundson concludes, "Our prayers can influence God" and "make a difference. God hears and responds."[17]

Jesus not only instructs others to offer petitionary prayers but himself offers up "prayers and supplications, with loud cries and tears" and is heard "because of his reverent submission" (Heb. 5:7). He frequently prays for others during his earthly ministry (e.g., Luke 22:32) and in his heavenly ministry, for "those who approach God through him, . . . he always lives to make intercession for them" (Heb. 7:25).

The rest of the New Testament also repeatedly instructs Christians to offer petitionary prayer and indicates that such prayer influences God's action (at least sometimes). For instance, Paul urges "that supplications, prayers, intercessions, and thanksgivings be made for everyone" (1 Tim. 2:1; cf. Phil. 4:6; Heb. 13:18–19). Elsewhere, Paul exhorts Christians to "persevere in prayer" (Rom. 12:12), to "pray without ceasing" (1 Thess. 5:17; cf. Col. 4:2), and to be ready to "stand against the wiles of the devil" in "our struggle . . . against the cosmic powers of this present darkness" and "the spiritual forces of evil in the heavenly places" (Eph. 6:11–12). Paul teaches, further, "Pray in the Spirit at all times in every prayer and supplication," and "always persevere in supplication for all the saints. Pray also for me" (6:18–19). Elsewhere, John

17. Simundson, *Where Is God?*, 60.

teaches that "if we ask anything according to his will, he hears us. And if we know that he hears us in whatever we ask, we know that we have obtained the requests made of him" (1 John 5:14–15).

Numerous other instances link divine deliverance to "belief" and "prayer." For example, in response to a man's plea to cast out a demon from his son (which Jesus's disciples fail to do), Jesus replies, "All things are possible for the one who believes" (Mark 9:23 NASB; cf. Matt. 17:20). The man replies, "I believe; help my unbelief," and Jesus casts the demon out (Mark 9:24). Afterward, the disciples wonder why they could not cast the demon out. Jesus answers, "This kind can come out only through prayer" (9:29). These factors of "faith" and "prayer" likewise appear in James: "If any of you is lacking in wisdom, ask God, who gives to all generously and ungrudgingly, and it will be given you. But ask in faith, never doubting. . . . For the doubter . . . must not expect to receive anything from the Lord" (James 1:5–7; see also Matt. 11:22–25).

Later, James teaches further, "You do not have because you do not ask. You ask and do not receive because you ask wrongly, in order to spend what you get on your pleasures" (James 4:2–3). Still later, James adds, "The prayer of faith will save the sick, and the Lord will raise them up, and anyone who has committed sins will be forgiven. Therefore confess your sins to one another and pray for one another, so that you may be healed. The prayer of the righteous is powerful and effective" (5:15–16; cf. Prov. 15:8, 29).

These and many other examples seem to indicate that petitionary prayer can influence God's action and that such influence is (partially) linked to factors including (but not limited to) faith, alignment with God's will, motives, humility and repentance, right relationship with God, and perseverance. We will revisit the striking implications of these passages (and many others) throughout this book. For now, suffice it to say that Scripture is filled with instructions and exhortations to offer petitionary prayers to God, and many seem to indicate that petitionary prayers can influence divine action. As Katherine Sonderegger puts it, "We cannot evade the impression that the Bible is a book of petition, a covenant history of prayer for earthly gifts of healing, of deliverance, of child-birth, of blessing."[18] Likewise, Esther Acolatse highlights "the deliverance from sin and temptation that occurs by prayer and the intervention of the divine, which is so basic to Scripture."[19]

In this regard, after extensive analysis of New Testament teachings on petitionary prayer, David Crump concludes that Scripture teaches that "prayer can

---

18. Sonderegger, "Act of Prayer," 151.
19. Acolatse, *Powers, Principalities, and the Spirit*, 60.

and does move God; it makes a difference. Some things in life occur, at least in part, because God's people asked him to act accordingly (2 Cor. 1:11; Phil. 1:19; Philem. 22)."[20] Later, he adds that Scripture teaches that "the sovereign Lord does some things precisely because we pray for them" and that "had we not prayed as we did, God would not have acted as he did."[21] I agree. For my part, I am convinced that many passages of Scripture indicate that (in at least some cases) human prayers influence divine action, and the remainder of this book will operate on this premise.

The Influence Aim Problem and the Problem of Seemingly Unanswered Prayer

Suppose these and other instances of Scripture do teach that (at least sometimes) petitionary prayer influences God to act in ways he otherwise would not have.[22] If so, a significant problem presents itself, which I call the "influence aim problem"—the problem of how to consistently affirm that (1) God is omniscient, (2) God is omnibenevolent, (3) God is omnipotent, and (4) petitionary prayer might *influence* God to bring about some good he otherwise would not have.[23]

Initially, it might seem that affirming that prayer might influence divine action entails that God is somehow informed by the prayer (contrary to omniscience), influenced to prefer some good he otherwise would not (contrary to omnibenevolence), or increased in power (contrary to omnipotence). Yet if God is omniscient, omnibenevolent, and omnipotent, then God would know all preferable goods he could bring about, prefer to bring about such goods, and possess the sheer power to do so. How, then, could it make sense to believe petitionary prayer might influence whether God brings about some

---

20. Crump, *Knocking on Heaven's Door*, 228. Fisher adds, "God uses intercessory prayer to accomplish results . . . he could not otherwise accomplish." Fisher, *Prayer in the New Testament*, 82.

21. Crump, *Knocking on Heaven's Door*, 290. Likewise, see Bloesch, *Struggle of Prayer*, 73; Brümmer, *What Are We Doing When We Pray?*, 33.

22. This and following sections draw from my article "Influence Aim Problem."

23. Many approaches assume that petitionary prayer is effective only if it influences God to bring about something he otherwise would not have (counterfactual dependence accounts). Some, however, have persuasively argued that petitionary prayer might be effective even if God would have actualized the prayed-for outcome apart from petitionary prayer, as long as "God brings about the thing in question at least in part because the person prays for it" (Davison, "Petitionary Prayer," 288; cf. Cohoe, "God, Causality, and Petitionary Prayer," 37–39; Davison, *Petitionary Prayer*, 26–42). Yet, as Cohoe notes, "many important cases of petitionary prayer do involve counterfactual dependence" (Cohoe, "God, Causality, and Petitionary Prayer," 38). This book focuses on a model for approaching cases that *do* involve counterfactual dependence.

good he otherwise would not bring about? Mark Gregory Karris argues that "petitionary prayers for others" aimed at influencing divine action might "unknowingly suggest a diminished view of God's loving nature," implying an "ignorant, ill-willed and manipulative God."[24]

This problem is even more troubling relative to prayers for basic needs or goods. David Basinger contends that "with respect to our basic needs [such as food, health, and shelter] it is never justifiable for God to withhold that which he can and would like to give us until petitioned."[25] If Basinger is right, then petitionary prayer aimed at influencing God to bring about a basic need he otherwise would not have brought about would be inconsistent with affirming God's perfect goodness (omnibenevolence).[26]

This would rule out, however, many of the petitionary prayers Christians offer and also conflict with any biblical passage that indicates petitionary prayer sometimes influences whether God provides a basic need, raising serious questions about Jesus's own instructions, such as to pray, "Give us today our daily bread" (Matt. 6:11). Might there be a way, then, to consistently affirm that (at least in some cases) petitionary prayer influences the omniscient, omnipotent, and omnibenevolent God to bring about some good he otherwise would not bring about—particularly regarding basic needs or preventing great evils?

Even if one arrives at a coherent understanding of how petitionary prayer aimed at influencing divine action might be consistent with God's perfect knowledge, will, and power, one still faces an equally difficult problem on the other side—the problem of seemingly unanswered prayer. If God does act in response to prayers, why do some prayers for goods (including prayers for basic needs) seem to go unanswered? Why does it sometimes seem that God is silent and hidden, unresponsive to our cries for sustenance, deliverance, and other goods?

In what follows, I seek to articulate an understanding of petitionary prayer that sheds light on both these problems: (1) how the influence aim of petitionary prayer might make sense (in a way consistent with prayers regarding basic needs and great evils) and (2) why God often does not answer our prayers in the ways we think he should.[27]

---

24. Karris, *Divine Echoes*, 53, 52.

25. Basinger, "God Does Not Necessarily Respond," 267; cf. Basinger, "Why Petition?"

26. Further, if God truly desires to save all (e.g., 1 Tim. 2:4–6; cf. 2 Pet. 3:9), would not God do everything he can to save each person regardless of our prayers? On this, see Wessling, "Interceding for the Lost."

27. In addition, some ask whether and how we might know "whether petitionary prayers have definitely been answered" (Davison, *God and Prayer*, 12). Though interesting, this question is not a focus of this brief book.

Some Common Ways of Addressing the Problems of Petitionary Prayer

Before moving to some avenues I find more helpful to address these problems, I will first introduce some avenues that I find unhelpful or less helpful, especially relative to prayer regarding basic needs or evils. Of course, one might sidestep the problem by simply denying the influence aim.[28] However, as seen (in part) earlier, numerous biblical passages appear to support the view that petitionary prayer can influence divine action (e.g., 2 Chron. 7:14; Mark 9:29; Luke 11:1–13). Accordingly, I seek an understanding of petitionary prayer that is consistent with affirming the influence aim, including relative to prayers regarding basic needs or great evils.

Denying Perfect Knowledge, Power, or Goodness

One might resolve the influence aim problem by simply denying that God is all-knowing, all-powerful, or perfectly good. First, one might claim that petitionary prayer informs God of human desires or needs, denying divine omniscience.[29] However, this would contradict many biblical passages—including those that teach God "knows everything" (1 John 3:20; cf. Ps. 147:5), knows what is in everyone's heart (Luke 16:15; cf. Pss. 44:21; 139:1–5; Heb. 4:13), and "knows what you need before you ask him" (Matt. 6:8; cf. 6:32).

Second, one might elude the problem by claiming that petitionary prayer might influence God to desire to bring about some good he otherwise would not have. However, if God is omnibenevolent—"good to all," "just in all his ways and kind in all his doings" (Ps. 145:9, 17; cf. James 1:17)—then God would *always* will what is good for all concerned. If so, it seems that prayer could not influence God to *desire* something good he previously did not desire.[30]

Third, one might escape the problem by claiming that God lacks the power to bring about some goods he wills to bring about but that petitionary prayer somehow increases God's power. As process theist Marjorie Hewitt Suchocki

---

28. For one discussion of Reformed approaches that take this approach, see Woznicki, "What Are We Doing When We Pray?"; see also Crisp, *Retrieving Doctrine*, 133–55.

29. Some argue that if God possesses exhaustive definite foreknowledge (EDF), the (counterfactual) influence aim of petitionary prayer would be pointless. This is a matter of considerable dispute, hinging on whether EDF entails that prayer could not counterfactually influence God's action. I do not believe EDF entails that, but adequate treatment of this issue is beyond this book's scope. For a discussion of the issues, see DiRoberts, *Prayer*; and Flint, *Divine Providence*, 212–28.

30. I understand omnibenevolence to entail that God wills all optimal compossible good(s), or, if there is no optimal set of compossible good(s), God wills a set than which no other set of compossible goods is morally better.

claims, "When God needs resources for any particular situation, God will give an impulse toward prayer to those open to such an impulse so that their praying may make a difference to what God can give in yet another place."[31] This, however, raises puzzling questions about *how* prayer could increase God's power. Further, this view that "God needs resources" or otherwise lacks power conflicts with the teaching that God needs nothing (cf. Acts 17:25) and is omnipotent (at least as traditionally understood), seemingly conflicting with Christ's teaching that "for God all things are possible" (Matt. 19:26) and many other biblical passages (e.g., Rev. 19:6; cf. Jer. 32:17).

Do other avenues fare better? Can one consistently affirm that prayer might influence divine action without entailing that God is ignorant, malevolent, or deficient in power?[32]

Other Prominent Avenues

One might argue there are other factors involved such that one can affirm the influence aim in a way that is consistent with divine omniscience, omnipotence, and omnibenevolence. Perhaps God's providence is ordered such that there are some good outcomes that God perfectly knows about, desires to bring about, and possesses the sheer power to bring about, but for some reasons compatible with God's perfect goodness, God will not bring about such goods without the "influence" of petitionary prayer.[33]

This, however, raises the question: Just what might these good reasons be, particularly concerning petitions that relate to basic needs and horrendous evils?

Skeptical Theism

One might contend that, given our limited perspective and cognitive capacity, we should not expect to be in a position to know *precisely* what God's reasons might be. Even if one "can't see what God's reason might be," it "doesn't follow that probably God doesn't have a reason."[34]

31. Suchocki, *In God's Presence*, 49. See also Griffin, *God, Power, and Evil*; Hartshorne, *Omnipotence*; Oord, *Uncontrolling Love*.

32. There are more nuanced proposals than can be adequately introduced here. I restrict the discussion to some representative proposals. For more, see Davison, *God and Prayer*; and Davison, *Petitionary Prayer*.

33. This is consistent with numerous understandings of God's providence, including the traditional understanding of primary and secondary causality. See Ashley Cocksworth's treatment of this as a noncompetitive relation between divine and human agency. Cocksworth, *Prayer*, 162–67. See also Crisp, *Retrieving Doctrine*, 150–55; and Woznicki, "Is Prayer Redundant?," 346.

34. Plantinga, *Warranted Christian Belief*, 497. Plantinga's comment refers to the problem of evil but also may apply to the problem of petitionary prayer. See, further, Dougherty and McBrayer, *Skeptical Theism*.

Imagine you are hiking and suddenly feel an insect bite. You look around but see no insects. Does the fact that you do not see any insects mean there are no insects around? Of course not. Just as tiny flies (no-see-ums) might be present but so small you "no see 'um," one might not be in a position to see or understand God's reasons for acting (or refraining from acting) as he does.[35]

Whatever else we conclude, we should recognize how little we know of God's ways. As Paul writes, "O the depth of the riches and wisdom and knowledge of God! How unsearchable are his judgments and how inscrutable his ways!" (Rom. 11:33; cf. Isa. 55:8–9; Job 38).

Value-Adding Approaches: True Friendship? Partnership with God?

Perhaps we can know some reasons, however. Some suggest that petitionary prayer is an important ingredient to foster true friendship between God and humans. Eleonore Stump posits that if no benefits depended on asking God to *freely* grant them (with no guarantee), either God might "completely dominate" the human in such a relationship or the human may be "spoiled" and relate to God as a "personal power source," either of which would undermine true friendship of the kind God values.[36]

This is one example of numerous approaches that suggest petitionary prayer is necessary to bring about some great value that (purportedly) cannot be achieved without it, such as partnership with God.[37] These value-adding approaches posit "some good which accrues as a result of the petition being made, a good significant enough to be worth forgoing the (lesser) good of the provision being made without the request."[38]

Value-adding approaches, however, face questions about whether petitionary prayer is actually necessary for such values. For instance, some critique approaches that claim petitionary prayer is necessary for the value of sustaining

---

35. Stephen J. Wykstra makes this argument in Wykstra, "Rowe's Noseeum Arguments," 126.

36. Stump, "Petitionary Prayer," 87; cf. Brümmer, *What Are We Doing When We Pray?*; and Reibsamen, "Divine Goodness," 131–44.

37. Interacting with Stump's proposal, Nicholas D. Smith and Andrew C. Yip offer an alternative that focuses on the additional value of "partnership with God," wherein God makes some goods contingent on petitionary prayer when those praying commit themselves to try to bring about the prayed-for outcome. Smith and Yip, "Partnership with God."

38. Murray and Meyers, "Ask and It Will Be Given to You," 313. Davison categorizes some of these as "consequentialist defenses," which he further distinguishes as those that add some value through "increased human responsibility for the nature of the world" (responsibility-based), "things that happen in response to reasons generated by requests," (request-based), "enhanced relationship with God along various dimensions" (relationship-based), and others. He also considers numerous deontological defenses. Davison, *God and Prayer*, 21–22.

right God-human relationships (e.g., Stump's approach) for tending "to over-look the possibility of achieving such relationships in ways other than prayer."[39] Numerous proposals attempt to overcome this kind of objection, with many arguing that God bringing about goods in partnership with creatures is more valuable than God doing so unilaterally.[40]

Even if petitionary prayer in general is somehow necessary relative to friendship or partnership with God, or some other great values (e.g., human responsibility), one might question whether petitionary prayer regarding basic needs or great evils is necessary to achieve such values. And, if so, would the addition of such values be enough to outweigh the detriment of God (some-times) refraining from providing basic needs or preventing horrendous evils in the absence of petitionary prayer?

At this juncture, Stump and many other advocates of value-adding accounts recognize that their approaches leave difficult questions unanswered relative to evils in our world.[41] Such accounts might successfully offer a proposal for how petitionary prayer might be necessary for some distinct and significant

39. Smith and Yip, "Partnership with God," 408; cf. Di Muzio, "Collaborative Model."

40. See, e.g., Howard-Snyder and Howard-Snyder, "Puzzle of Petitionary Prayer"; and Smith and Yip, "Partnership with God." Martin Pickup, however, questions the viability of value-adding accounts of counterfactual dependence, arguing that such proposals suppose that "God will choose to actualise an event if and only if it is overall better that it occurs than not," but this means (he argues) that "on these models petitionary prayer only has a self-fulfilling benefit: prayer is effective [relative to counterfactual dependence] simply because of the benefits that answered prayer has, independent of the outcomes prayed for," which is "unsatisfying" and "wildly at odds with the actual practice of petitionary prayer." Pickup, "Answer to Our Prayers," 93–94.

He further notes that some outcomes may be of incommensurable value from God's per-spective, raising further questions for value-adding accounts. His solution is that, in such cases, "prayer" itself "might give God a reason to choose that the event occur rather than not" (Pickup, "Answer to Our Prayers," 98; cf. Cohoe, "God, Causality, and Petitionary Prayer"; Cohoe, "How Could Prayer Make a Difference?"; Parker and Rettler, "Possible-Worlds Solution"). However, as Pickup himself recognizes, in many cases the value of whether an event occurs or not is not incommensurable (e.g., in *at least* most cases, it would be better if a starving child had food). Pickup's account thus does not provide help with respect to petitionary prayers regarding great evils or basic needs. Further, Pickup's account does not consider that it might be better for an event to occur in itself, but it might be worse for God to make that event occur, and this might depend (somehow) on human actions—including petitionary prayer. Further, one might elude Pickup's critique of value-adding accounts not by treating God's decision whether to bring about an event strictly in terms of what amounts to more value overall but by affirming instead that God's decisions depend on whether it would be morally good or evil (all things considered) for God to perform or refrain from performing some action (while recognizing that some cases might be morally ambivalent).

41. See, e.g., Cohoe, "God, Causality, and Petitionary Prayer," 40; Smith and Yip, "Partner-ship with God," 396; and Stump, "Petitionary Prayer," 89–90. For Stump's broader accounts regarding the problem of evil, see Stump, *Image of God*; and Stump, *Wandering in the Darkness*.

values, then, but seem inadequate to address the influence aim problem when it comes to prayers regarding basic needs or great evils.[42] Such prayers, however, repeatedly appear in Scripture and amount to a significant portion of the petitionary prayers of Christians today.

Free Will and Other Factors That Might Morally Prevent Divine Action

One might propose an additional premise compatible with some value-adding proposals. Perhaps some other factors *morally* prevent God from bringing about what he already otherwise prefers to bring about, but petitionary prayer makes a difference relative to such factors.

One such factor might be creaturely free will.[43] Perhaps, for some good reason (e.g., the value of love), God has committed to grant creatures free will of the kind such that some divine "interventions" may occur only in response to petitionary prayer. As W. Paul Franks suggests, perhaps "God has restricted his powers of interaction with humankind in such a way that those powers are exercised only in response to promptings from humankind."[44] This would not entail any limit to God's sheer power and thus would be consistent with divine omnipotence. "If we understand" this "to be a self-imposed restriction, then there is no inconsistency between it and God being all-powerful. It is not that God *cannot* interact with humankind without being prompted to do so; it is that he has decided not to do so."[45]

Perhaps God wishes to bring about some good and has the sheer power to do so, but doing so would contravene the kind of free will God has granted (for some sufficiently good reason), *unless* someone asks God to intervene. According to many theologians, free will of the kind necessary for love requires the possibility of evil.[46] As C. S. Lewis puts it, "Free will, though it makes evil possible, is also the only thing that makes possible any love or goodness or joy worth having. A world of automata—of creatures that worked like machines—would hardly be worth creating. The happiness which God designs

---

42. Davison concludes, "No single defense seems to explain, all by itself, why people might find it reasonable to offer petitionary prayers across the full range of ordinary circumstances in which people commonly hold that such prayers would be appropriate," especially "in cases where a great deal is at stake." Davison, *God and Prayer*, 16, 22.

43. See Brümmer, *What Are We Doing When We Pray?*, esp. 74–81.

44. Franks, "Why a Believer Could Believe," 322. This follows the lines of Alvin Plantinga's free will defense relative to evil (see Plantinga, *God, Freedom, and Evil*; cf. D. Morris, *Believing Philosophy*, 177–93).

45. Franks, "Why a Believer Could Believe," 322.

46. "It was not necessary that evil exist," but the "possibility of freely doing evil is the inevitable companion of the possibility of freely doing good." Davis, "Free Will and Evil," 75.

for His higher creatures is the happiness of being freely, voluntarily united to Him and to each other. . . . And for that they must be free."[47]

Even if such an approach might explain how *some* petitionary prayers might influence divine action in ways consistent with God's omnipotence, omniscience, and omnibenevolence, it seems to account only for petitionary prayers offered by persons in a position to grant God permission regarding whoever's free will would otherwise be contravened. This might work relative to some petitionary prayers offered regarding oneself, but it is unclear how it could account for many other kinds of petitionary prayer, especially prayer for others (intercessory prayer). Perhaps in some cases one might be in a position to grant God permission relative to the free will of another insofar as that other person is incapable of doing so for themself (e.g., a mother for her very young child). Even if so, only a narrow set of intercessory prayers would fall within these parameters, leaving the vast majority of intercessory prayers found in Scripture and Christian practice unaccounted for.

Of course, many intercessory prayers request benefits for other persons that presumably would not contravene those other persons' free will—such as asking for a loved one's safety in an approaching storm, which God might accomplish in numerous ways without impinging on that person's free will (e.g., calming or diverting the hurricane, miraculously shielding that person, or providing advance warning through special revelation). However, by definition, prayers for things that would not contravene anyone's free will in the first place would not be accounted for by a free will approach and thus remain subject to the question of how such petitionary prayers could influence the action of an omniscient, omnibenevolent, and omnipotent God.

Some further approach is still needed to account for many kinds of petitionary prayer common in Scripture and Christian practice, especially prayers for others regarding basic needs and great evils.

More to the Story: A Cosmic Conflict Context

Beyond a basic free will approach, perhaps God has some morally sufficient reasons for committing himself to consistently operate in a way that, at least on many occasions, God is morally prevented from bringing about certain goods in certain cases in the absence of petitionary prayer.[48] Perhaps, to extend

---

47. Lewis, *Mere Christianity*, 48.

48. Cohoe suggests that perhaps "God must allow the things he has created to exercise their causal powers, since a world in which God denied these created things the exercise of their powers would not be as well ordered." Cohoe, "God, Causality, and Petitionary Prayer," 31.

some of the accounts introduced earlier, God so commits himself because that mode of operating is necessary for true friendship, partnership with God, or some other preferable good outcome.

Since it would be immoral for God to break any commitment he makes, if God has committed himself along such lines, then petitionary prayer might make a difference such that (at least in some cases) God is no longer morally prevented from bringing about those goods. This kind of approach would face many questions, however, including what kind of morally sufficient reason God could have for committing himself in this fashion. Further, absent broader context, such an approach would still not account for petitionary prayers regarding basic needs and great evils.

But what if there is more to the story? What about the broader context provided by the overarching story of a cosmic conflict between good and evil throughout Scripture (a behind-the-scenes conflict between God's kingdom of light and a demonic realm of darkness), in which (at least in some cases) prayer makes a difference relative to what avenues of action are (morally) available to God, in which prayer might unlock avenues for God to do what he already wanted to do?[49] Perhaps in this context God has committed himself such that (at least in some cases) petitionary prayer unlocks avenues (morally) for God to bring about some good or prevent some evil regarding which God would otherwise be (morally) prevented from intervening. If so, petitionary prayer might (at least in some cases) provide God with moral license to act more directly in response to petitionary prayers.

As discussed later in this book, Scripture sets forth a cosmic conflict between God's kingdom and the kingdom of darkness governed by the devil and his minions (see, e.g., Rev. 12:7–10; cf. Matt. 12:24; 25:41), fallen angels who rebelled against God's government (cf. Col. 1:16–17; 2 Pet. 2:4). This conflict is not one of sheer power, however. Since God is all-powerful, that would be impossible. Instead, this conflict is primarily one of character, revolving around slanderous allegations raised by the devil against God's goodness, justice, and government (see, e.g., Job 1–2; Zech. 3:1–3; Matt. 13:27–29; John 8:44; Rom. 3:3–8, 25–26; Jude 9; Rev. 12:9–11; 13:4–6; cf. Gen. 3:1–6). Within this conflict, the devil—whom Jesus himself repeatedly calls the "ruler of this world" (John 12:31; 14:30; 16:11; cf. 2 Cor. 4:4)—possesses some real (but limited and temporary) rulership in this world, though his power is quickly approaching

---

49. Plantinga raises cosmic conflict as a possibility (drawing on Augustine), particularly regarding natural evil (Plantinga, *Nature of Necessity*, 192). However, most scholarly discussions of prayer do not consider cosmic conflict. Terrance Tiessen discusses something like it—the "church dominion model"—but this model "is represented in popularly written works on prayer rather than in scholarly treatises on providence." Tiessen, *Providence and Prayer*, 119.

its end (Rev. 12:12).[50] This portrait of a cosmic conflict set forth in Scripture (and recognized in the Christian tradition) may provide a broader context in which the all-powerful God is sometimes morally impeded from bringing about goods he wishes to bring about, unless petitionary prayer is offered (alongside other fluid conditions that God does not unilaterally determine).

Throughout Scripture, prayer is embedded in the context of cosmic conflict, with significant implications for both the influence aim problem of petitionary prayer and the problem of seemingly unanswered prayer, discussed further in later chapters. In short, it might be that God has committed himself to some parameters or boundaries in the cosmic conflict such that God is morally prevented from bringing about some goods (that God is aware of, otherwise would like to bring about, and possesses the sheer power to bring about) unless he is petitioned to do so by an appropriate party or parties.

To even begin to understand and recognize the implications of this possibility, however, we need to take a few steps back, beginning first with a discussion of what God must be like in order for it to make sense to pray with the influence aim (chap. 2). This is followed by a discussion of Christ's most famous teachings about prayer, found in the Lord's Prayer, where I draw out what is revealed therein about the nature and practice of petitionary prayer in the midst of cosmic conflict (chap. 3). Against this background, chapter 4 further introduces the biblical motif of cosmic conflict, focusing on what I call the rules of engagement in relation to the (influence aim) problem of petitionary prayer. Chapter 5 builds on this rules of engagement framework to further address the problem of seemingly unanswered prayer and effective prayer in light of numerous biblical teachings. Chapter 6 concludes by drawing together implications of this cosmic conflict approach to petitionary prayer for the problem of divine hiddenness and regarding injustice in the world, highlighting the biblical pattern of lament by God and his followers in the face of injustice, alongside the assurance of the intercessory work of Christ and the Holy Spirit on our behalf and God's final victory.

---

50. See Peckham, *Theodicy of Love*.

2

If My People Pray

*The Covenantal God of Scripture
to Whom We Pray*

Desperately wanting a child, Hannah "prayed to the LORD and wept bitterly," vowing, "If only you will look on the misery of your servant and remember me" and "give to your servant a male child, then I will set him before you as a nazirite until the day of his death" (1 Sam. 1:10–11). Alongside the massive problems facing Israel at the time, Hannah's prayer might have seemed insignificant, but God answers her prayer and she bears a son whom she names Samuel, saying, "I have asked for him of the LORD." Later, she praises God, saying, "For this boy I prayed, and the LORD has granted me my request which I asked of Him" (1:20, 27 NASB; cf. Gen. 25:21).[1] In direct answer to Hannah's prayer, God raises up Samuel—a great prophet and judge who changes history for God's covenant people (and beyond).

Long before, God had responded to the distressed cries of another woman in a seemingly hopeless situation. Hagar cried to God after she and her son Ishmael were cast from their home. In the wilderness, she ran out of water and cried out, "May I not see the boy die!" Then, she "raised her voice and wept. God heard the boy crying; and the angel of God called to Hagar from

---

1. Hannah's words include "almost verbatim the repetition of Eli's blessing in 1 Sam. 1:17." Tsumura, *First Book of Samuel*, 132.

heaven," saying, "Do not fear, for God has heard the voice of the boy where he is. Get up, lift up the boy, and hold him by the hand, for I will make a great nation of him" (Gen. 21:16–18 NASB). God preserves them in the wilderness and makes a great nation of Ishmael, just as he had promised.

These and many other biblical stories wherein God hears and responds to human pleas raise numerous disputed questions about God's nature and relation to the world. As Vincent Brümmer puts it, the view that petitionary prayer can actually influence God's actions "raises various problems in connection with" the common "claim[s] that God is omnipotent, immutable, omniscient and perfectly good as well as with our understanding of his agency in the world."[2]

Beyond the problem of how petitionary prayer could make any difference to an all-powerful, all-knowing, and perfectly good God, some question whether God can be *affected* or *influenced* in the first place. Specifically, many theologians maintain that God "exists independently of all causal influence from his creatures," such that creatures *cannot* impact God or his actions, by prayer or otherwise.[3] In this and other respects, one's beliefs about God's nature hold massive implications regarding whether and in what ways it makes sense to pray. As Peter Baelz writes, "At the heart of all our difficulties concerning Christian prayer, both theoretical and practical, is the problem of understanding the being of God in general, and the relation of God to the world and to ourselves in particular."[4]

Before we can address the problems of petitionary prayer introduced in chapter 1, however, we must first address the prior question, Who is the God to whom we pray? This chapter takes up this and other related questions such as, Can prayer affect God or influence God's actions? Can God truly respond to prayer? To what kind of God does it make sense to offer petitionary prayers?

Can Prayer Influence God?

The way one prays expresses what one believes and, in turn, how one lives out one's faith (*lex orandi, lex credendi, lex vivendi*). Indeed, one's "belief about prayer," Baelz writes, displays "the distinctively religious character" of one's "belief in God."[5] Accordingly, "it is no exaggeration to say that intercession provides a test-case for theological understanding."[6] As Katherine

---

2. Brümmer, *What Are We Doing When We Pray?*, 33.
3. Dolezal, "Strong Impassibility," 18.
4. Baelz, *Prayer and Providence*, 15.
5. Baelz, *Prayer and Providence*, 12.
6. Baelz, *Prayer and Providence*, 14. So also Brümmer, *What Are We Doing When We Pray?*, 16; and Crump, *Knocking on Heaven's Door*, 280.

Sonderegger puts it, "The creaturely act of prayer and the Doctrine of God belong together; they are a natural pair."[7] Georgia Harkness adds that "all prayer rests back upon our understanding of the nature of God and his relation to the world."[8]

Along these lines, William Alston identifies one's "understanding of prayer" as "one of the prime loci of the pervasive tension in Christian thought between 'the God of the philosophers and the God of the Bible,' between God as 'wholly other' and God as a partner in interpersonal relationships, between God as the absolute, ultimate source of all being and God as the dominant actor on the stage of history."[9] This is because "divine-human dialogue is an essential component of at least the more developed Christian spiritual life" and because "the conditions of the possibility of such dialogue put a significant constraint on our conception of God." This raises the crucial question of "what God must be like if divine-human dialogue is to be possible."[10]

Some theologians maintain that such back-and-forth "divine-human dialogue" is *not* possible. According to a view of God known as (strict) classical theism (heavily influenced by Platonic and Aristotelian philosophy), it is metaphysically impossible that prayer could affect God or have any genuine influence on what God brings about.[11] According to (strict) classical theism, God cannot change in any way (strict immutability) and, thus, cannot be affected by creatures in any way (strict impassibility)—including by prayer.[12] Rather, God "exists independently of all causal influence from his creatures."[13] Thus, prayer (or any other creaturely action) *cannot* influence God or his actions.

This view of God lends itself to an approach to prayer that some call "classical mysticism," in which "the emphasis is on the [noncognitive] experience of unity with the divine presence" such that one "is taken up beyond [one-]self into a blissful union with the One or the Absolute or the World Soul."[14] In this respect, Donald Bloesch lays out a sharp distinction between classical mysticism, which involves "a synthesis of Christian and Neo-Platonic

7. Sonderegger, "Act of Prayer," 139.
8. Harkness, *Prayer*, 36.
9. Alston, *Divine Nature*, 147.
10. Alston, *Divine Nature*, 147.
11. See the brief discussion in Arcadi, "Prayer in Analytic Theology," 542.
12. (Strict) classical theism maintains God is (among other things) *strictly* simple, timeless, immutable, and impassible. It is beyond the scope of this book to delve more deeply into this debate. For more, see Peckham, *Divine Attributes*.
13. Dolezal, "Strong Impassibility," 18.
14. Bloesch, *Struggle of Prayer*, 100.

motifs" (while also drawing "from the Greek mystery religions" and Eastern philosophies) and the biblical view of God as personal, which "has its source in the prophetic tradition of biblical history."[15]

In contrast to classical mysticism and (strict) classical theism more broadly, many theologians point out that "if God is immutable in the traditional [strict] sense He cannot be the God of biblical revelation, a God who is a person and an agent, who loves His people, who responds to prayer."[16] Emil Brunner writes, "The God of [biblical] revelation is the God who hears prayer. The God of Platonism does not hear prayer. To hear prayer means to be concerned about that which ascends to God from the world; it means that God is interested in what happens upon earth."[17] Vincent Brümmer adds that the view that petitionary prayer can influence God requires that we "presuppose a personal relation between God and ourselves . . . in which both God and we are personal agents."[18] However, "these presuppositions seem to conflict with" some strict understandings of "God's omnipotence, immutability and omniscience."[19]

How should we understand the God of the Bible, then, particularly when it comes to whether God can be genuinely influenced by and respond to prayer? Toward addressing this question, we turn to briefly consider some striking biblical narratives that shed considerable light on who God is, how God relates to humans, and how God hears and responds to petitionary prayers.

The God of Scripture Invites, Hears, and Answers Petitionary Prayer

Can God hear and answer prayer? Does prayer make any difference to God? Who is the God of Scripture to whom Christians pray? Earlier, we briefly considered the cases of Hannah and Hagar. In both cases, God hears and responds to the petitions and cries of ordinary humans. Many other striking instances likewise depict God being affected by and responding to prayer. Among these are God's amazing responses to the petitionary prayers of Abraham, Moses, and Solomon, to which we now turn.

---

15. Bloesch, *Struggle of Prayer*, 98–99. So also Baelz, *Prayer and Providence*, 72; Crump, *Knocking on Heaven's Door*, 284; and Harkness, *Prayer*, 37.

16. Rogers, *Perfect Being Theology*, 46. Rogers affirms (strict) classical theism but here summarizes opponents.

17. Brunner, *Christian Doctrine of God*, 269.

18. Brümmer, *What Are We Doing When We Pray?*, 54.

19. Brümmer, *What Are We Doing When We Pray?*, 54.

Will Not the Judge of the Earth Do What Is Right?

Seemingly out of nowhere, three visitors appear to Abraham. Among these is God, appearing in the form of a man (Gen. 18:1; cf. 18:13, 22, 26). God tells Abraham that the wicked city of Sodom, where Abraham's nephew lives, will soon be destroyed. In response, Abraham audaciously prays, "Will You indeed sweep away the righteous with the wicked? Suppose there are fifty righteous people within the city; will You indeed sweep it away and not spare the place for the sake of the fifty righteous who are in it? Far be it from You to do such a thing, to kill the righteous with the wicked, so that the righteous and the wicked are treated alike. Far be it from You! Shall not the Judge of all the earth deal justly?" (18:23–25 NASB). With "a profound mix of audacity and humility," this question "appeals to the character and reputation of God," a common appeal "in the intercessory prayers of the Bible."[20]

God answers, promising to "spare the entire place" if he finds even "fifty righteous" therein (Gen. 18:26 NASB). Yet Abraham humbly presses further: What if there are only forty-five righteous persons or as few as forty, thirty, twenty, or even ten? "For the sake of ten I will not destroy it," God replies (18:32).

In this striking narrative, God engages in back-and-forth dialogue with Abraham, agreeing to each of Abraham's requests. But not even ten righteous were found, so the city was nevertheless destroyed (Gen. 18:24–25; 19:24–25; cf. Amos 7:1–9). What did Abraham's intercession accomplish, then?

In some ways, this story raises more questions than it answers. Yet the dialogue reveals much about God's character, highlighting that God had no intention to "sweep away the righteous with the wicked" but was willing to spare the city were it not beyond remedy (cf. 2 Chron. 36:16). Indeed, Miller writes, "the dialogue as a whole indicates that God will go as far as God can in behalf of the innocent even if that means pardon and forgiveness of the wicked."[21] And God sends two angels to rescue Abraham's nephew Lot and those in his family willing to heed the warning (Gen. 19:16–17, 29).

While leaving many questions, this story puts on the table numerous pieces of the puzzle regarding how God relates to human petitions. Here, I will highlight just three:

1. Sometimes, God does not answer our prayers the way we think he should at the time. Yet God is the judge of the earth who always does what is just in light of all factors (cf. Gen. 18:25; Deut. 32:4)—including factors

20. P. Miller, *They Cried to the Lord*, 268, 269.
21. P. Miller, *They Cried to the Lord*, 269.

invisible to us—so God can be trusted even when prayers seem to go unanswered.

2. God welcomes honest questions and pleas, even if God does not answer as we have in mind. God is willing to engage in dialogue with humans even though, in his perfect wisdom, God has already taken into account the very things humans are inquiring about or requesting.

3. God works to save us far beyond what we deserve or merit. Whatever else petitions might accomplish, they do not make God more benevolent toward us—God already wishes to deliver each person (cf. Ezek. 18:32; 33:11; 2 Pet. 3:9).

Show Me Your Glory, I Pray

In the aftermath of Israel's golden-calf rebellion, all seemed lost. It seemed that Israel would no longer be God's covenant people—an unimaginably awful prospect, leaving them at the mercy of a barren wilderness and hostile surrounding nations, with no hope of survival.

"Let me alone so that my wrath may burn hot against them and I may consume them," God told Moses (Exod. 32:10). In response, Moses implored God to *relent* from judgment—appealing to God to *remember* his covenantal promises, noting that otherwise, onlooking nations would doubt God's character, bringing disrepute on God's name (32:11–14).[22]

What audacity! Did Moses really think his petitions could make any difference to the almighty God? According to Scripture, they did. In response, God relented "from the disaster that he had spoken of bringing on his people" (Exod. 32:14 ESV; cf. Jer. 7).

Then Moses came down from the mountain and saw "the calf and the dancing" (the depraved, sexual rituals of idol worship) (Exod. 32:19). Furious, Moses threw down and shattered the tablets of the Ten Commandments, destroyed the golden calf, and called those "on the LORD's side" to execute judgment against the revelers (32:26).

The following day, Moses again intercedes for the people, seeking to make atonement for the people's great rebellion—"if You will forgive their sin, very well; but if not, please wipe me out from Your book which You have written!"

---

22. Here again, "as in many prayers for help, Moses' pleas for the people contain an appeal to the reputation" of God and "call for the vindication" of God (P. Miller, *They Cried to the Lord*, 272; see Exod. 32:12; Num. 14:15–16; Deut. 9:28; cf. Millar, *Calling on the Name of the Lord*, 40–41). Seitz even suggests that God is "held hostage, Moses insists, to his own prior promises." Seitz, "Prayer in the Old Testament," 16.

(Exod. 32:32 NASB). God proclaims that he will punish the guilty for their sin but also instructs Moses to lead the people to the promised land, promising that his angel will go before them (32:33–35).

This is good news, but it leaves significant questions because God also says, "I will not go up in your midst, because you are an obstinate people, and I might destroy you on the way" (Exod. 33:3 NASB). If God will not go with them himself, is the covenant irreparably broken? If so, what hope can they have?

Accordingly, Moses further implores God to go with Israel—in their midst (Exod. 33:12–13). "My presence shall go with you," God replies, "and I will give you rest" (33:14 NASB). To this, Moses presses further, asking God to confirm that he will indeed go with the people, in their very midst (33:15–16). In response, God further assures Moses, "I will also do this thing of which you have spoken; for you have found favor in My sight and I have known you by name" (33:17 NASB).

Here (and elsewhere), God welcomes and even elicits intercession. Had God actually wanted to destroy Israel, he need not have spoken to Moses in the first place. God's words "let me alone" (Exod. 32:10) are "a rhetorical way of saying to Moses: 'Here is what I will do unless you intervene.'"[23] God's words thus evoke Moses's intercession (as God knew they would), providing legal/moral grounds for God to justly forgive his covenant people, renew the covenant, and dwell with them. This was not just for show but made an actual difference. Psalm 106:23 declares,

> He said that He would destroy them,
> If Moses, His chosen one, had not stood in the gap before Him,
> To turn away His wrath from destroying them. (NASB)[24]

J. Richard Middleton comments that Moses "decisively changed the outcome for Israel by his prayer."[25] Terence Fretheim adds, "This text reveals *an amazing picture of God*, a God who enters into genuine dialogue with chosen leaders and takes their contribution to the discussion with utmost

---

23. Stuart, *Exodus*, 670. He adds that God's announcing to a prophet "his intention to do something as a way of inviting intercession has many parallels" (670; cf. Amos 7:1–6; Jon. 3:4). See, further, Peckham, "Show Me Your Glory."

24. On Moses's intercession as a type of Christ, see Seitz, "Prayer in the Old Testament," 17–21. Note especially his discussion of "the servant" who "is introduced before the heavenly council" in Isa. 42 (p. 19).

25. Middleton, *Abraham's Silence*, 54. Middleton points out that many other "prophets stand in the breach between God and the people," such as Amos, Micah, Jeremiah, and Ezekiel (56).

seriousness."[26] Indeed, "Moses is responsible for shaping a future other than what would have been the case had he been passive and kept silent."[27]

Much later, Revelation 12 reveals that the devil continually raises accusations against God and his people, identifying Satan as "the accuser of our brothers and sisters . . . who accuses them before our God day and night" like a malevolent prosecuting attorney (Rev. 12:10 NASB). This is on full display in Job (see chap. 4) and in Zechariah's vision of "Joshua the high priest standing before the angel of the LORD, and Satan standing at his right to accuse him," wherein "the Lord said to Satan, 'The Lord rebuke you, Satan! Indeed, the Lord who has chosen Jerusalem rebuke you!'" (Zech. 3:1–2 NASB; cf. Luke 22:31–32; Jude 9).[28] In light of the devil's continual accusations, it is no surprise that God elicits intercession, seeking legal/moral grounds to justly provide forgiveness and defeat Satan's accusations (see, further, chap. 4).

Scripture repeatedly teaches that God *wants* to forgive. He "longs to be gracious" and "waits on high to have compassion" (Isa. 30:18 NASB) but often *waits* on repentance and/or intercession to provide (moral/legal) license for him to do so *while upholding justice*. The supreme example of this is Christ's intercession—so God can remain just even as he justifies sinners (see Rom. 3:25–26; Rev. 5). Yet God seeks others (such as Moses) to intercede for his people—prefiguring Christ's intercessory work.[29] As God himself states in Ezekiel 22:30, "I searched for a man among them who would build up a wall and stand in the gap before Me for the land, so that I would not destroy it; but I found no one" (NASB; cf. Isa. 63:5; Jer. 5:1; 33:3; Ezek. 13:5). Lamar Eugene Cooper comments, "Whenever such moral and spiritual crises have gripped nations, God has sought for a solitary individual who would be willing to be used ([Ezek. 22] v. 30). He found such a person in Noah, in Moses, in Deborah, in Daniel, and in Ezekiel."[30]

Such intercession does not make God want to do good for us (God already wants to bless and deliver us), but intercession opens up avenues for God to *justly* bring about the good he already wanted to bring (more on this later, especially in chap. 4). In the end, we are promised, God "will certainly be gracious to you at the sound of your cry; when He hears it, He will answer you" (Isa. 30:19 NASB; cf. Ps. 81:11–14; Jer. 33:3).

---

26. Fretheim, *Exodus*, 291.
27. Fretheim, *Exodus*, 292.
28. Whether this figure ("the *śāṭān*") corresponds to the devil in the New Testament is disputed. Elsewhere, I have made a case in the affirmative. See Peckham, *Theodicy of Love*, 76–82.
29. See P. Miller, *They Cried to the Lord*, 273.
30. Cooper, *Ezekiel*, 224; cf. Block, *Ezekiel*, 727–28; Seitz, "Prayer in the Old Testament," 21.

Moses's intercession thus highlights that

1. God responds to prayer—even audacious petitions like those of Moses—
   and even elicits intercession as a crucial factor that might provide moral
   grounds for God to act (as he already wanted to) in favor of his people.

And, in the following section, we will see that Moses's intercession further
reveals that

2. God's name (in terms of his reputation and character of compassion
   and grace) is inextricably linked to God's glory and goodness, and God
   responds to prayer in accordance with his name, manifesting his glory
   and goodness to the nations.

I Will Make All My Goodness Pass before You

Though God has promised to do just as Moses asks, Moses nevertheless
makes one more daring request: "Show me your glory, I pray" (Exod. 33:18
NRSV). "I Myself will make all My goodness pass before you," God replies,
"and will proclaim the name of the LORD before you; and I will be gracious
to whom I will be gracious, and will show compassion to whom I will show
compassion" (33:19 NASB). Moses asks to see God's glory. In response, God
promises to show his goodness and proclaim his name. The Hebrew word
translated as "glory" (*kābôd*) often refers to "honor" or "dignity" and is
repeatedly linked to God's name or reputation (relative to his goodness and
justice).[31] To see God's glory is to see God's goodness, which corresponds to
his *name* (his character or reputation).

In this encounter with Moses, God expands on the earlier proclamation
of his name as "I AM WHO I AM" (Exod. 3:14 NASB), explaining his name
(character) in terms of his compassion, graciousness, long-suffering patience,
steadfast love, faithfulness, and justice. Specifically, God "passed by in front
of [Moses] and proclaimed, 'The LORD, the LORD God, compassionate and
merciful, slow to anger, and abounding in faithfulness and truth; who keeps·
faithfulness for thousands, who forgives wrongdoing, violation of His Law,
and sin; yet He will by no means leave the guilty unpunished'" (34:6–7 NASB).[32]
Whatever else we conclude about how petitionary prayer operates, we can be

31. "The noun *kābôd* derives from *kbd*, which denotes 'heaviness' in the physical sense as
well as 'gravity' and 'importance' in the spiritual sense—i.e., 'honor' and 'respect'" (Weinfeld,
"כָּבוֹד," 23). Cf. Finkel, "Prayer in Jewish Life," 46.

32. For more on these attributes, see Peckham, *Love of God*.

assured that God always acts according to his name—his character of perfect love and justice.

God's name is a crucial theme throughout Scripture, inextricably linked to God's goodness and glory/honor, with emphasis on the vindication of God's character/reputation against slander and defamation. In his intercessions, Moses repeatedly appeals to God's name or reputation among the nations (cf. Exod. 32:11–13), expressing that "Yahweh's reputation is on the line" with respect to how he deals with his people.[33] Elsewhere, God declares,

> For my name's sake I defer my anger;
>> for the sake of my praise I restrain it for you,
>> so that I may not cut you off. . . .
>> For why should my name be profaned?
>> My glory I will not give to another. (Isa. 48:9, 11; cf. 66:18)

Here, and in many other cases, Scripture directly links God's acting for his "name's sake" with God defending his character before the nations against charges of unfairness. As God declares elsewhere, "I acted for the sake of My name, that it would not be defiled in the sight of the nations" (Ezek. 20:9 NASB; cf. 18:25; 20:14, 22, 44). As Carmen Joy Imes puts it, commenting on this text, "Yahweh's own reputation is at stake."[34]

Likewise, Psalm 79:9–10 records this prayer:

> Help us, God of our salvation, for the glory of Your name;
> And save us and forgive our sins for the sake of Your name.
> Why should the nations say, "Where is their God?" (NASB; cf. Jer. 12:1–4)

Moshe Weinfeld comments, "Biblical prayers often request God to deliver Israel for the sake of God's *kābôd*, i.e., for the sake of his reputation among the nations."[35] As Psalm 115:1–2 states,

> Not to us, O Lord, not to us, but to your name give glory,
>> for the sake of your steadfast love and your faithfulness.
> Why should the nations say,
>> "Where is their God?"

---

33. Imes, *Bearing God's Name*, 65. N. T. Wright likewise comments, "It was the honor and reputation of YHWH's name that Moses [used] . . . as the fulcrum in his great prayer for Israel's forgiveness after the episode of the golden calf." Wright, "Lord's Prayer," 140–41.

34. Imes, *Bearing God's Name*, 123.

35. Weinfeld, "כָּבוֹד," 26.

Psalm 106 says of the exodus,

> He saved them for the sake of His name,
> So that He might make His power known. (Ps. 106:8 NASB; cf. Exod.
>   32:12; Num. 14:15–16; Deut. 9:28; Josh. 7:7–9; 1 Chron. 17:21,
>   23–24)

Many other instances likewise describe God's benevolent actions as for his "name's sake" (e.g., Pss. 23:3; 25:11; 31:3; Jer. 14:7, 21; Dan. 9:19; cf. Isa. 48:9–11; 66:5). The psalmist prays,

> Lord, deal kindly with me for the sake of Your name;
> Because Your mercy is good, rescue me. (109:21 NASB)

Likewise, Psalm 143:11 records the prayer,

> For the sake of Your name, LORD, revive me.
> In Your righteousness bring my soul out of trouble. (NASB)

It is no coincidence that Scripture repeatedly identifies prayer as "at bottom line, a 'calling on the name of the LORD'" (e.g., Gen. 4:26; think of the concept of praying "in God's name").[36] As Joel Green comments, "Prayer grows out of a recognition of God's character, as his character is manifest in history and especially in the person and ministry of Jesus."[37] Millar adds, "'Calling on the name of Yahweh' is the definitive mark of the people of God," especially calling on God to fulfill his promises.[38] Thus, God proclaims regarding his people,

> They will call on My name,
> And I will answer them;
> I will say, "They are My people,"
> And they will say, "The LORD is my God." (Zech. 13:9 NASB)

Throughout Scripture, God is concerned about vindicating his name—not because he *needs* to do so but for the well-being of the universe, which can flourish in perfect harmony only if all creatures trust God's goodness. As Millar extensively shows, to call on God's name is to call on God to act and

---

36. Seitz, "Prayer in the Old Testament," 6. Millar traces this theme throughout Scripture in *Calling on the Name of the Lord*.

37. J. Green, "Persevering Together," 200–201.

38. Millar, *Calling on the Name of the Lord*, 24.

thus manifest and vindicate his character through his righteous deeds.[39] As Psalm 98:2 puts it,

> The LORD has made His salvation known;
> He has revealed His righteousness in the sight of the nations. (NASB)

And in the plan of salvation, especially through Christ's work, God supremely demonstrates his righteousness and love (Rom. 3:25–26; 5:8; cf. 1 Cor. 4:9; 6:2–3; Isa. 5:1–5), defeating the devil's slanderous allegations (Rev. 12:10–11; see chap. 4). Thus Christ prays of his impending death, "'Father, glorify your name.' Then a voice came out of heaven, 'I have both glorified it, and will glorify it again'" (John 12:28 NASB).

In the end, all will recognize the perfect justice and righteousness of God: "Every knee will bow to" God "and every tongue will give praise to God" (Rom. 14:11 NASB; cf. Isa. 45:23; Phil. 2:10–11). And a throng of the redeemed will sing

> the song of Moses . . . and the song of the Lamb, saying,
>
> > "Great and marvelous are Your works,
> > Lord God, the Almighty;
> > Righteous and true are Your ways,
> > King of the nations!" (Rev. 15:3 NASB; cf. 5:13; 19:1–6)

If My People Pray, I Will Hear Them

One night, God appears to King Solomon, saying, "Ask what you wish Me to give you" (1 Kings 3:5 NASB). In response, Solomon praises God for his "great and steadfast love" and humbly prays for "an understanding mind to govern your people, able to discern between good and evil" (3:6, 9). Invited by God to ask for anything, Solomon prays for wisdom. Pleased by this, God replies,

> Because you have asked this thing, and have not asked for yourself a long life, nor have asked riches for yourself, nor have you asked for the lives of your enemies, but have asked for yourself discernment to understand justice, behold, I have done according to your words. . . . I have also given you what you have not asked, both riches and honor, so that there will not be any among the kings like you all your days. And if you walk in My ways, keeping My statutes and commandments, as your father David walked, then I will prolong your days. (3:10–14 NASB; cf. James 1:5–7)

---

39. Millar, *Calling on the Name of the Lord.*

God answers Solomon's prayers in ways far beyond what he has asked. Later, Solomon petitions God again in a corporate prayer on behalf of Israel at the dedication of the temple. He first praises God for his covenant faithfulness and steadfast love, then prays, "LORD, God of Israel, keep to Your servant David, my father, that which You promised him, saying, 'You shall not lack a man to sit on the throne of Israel, if only your sons pay attention to their way, to walk in My Law as you have walked before Me.' Now then, LORD, God of Israel, let Your word be confirmed which You have spoken to Your servant David" (2 Chron. 6:16–17 NASB).

After extolling God again, Solomon prays further,

> Turn Your attention to the prayer of Your servant and to his plea, LORD, my God, to listen to the cry and to the prayer which Your servant prays before You; that Your eye will be open toward this house day and night, toward the place of which You have said that You would put Your name there, to listen to the prayer which Your servant shall pray toward this place. Listen to the pleadings of Your servant and of Your people Israel when they pray toward this place; hear from Your dwelling place, from heaven; hear and forgive. (2 Chron. 6:19–21 NASB)

Solomon then asks about future pleas for deliverance from enemy nations, "If Your people . . . return to You and praise Your name, and pray and plead before You in this house, then hear from heaven and forgive the sin of Your people Israel, and bring them back to the [promised] land" (6:24–25 NASB; cf. 6:36–39). Solomon prays likewise about future pleas in the midst of drought, famine, plagues, and enemy sieges: "Whatever prayer or plea is made by anyone or by all Your people Israel." He asks God to "hear," "forgive," and "render to each according to all his ways, whose heart You know" (6:29–30 NASB; cf. 6:34–35).

Solomon's prayer also includes the foreigner who "comes from a far country on account of Your great name . . . when they come and pray toward this house, then hear from heaven, from Your dwelling place, and do according to all for which the foreigner calls to You, so that all the peoples of the earth may know Your name, and fear You" (2 Chron. 6:32–33 NASB). Here, "fear" does not connote being afraid but connotes being in awe of God and revering him accordingly. Solomon prays that God's response to foreigners' prayers will reveal God's character so that they may "know" God's "name" and revere him.

Finally, Solomon prays, "Now, my God, please, let Your eyes be open and Your ears attentive to the prayer offered in this place" (2 Chron. 6:40 NASB).

In response, "fire came down from heaven and consumed the burnt offering and the sacrifices, and the glory of the LORD filled the" temple (7:1 NASB). Afterward, God again appears to Solomon in the night, saying, "I have heard your prayer." He continues: "[If] My people who are called by My name humble themselves, and pray and seek My face, and turn from their wicked ways, then I will hear from heaven, and I will forgive their sin and will heal their land. Now My eyes will be open and My ears attentive to the prayer offered in this place" (7:12–15 NASB). In response to Solomon's prayer, then, God invites and gives specific instructions for the people to petition him, promising to hear and respond *if* his people (1) humble themselves, (2) pray, (3) seek his face, and (4) turn from their wicked ways.

Among other things, this case highlights that

1. God *invites* prayers from individuals and groups (corporate prayer), including foreigners, signaling that God is already willing to bless people.
2. God already knows the hearts of all who pray (2 Chron. 6:30) and, yet, hears and responds to the specifics of petitionary prayers, according to his perfect character of steadfast love.
3. God's promised blessings in response to petitionary prayers are conditional (at least in part) on the people's dispositions and actions (e.g., humble, repentant prayer; see chap. 5).

Here and elsewhere, God *commits himself* to operating in ways that are (partially) tied to prayer, specifically *fervent* prayer offered in humble faith. Elsewhere, God likewise promises his covenant people, "Call to Me and I will answer you" (Jer. 33:3 NASB). Likewise, Isaiah writes, "the LORD longs to be gracious to you. . . . He will certainly be gracious to you at the sound of your cry; when He hears it, He will answer you" (Isa. 30:18–19 NASB).

The instances briefly surveyed above (and many others) depict God being affected by prayers, even eliciting prayers as if they might "unlock" avenues of divine action. God responds to Abraham's petitions and to Hagar's desperate pleas (Gen. 21:17), answers Eliezer's prayer to find the right wife for Isaac (24:12–15), hears the groans of Israel under Egyptian slavery and delivers them (Exod. 2:24), positively responds to intercession by Moses (33:12–34:10), is repeatedly "moved to pity by" his people's "groaning because of those who tormented and oppressed them" (Judg. 2:18 NASB; cf. 10:16), is "moved by prayer for the land" (2 Sam. 21:14; 24:25 NASB95), answers Solomon's prayers (1 Kings 3:10–14), grants Hezekiah's prayer for healing (2 Kings 20:5–6), and directly responds to the petitionary prayers of prophets like Amos,

Daniel, and many others (Amos 7; Dan. 9–10; cf. Neh. 2:4–6; Isa. 30:19; Jer. 33:3).[40]

In these and other instances throughout Scripture, God responds to the prayers of people—from outcasts to kings—often changing his course of action in *direct* response to human petitions. Insofar as we seek an understanding ruled by Scripture, whatever we conclude regarding petitionary prayer must be consistent with these and other biblical teachings and depictions of God's responses to petitionary prayers.

The Covenantal God Who Responds to Petitionary Prayer

This brings us back to the main question of this chapter: Who is the God of Scripture to whom we pray? "According to the Bible," Crump comments, "prayer makes sense only in a certain kind of universe with a certain kind of God."[41] But what is this God like? What do biblical portrayals and teachings about God's responsiveness to petitionary prayer reveal about God's nature and character?

Scripture repeatedly portrays God as speaking, hearing, willing, covenanting, grieving, relenting, responding to prayer, dwelling with creatures, and otherwise engaging in back-and-forth relationship with creatures.[42] As Michael Horton puts it, "The biblical testimony to a living history with a living God in a covenant with genuine interaction resists all Stoic and Platonic conceptions of a nonrelational and nonpersonal One. In the unfolding drama there are suits and countersuits, witnesses and counterwitnesses, and God is represented as repenting, relenting, and responding to creatures."[43]

Some claim, however, that biblical depictions of God engaging in back-and-forth relationship and responding to prayer consist of language that accommodates our limited human understanding (accommodative language) and thus do not actually correspond to God as he is. In this regard, I agree with Justo González that God's "revelation must come to us in terms and categories we can somehow grasp—that is, in human terms and categories."

---

40. Relative to many cases in Nehemiah (e.g., 4:9; 5:19; 13:14, 22, 29; 13:31), Millar comments, "If the work of Yahweh in Jerusalem is to progress, it will be in large measure down to the prayers of the people." Millar, *Calling on the Name of the Lord*, 123.

41. Crump, *Knocking on Heaven's Door*, 294.

42. See Peckham, *Divine Attributes*, 1–17. Miller adds that biblical "prayers reveal that the relationship with God is highly dialogical" (P. Miller, *They Cried to the Lord*, 133). Likewise, Crump notes that Scripture depicts God engaging "in a two-way relationship of personal give and take." Crump, *Knocking on Heaven's Door*, 285.

43. Horton, *Christian Faith*, 240.

But "the fact that a theological statement" is given in accommodative language "is no valid reason for rejecting that statement—unless one is willing to abandon God-talk altogether."[44] Indeed, I often explained things about God to my young son in ways that accommodated his limited understanding at the time, while nevertheless conveying truths about God. If I can do so, surely God can use accommodative language that communicates truths in ways we can understand.

Elsewhere, I have addressed these and other issues in more detail and made a canonical case that the God of Scripture is the covenantal God who freely commits himself to back-and-forth relationship with creatures—who *always* keeps his promises.[45] He acts in the world, intervenes, speaks, communes, covenants, and hears and answers prayer in accordance with his perfect power, wisdom, goodness, and love. In the words of Amos Yong, the God of Scripture is "not only the covenant-making but also covenant-keeping God who enters into and is involved with the history of the people of God, who seeks to accomplish what is just on their behalf, and who liberates the people of God from their plight in order to reestablish—redeem or restore—the relationship between creation and the creator."[46]

We have seen many biblical examples wherein God *actually* hears and responds to human prayers—the God of Scripture is repeatedly "moved by prayer" (e.g., 2 Sam. 24:25 NASB95). As Paul Copan writes, the God of Scripture "isn't the static, untouchable deity commonly associated with traditional Greek philosophy. He's a prayer-answering, history-engaging God."[47] The very possibility that God *hears* and *responds* to human prayers such that petitionary prayer might actually influence God's actions, however, hinges on what is true about God and the God-world relationship.

Elsewhere, I have made a more extensive case for what I call covenantal theism, which cannot be rehearsed here.[48] Instead, in what follows I briefly lay out what I take to be the biblical teaching in a number of respects that are crucial to the very possibility that petitionary prayer might influence God's action in the world.

---

44. González, *Mañana*, 91. Of the tendency to suggest that biblical depictions of God are simply "speak[ing] in our lowly tongue" and "offer[ing] us a human God," Sonderegger cautions that "we have reason to be wary of solving the riddles of Holy Writ in this way; of dissolving them, in truth." Sonderegger, "Does God Pray?," 140.

45. See Peckham, *Divine Attributes*. I use the term "covenantal" in the broader sense of engaging in back-and-forth relationships with creatures in which God makes and keep promises.

46. Yong, *Spirit of Love*, 81–82.

47. Copan, *Loving Wisdom*, 94.

48. See Peckham, *Divine Attributes*.

Specifically, the covenantal God of Scripture

1. hears, can be "affected," and responds accordingly—willingly engaging in back-and-forth relationship with creatures.

2. is perfectly good and loving (omnibenevolent)—willing only good to all in accordance with his character of abundant compassion, grace, and lovingkindness.

3. possesses perfect knowledge (omniscience) and thus always knows what is preferable, all things considered.

4. possesses perfect power (omnipotence) and is thus powerful enough to respond to whatever one might ask of him.

5. is present *with us* wherever we may be, though not as intimately as he would like due to the separation caused by sin.

6. is eternal and self-existent, such that God works historically, but his timing is not our timing; and we need God, but he does not need us.

7. always keeps his promises. As such, when God makes a promise or commitment (in a formal covenant or otherwise), God's future action is thereby *morally* bound to be in keeping with that promise or commitment (see chap. 4).

To a brief discussion of these points we now turn, with special emphasis on numerous psalms that exemplify the connection between the way we pray and what we believe about God.

God Cares, Hears, and Responds

If God is entirely immutable (changeless) and strictly impassible, God could not be influenced or affected by anything, including prayer.[49] On one hand, God himself states in Malachi 3:6, "For I, the LORD, do not change; therefore you, the sons of Jacob, have not come to an end" (NASB; cf. Ps. 102:24–27; James 1:17). On the other hand, in the very next verse God urges his people, "Return to me, and I will return to you" (Mal. 3:7 NASB), one among many biblical examples wherein God changes course in response to human repentance (e.g., Exod. 32:14; Jon. 3:10; cf. Jer. 18:7–10). Elsewhere, Scripture

---

49. As James Arcadi puts it, "If God is simply unchanging and unchangeable then there is clearly no point to human effort to change God. Rather, human petitions only seem effective when it just so happens that one requests what God was going to do anyway." Arcadi, "Prayer in Analytic Theology," 542.

repeatedly teaches that God undergoes relational changes—that is, changes responsive to humans such as doing new things, entering into back-and-forth relationships, and responding to prayer (e.g., 2 Sam. 24:25; 2 Chron. 7:14). As Patrick Miller explains, prayers throughout Scripture assume that "the ears of God are open to the cries of people in distress and need of help."[50]

The God of Scripture both engages in genuine back-and-forth relationship with creatures that involves relational changes and yet always remains the same with respect to his essential nature and character. Thus, in the midst of petitionary prayer, the psalmist declares to God, "You are the same / And Your years will not come to an end" (Ps. 102:27 NASB). Then, Psalm 103 further teaches, "Just as a father has compassion on his children / So the LORD has compassion on those who fear Him," for "the mercy of the LORD is from everlasting to everlasting for those who fear Him" (Ps. 103:13, 17 NASB; cf. Isa. 49:15–16; 66:13; Luke 1:78).[51] The God to whom we pray both remains "the same" throughout all years and is deeply compassionate, being moved by the plights and pleas of his people according to his steadfast love.

In this respect, Scripture repeatedly indicates that God undergoes emotional changes, such as taking "pleasure in His people" (Ps. 149:4 NASB), being "moved to pity" and compassion (Judg. 2:18 NASB; cf. 10:16; Luke 19:41), deeply grieved by evil (e.g., Gen. 6:6; Ps. 78:40–41), or "provoked" to anger (Ps. 78:58; cf. Deut. 9:7; 32:16), even describing himself as changing from one emotional state to another in response to humans (e.g., Zech. 1:15–16; Hosea 11:8; Jer. 31:20).[52] Over and over again, God laments over the state of his beloved people, saying in one instance,

> My heart recoils within me;
>   my compassion grows warm and tender. (Hosea 11:8)

As Nicholas Wolterstorff writes, "God's love for his world is a rejoicing and suffering love."[53] Accordingly, Walter Brueggemann concludes, the strictly

---

50. P. Miller, *They Cried to the Lord*, 133.

51. The Hebrew word translated as "compassion" (*raham*) is believed to be derived from the Hebrew word for "womb" (*rehem*). God's compassion, then, might be described as a "womblike mother love." See Trible, *God and the Rhetoric of Sexuality*, 31–59. See also Stoebe, "רחם," 1226–28; cf. Koehler, Baumgartner, and Stamm, *Hebrew and Aramaic Lexicon*, 3:1217–18; Butterworth, "רהם," 1093.

52. Yet God is the unique Creator such that God's "emotions" should not be thought of as identical to faulty human emotions—God is "not a man" but is "the Holy One" (Hosea 11:9 NASB). See Peckham, *Divine Attributes*, 39–72.

53. Wolterstorff, *Inquiring about God*, 219. James Cone adds, "God is not indifferent to suffering" but is "a *Servant* who suffers on behalf of the people. He takes their pain and affliction

"immutable God" of "scholastic theology . . . stands in deep tension with the biblical presentation of God."[54]

Elsewhere I have made a broader case that Scripture teaches that God does not change with respect to his essential nature and character (see, e.g., Ps. 102:24–27; Mal. 3:6; James 1:17) but may undergo relational changes in ways consistent with his nature (qualified immutability) and voluntarily engages in back-and-forth relationship with creatures in which God experiences changing emotions such as pleasure or displeasure (qualified passibility).[55] Put simply, with respect to his character and essential nature, God is changeless or immutable. But God can and does change relationally, freely entering into back-and-forth relationship with creatures that deeply affects God. As Thomas Oden puts it, "Precisely because God is unchanging in the eternal character of his self-giving love, . . . God is free in responding to changing historical circumstances, and versatile in empathy."[56] Baelz adds, "God's love is perfect and unchanging; but the created objects of his love, and consequently his relations with them, do change."[57]

This fits with Scripture's consistent and emphatic teaching that God hears and responds to prayer, including being moved to compassionate action in response to human petitions (e.g., Judg. 2:18; 10:16; 2 Sam. 21:14; 24:25; cf. Luke 1:78).[58] Elsewhere, Scripture teaches that our prayers might please or displease God:

> The sacrifice of the wicked is an abomination to the LORD,
> But the prayer of the upright is His delight. (Prov. 15:8 NASB; cf.
>   11:20; 12:22)

---

upon himself, thereby redeeming them *from* oppression" (Cone, *God of the Oppressed*, 8–9, 75). Cf. González, *Mañana*, 92.

54. Brueggemann, "Book of Exodus," 932. See, further, Mullins, *God and Emotion*; Peckham, *Love of God*, 147–90.

55. Peckham, *Divine Attributes*, 39–72. Vincent Brümmer comments, "There is nothing incoherent in maintaining on the one hand that God is a person and therefore capable of change in certain respects (e.g., by really responding to contingent events and human actions), and yet to hold that he is immutable in certain other respects," being "faithful to his character." Brümmer, *What Are We Doing When We Pray?*, 45.

56. Oden, *Classic Christianity*, 68. So also Davis, *Logic and the Nature of God*, 141; Feinberg, *No One Like Him*, 271; Padgett, "Eternity as Relative Timelessness," 109.

57. Baelz, *Prayer and Providence*, 140.

58. Christian theists generally affirm that God responds to prayer, but as Rogers puts it, "The concept of a response requires that there be a certain sort of causal connection such that . . . prayer 'prompts' the response, and the response 'answers' the prayer" (Rogers, *Perfect Being Theology*, 66). If so, it is difficult (if not impossible) to see how God could respond to prayer if God is strictly immutable and impassible.

Further, some biblical cases indicate that God's action might be impeded by lack of genuine faith (e.g., Mark 6:5) or prayer (9:29), which raises numerous highly puzzling and important questions (discussed in chap. 5).

In this regard, David Crump concludes, "Despite certain Christian traditions disputing this claim," God "enters into true reciprocity with us in such a way that he allows himself to be affected by our words and decisions. Christian petition requires believing that the Father is honestly listening, is willing to be influenced, and is thus engaged in authentic two-way communication with the one who prays."[59] Indeed, "God not only listened to his people but enlisted them as genuine partners in accomplishing his purposes for the world."[60] Patrick Miller adds that, throughout Scripture, "the structure of prayer and divine response . . . is the structure of faith itself."[61]

Not only does God hear and respond to prayer, but the persons of the Trinity themselves intercede for us in special ways (see, further, chap. 5). The Son "always lives to make intercession for [us]" (Heb. 7:25 NASB), and "the Spirit also helps our weakness; for we do not know what to pray for as we should, but the Spirit Himself intercedes for us with groanings too deep for words" (Rom. 8:26 NASB).

Knowing that God cares, hears, responds, and even intercedes may give us confidence to bring our petitions to him. We can trust that God cares about and hears us, even when our prayers are seemingly unanswered, which might tempt us to think that God "is a distant God, or an absent God, who does not really care for his creatures" (see chap. 6).[62] As Scripture consistently teaches, God truly "cares about you" (1 Pet. 5:7 NASB).

Before proceeding, I invite you to pause and prayerfully read Psalm 103.

God Is Eternal and Self-Existent

Because God's character and essential nature are unchanging, humans can pray to God with confidence that he will never change from caring to uncaring or from loving to unloving, but, rather, he is eternally the same God of unwavering goodness and love.[63] In this regard, Psalm 102 offers a prayer for

---

59. Crump, *Knocking on Heaven's Door*, 285. Brümmer likewise contends that an "absolutely immutable God would be more like the neo-platonic Absolute than like the personal being the Bible represents him to be" and "would not be able to react to what we do or feel, nor to the petitions that we address to him." Brümmer, *What Are We Doing When We Pray?*, 40.

60. Crump, *Knocking on Heaven's Door*, 130.

61. P. Miller, *They Cried to the Lord*, 176–77.

62. Baelz, *Prayer and Providence*, 128.

63. For more on this, see Peckham, *Divine Attributes*, 73–110.

help based on confidence in God as the eternal Creator who ever remains the same:

> You, LORD, remain forever,
> And Your name remains to all generations. . . .
> Your years are throughout all generations.
> In time of old You founded the earth,
> And the heavens are the work of Your hands.
> Even they will perish, but You endure;
> All of them will wear out like a garment;
> Like clothing You will change them and they will pass away.
> But You are the same,
> And Your years will not come to an end. (Ps. 102:12, 24–27 NASB)

This psalm begins with the plea,

> Hear my prayer, LORD!
> And let my cry for help come to You.
> Do not hide Your face from me on the day of my distress;
> Incline Your ear to me;
> On the day when I call answer me quickly. (102:1–2 NASB)

This psalm, then, offers petitionary prayer with the expectation that God will hear ("incline" his ear) and answer quickly because God is eternally "the same" (eternity and qualified immutability). The psalm thus confidently claims that God

> has turned His attention to the prayer of the destitute
> And has not despised their prayer. (102:17 NASB)

"A people yet to be created" are called to "praise the LORD,"

> For He looked down from His holy height . . .
> To hear the groaning of the prisoner,
> To set free those who were doomed to death. (102:19–20 NASB)

In this psalm and elsewhere, Scripture repeatedly teaches that God is eternal—that is, God has no beginning and no end (Isa. 40:28; 57:15; Ps. 90:2; Rom. 16:26). As such, God's timing is not our timing. For humans, a year—or even a month, week, or day—might seem like a long time, *especially when praying for deliverance.* But "with the Lord one day is like a thousand years, and a thousand years like one day" (2 Pet. 3:8 NASB; cf. Ps. 90:2–4).[64]

As the unique Creator of all (cf. Rev. 4:11), God does not depend on anything for his existence but is the source of all things (Rom. 11:36) and thus is self-existent. It makes sense to place all our confidence in this God because *everything* depends on him—he "upholds all things by the word of His power" (Heb. 1:3 NASB). We need God for everything, but God needs nothing (cf. Acts 17:25).[65] It is no coincidence that, when tragedy strikes, even many atheists feel the urge to cry out to a higher power in prayer.[66] As creatures of a loving God who invites us to pray, we are "wired" to call out to our Maker (who himself first calls to us), particularly when we or a loved one are in need or are facing great suffering.

We wait, often anxiously, but God "waits" in his perfect timing, knowing the end from the beginning (cf. Isa. 46:10). We may wonder what is taking so long for our prayers to be answered, often failing to realize that God operates on different timing. Just after declaring that "with the Lord one day is like a thousand years, and a thousand years like one day," Peter explains further, "The Lord is not slow about His promise, as some count slowness, but is patient toward you, not willing for any to perish, but for all to come to repentance" (2 Pet. 3:8–9 NASB).

We often get caught up in the here and now and forget to consider the bigger story, but God is both concerned with everything that takes place here and now and also takes the long view, concerned about all creatures now and in the future. Thus, while himself familiar with the great suffering of this present time, Paul proclaims that "the sufferings of this present time are not worthy to be compared with the glory that is to be revealed to us" (Rom. 8:18 NASB), which he elsewhere calls "an eternal weight of glory far beyond all comparison" (2 Cor. 4:17 NASB).

Before proceeding, I invite you to pause and prayerfully read Psalm 102.

God Is Perfectly Good and Loving

God is not only eternal but eternally good—in every way.[67]

> The LORD is gracious and compassionate;
> Slow to anger and great in mercy.

---

64. The debate over the relationship between God and time cannot be adequately addressed in this brief book. As I have explained elsewhere, however, I am convinced Scripture indicates that God is *analogically* temporal (see Peckham, *Divine Attributes*, 73–110). For an excellent case for divine temporality, see Mullins, *End of the Timeless God*; cf. Baelz, *Prayer and Providence*, 137–38.
65. On humanity's great need, see McKirland's excellent book, *God's Provision, Humanity's Need*.
66. Wicker, "Do Atheists Pray?"
67. For more on this, see Peckham, *Divine Attributes*, 175–208; Peckham, *Love of God*.

> The LORD is good to all,
> And His mercies are over all His works. . . .
> The LORD is righteous in all His ways,
> And kind in all His works.
> The LORD is near to all who call on Him,
> To all who call on Him in truth.
> He will fulfill the desire of those who fear Him;
> He will also hear their cry for help and save them. (Ps. 145:8–9, 17–19
> NASB; cf. Exod. 34:6)

Humans regularly fail, but God "is a righteous judge" (Ps. 7:11 NASB; cf. Rom. 2:5) who "does no wrong" (Zeph. 3:5).

> [God's] work is perfect,
> For all His ways are just;
> A God of faithfulness and without injustice,
> Righteous and just is He. (Deut. 32:4 NASB; cf. Ps. 92:15; 129:4)

First John 1:5 tells us that "God is Light, and in Him there is no darkness at all" (NASB; cf. Ps. 5:4). Accordingly,

> All His work is done in faithfulness.
> He loves righteousness and justice;
> The earth is full of the goodness of the LORD. (Ps. 33:4–5 NASB)

God's "steadfast love is established forever," his "faithfulness is as firm as the heavens" (89:2). He is the utterly holy one.

Being utterly holy and good, God is not the cause of evil in this world. Rather, as Jesus explains in the parable of the wheat and tares, "An enemy [the devil] has done this" (Matt. 13:28 NASB). The evil in this world is alien to God's entirely good wishes. God wants only what is good for *all* of creation. Thus we can unreservedly trust him—in prayer and otherwise— knowing that our "Father who is in heaven" will "give good things to those who ask him!" (7:11). Indeed, "Every generous act of giving, with every perfect gift, is from above, coming down from the Father of lights, with whom there is no variation or shadow due to change" (James 1:17). As I. Howard Marshall explains, "The really important factor in prayer is the character of God as the One who wants to do good for his people and to accomplish his own purpose, which will also be for their good. Petition- ary prayer depends on the character of the one petitioned rather than on the effort of the petitioner to have the right attitude of faith. Prayer is the expression of a relationship with a God whom we are learning to trust because he is faithful and good."[68]

Before proceeding, I invite you to pause and prayerfully read Psalm 145.

God Is All-Knowing and Perfectly Wise

God not only wants but also perfectly *knows* precisely what is good for all creation—now and in the future. God "knows what you need before you ask Him" (Matt. 6:8 NASB) because God "knows all things" (1 John 3:20 NASB; cf. Ps. 147:5). God knows all present and future factors such that his plans and counsels are perfectly wise (cf. Isa. 46:10).[69] We can thus pray, "Your will be done" (Matt. 6:10 NASB), with full confidence that God knows what he is doing, having already taken into account all factors.

Sometimes, people pray as if God does not know everything about us already—a bit like a child in a game of hide-and-seek who hides behind a slim tree with his limbs sticking out on both sides but thinks you cannot see him. But nothing is hidden from God's sight (Heb. 4:13). Thus in a prayer for help, it is written that God "knows the secrets of the heart" (Ps. 44:21 NASB), and elsewhere the psalmist prays,

> LORD, You have searched me and known me.
> You know when I sit down and when I get up;
> You understand my thought from far away. . . .
> Even before there is a word on my tongue,
> Behold, LORD, You know it all. . . .
> And in Your book were written
> All the days that were ordained for me,
> When as yet there was not one of them. (Ps. 139:1–2, 4, 16 NASB; cf.
>   1 Kings 8:39; 1 Chron. 28:9; Jer. 20:12; Luke 16:15)

This is good news. God already knows my sins and flaws and loves me nonetheless, promising to forgive, cleanse, and heal me *if I am willing*. There is no point in putting up a facade with God. Hold nothing back, for God already knows you better than you know yourself—and loves you more than you can imagine. As Linda Zagzebski notes, God's omniscience holds "radical consequences for the way God hears prayers," since "God would know your

---

68. Marshall, "Jesus," 122–23.

69. Addressing the debate over God's foreknowledge is beyond this work's scope. For my view that Scripture teaches that God does possess exhaustive definite foreknowledge, see Peckham, *Divine Attributes*, 111–40.

prayers the way you know them, when you first have the desire, then possibly struggle for the words, and perhaps use the wrong words" (cf. Rom. 8:26–27).[70]

Before proceeding, I invite you to pause and prayerfully read Psalm 139.

God Is All-Powerful

Scripture presents the God to whom we pray as all-powerful (2 Cor. 6:18; Rev. 1:8; 11:17; 16:14; 19:15; 21:22; cf. Eph. 1:19).[71] Indeed, while praying to God, Jeremiah declares, "Nothing is too hard for" the "great and mighty God," who "showed signs and wonders in the land of Egypt, and to this day in Israel and among all humankind" (Jer. 32:17–20; cf. 32:27; Ps. 147:5; Job 42:2). Accordingly, David identifies God as "my rock and my fortress and my savior" and "my stronghold" (Ps. 18:2 NASB), writing further,

> In my distress I called upon the LORD,
> And cried to my God for help; He heard my voice from His temple,
> And my cry for help before Him came into His ears. . . .
> He saved me. (Ps. 18:6, 17 NASB)

Does omnipotence mean, however, that God can do anything whatsoever? Notably, Christ prays in Gethsemane, "Father! All things are possible for You" (Mark 14:36 NASB; cf. Luke 1:37; Matt. 19:26; Mark 9:23; 10:27). Yet Christ also prays in Gethsemane, "If it is possible, let this cup pass from Me" (Matt. 26:39 NASB; cf. Mark 14:35). In some sense, then, for God all things are possible, while in another sense some things might not be possible, even for God. Since God is all-powerful (see Rev. 1:8), anything *not* possible for God could not be due to any lack of divine power but must be due to some other factor(s). Regarding Christ's prayer in Gethsemane, it was possible (in and of itself) for the Father to save Christ from the cross, but it was not possible if God was to keep his promises to save sinners while remaining perfectly just (cf. Rom. 3:25–26). This is consistent with omnipotence since, as Richard Swinburne explains, omnipotence entails only the "power to do what is possible," that which involves no actual contradiction.[72]

---

70. Zagzebski, "Omnisubjectivity," 245.

71. For more on this, see Peckham, *Divine Attributes*, 141–74.

72. Swinburne, *Coherence of Theism*, 153. So also Brümmer, *What Are We Doing When We Pray?*, 34–35. As C. S. Lewis explains, "Omnipotence means power to do all that is intrinsically possible, not to do the intrinsically impossible. . . . It is no more possible for God than for the weakest of his creatures to carry out both of two mutually exclusive alternatives; not because his power meets an obstacle, but because nonsense remains nonsense even when we talk it about God." Lewis, *Problem of Pain*, 18.

Accordingly, Scripture identifies some things God *cannot* do. God "cannot deny Himself" (2 Tim. 2:13 NASB) and "cannot be tempted by evil" (James 1:13 NASB).[73] Further, God "cannot lie" (Titus 1:2 NASB; cf. Num. 23:19), and God's promises are unchangeable, for "it is impossible for God to lie" (Heb. 6:18 NASB; cf. Ps. 89:34). Thus while God is all-powerful such that he can do anything that can possibly be done, he also operates within some parameters due to commitments he has made. Since God never breaks his promises, his future action is (morally) limited to accord with whatever he promises.[74]

God grants creatures real agency in the world. As Bloesch writes, "Scripture makes clear that God has chosen to work out his purposes in cooperation with his children."[75] Thus, "God makes us covenant partners in the working out of his purposes in the world," though we are certainly "not equal partners"—not even close.[76] Speaking of prayer specifically, Bloesch affirms that "prayer cannot change God's purpose, but prayer can release it."[77] Yet "the way in which God implements his will is contingent on our prayers, and in this sense we can change God's will."[78] As Philip Yancey puts it, "From the very beginning God has relied on human partners" as "kingdom partners," and prayer itself is a significant part of such partnership with God.[79]

Though all-powerful, God does not use his power to make everyone do what he wants but grants creatures genuine agency in the world to do otherwise than he prefers (see chap. 3).[80] Baelz writes, "There is much that is contrary to God's positive will. He may permit, but he does not countenance or condone. Angels and men are in open rebellion against him."[81] Further, there is a "conflict between God and the powers of this world," but these are mere creatures while God "remains the sole creator. . . . Nevertheless, the conflict

---

73. God's "power does not violate his love. . . . The God of the Bible does not contradict his own nature." Bloesch, *Struggle of Prayer*, 30.

74. Brümmer writes, "Divine self-limitation is given in the fact that God chooses to establish a relation of loving fellowship with us humans," entailing that he grant creatures free will since "love can only be freely given and freely received," and this "necessarily entails that [God] limits his own power in relation to" humans (*What Are We Doing When We Pray?*, 36). God "will not act in ways which seriously violate the natural order and the free agency of human beings" (79). Likewise, see Baelz, *Does God Answer Prayer?*, 63.

75. Bloesch, *Struggle of Prayer*, 74.

76. Bloesch, *Struggle of Prayer*, 55. Likewise, see Crump, *Knocking on Heaven's Door*, 275.

77. Bloesch, *Struggle of Prayer*, 74, quoting Fosdick, *Meaning of Prayer*, 63.

78. Bloesch, *Struggle of Prayer*, 74.

79. Yancey, *Prayer*, 109.

80. For a survey of numerous models of divine providence in relation to prayer, see Tiessen, *Providence and Prayer*.

81. Baelz, *Prayer and Providence*, 81.

between the rule of God and the rule of Satan in the world is a real and ter-rible conflict" (discussed further later in this book).[82]

Yet God remains all-powerful and, as such, can respond to our prayers in ways beyond what we can imagine. This is crucial since, as Tom Morris writes, "unless [God] is sufficiently powerful, we cannot be confident that he will succeed" in keeping his promises.[83] Because God is all-powerful, we can be confident God that will bring about all he has promised. He is able to heal the brokenhearted, set captives free, make the lame to walk again, cause the blind to see, feed the hungry, restore justice, and raise the dead to eternal life.

Before proceeding, I invite you to pause and prayerfully read Psalm 18.

God Is Omnipresent

The God to whom we pray is also present with us wherever we may be.[84] As the psalmist prays,

> Where can I go from Your Spirit?
> Or where can I flee from Your presence?
> If I ascend to heaven, You are there;
> If I make my bed in Sheol, behold, You are there.
> If I take up the wings of the dawn,
> If I dwell in the remotest part of the sea,
> Even there Your hand will lead me,
> And Your right hand will take hold of me. (Ps. 139:7–10 NASB; cf.
>   Prov. 15:3)

God is somehow present to all creation; God fills heaven and earth (Jer. 23:24) and "upholds all things by the word of His power" (Heb. 1:3 NASB). God is thus

> our refuge and strength,
> A very ready help in trouble. (Ps. 46:1 NASB)

Accordingly, David proclaims,

> Even though I walk through the valley of the shadow of death,
> I fear no evil, for You are with me. (23:4 NASB)

---

82. Baelz, *Prayer and Providence*, 80.
83. T. Morris, *Our Idea of God*, 65–66.
84. For more on this, see Peckham, *Divine Attributes*, 73–110.

While God may be specially present in particular locations and "dwell on the earth," God is Spirit and cannot be contained in any particular location: "Even heaven and the highest heaven cannot contain [God]" (1 Kings 8:27; cf. Isa. 66:1; John 4:21–24; Acts 7:49). God remains transcendent even as he condescends to be with us personally.[85] However, "personal communion" involving God's special, personal presence is conditional upon (among other things) whether humans are "willing to grow in intimacy with God" (see chap. 5).[86]

Sin has ruptured the God-human relationship (cf. Isa. 59:2), requiring mediation. But God promises to be with his people in special ways. Indeed, God promises his covenant people,

> When you pass through the waters, I will be with you;
>   and through the rivers, they shall not overwhelm you;
> when you walk through fire you shall not be burned,
>   and the flame shall not consume you. (Isa. 43:2)

Further, Jesus promises his disciples, "I am with you always, to the end of the age" (Matt. 28:20; cf. 18:20).

God promises his covenant people, "The LORD your God is the One who is going with you. He will not desert you or abandon you" (Deut. 31:6 NASB; cf. 31:8). Again, God promises Joshua, "Just as I have been with Moses, I will be with you; I will not desert you nor abandon you. . . . Be strong and courageous! Do not be terrified nor dismayed, for the LORD your God is with you wherever you go" (Josh. 1:5, 9 NASB). Hebrews 13:5 also declares this promise to believers in Christ, teaching that the Lord "himself has said, 'I will never leave you or forsake you.'" God's people can thus

say with confidence,

> "The Lord is my helper;
>   I will not be afraid.
> What can anyone do to me?" (13:6)

Before proceeding, I invite you to pause and prayerfully read Psalm 23.

85. The "gods in Greek religion were frequently invoked to 'come'" because they were not "omnipresent and therefore must 'come' in order to be present and actually hear the supplicant" (Aune, "Prayer in the Greco-Roman World," 32). In contrast, the God of Scripture is omnipresent—"both intimately present within the world and utterly beyond, other, and different from it." Wright "Lord's Prayer," 132–33.

86. Reibsamen, "Divine Goodness," 140. See Eleonore Stump's discussion of how significant personal presence requires closeness and (conscious, intentional) shared attention. "God is always and everywhere in a position to share attention with any creature able and willing to share attention with God." Stump, *Wandering in the Darkness*, 117.

God Is the Faithful, Covenantal God

Since God's perfectly good character never changes and since he will never break his word, we can confidently call on God's promises.[87] God's promises are "unchangeable," for "it is impossible for God to lie" (Heb. 6:18 NASB; cf. Num. 23:19; Titus 1:2), for God "cannot deny Himself" (2 Tim. 2:13 NASB). As God proclaims relative to his covenant promises to David,

> I will not violate My covenant,
> Nor will I alter the utterance of My lips. (Ps. 89:34 NASB)[88]

Since God's promises are "unchangeable" (Heb. 6:18), when God makes a commitment (in a formal covenant or otherwise), God's future action is thereby morally bound in keeping with that commitment. As Scott Hahn puts it, "In the context of covenant, the justice of God does not consist merely in enforcing obedience to the law, but also in fidelity to his own sworn covenant commitments."[89] God is "the faithful God, who keeps His covenant and His lovingkindness to a thousandth generation with those who love Him and keep His commandments" (Deut. 7:9 NASB95; cf. Exod. 20:6; 1 Kings 8:23; Dan. 9:4).

As seen earlier, prayer might be minimally defined as calling on the name of the Lord, "calling on God to do what he has promised and to advance his agenda in the world."[90] Of course, keeping his promises is necessary relative to his character, and it has implications for his reputation. Thus God's covenant people prayed,

> Do not despise us, for the sake of Your own name;
> Do not disgrace the throne of Your glory.
> Remember and do not annul Your covenant with us. (Jer. 14:21 NASB;
>   cf. 14:7; 1 Chron. 17:21, 23–24)

God's people also pray "that his plans for [them] will come to fruition, and that his name will therefore be honoured."[91]

Before proceeding, I invite you to pause and prayerfully read Psalm 89.

87. For more on this, see Peckham, *Divine Attributes*, 175–208.
88. Scripture is filled with "God's keeping the promises he made" and "the characterization of God as a covenant-keeping God." Millar, *Calling on the Name of the Lord*, 61.
89. Hahn, *Kinship by Covenant*, 336. Michael Horton adds that God "has bound himself to us . . . by a free decision to enter into covenant with us" and that "God is not free to act contrary to such covenantal guarantees." Horton, *Lord and Servant*, 33.
90. Millar, *Calling on the Name of the Lord*, 228.
91. Millar, *Calling on the Name of the Lord*, 70.

Conclusion

The biblical stories of Hannah, Hagar, and many others manifest (among other things) that God cares about and hears the prayers of suffering people and that one person's prayer, however insignificant it might seem to onlookers at the time, can significantly change the course of history. Knowing that God cares and acts in response to prayers might give us confidence to pray like Hannah and Hagar and so many others, particularly when facing problems far beyond our means.

According to his great love and compassion, the God of Scripture hears and responds to prayer, inviting us to fervently bring our cares and needs to him—to call on the name of the Lord, which indirectly calls on God to act in accordance with his perfect goodness and wisdom, just as he has promised. It makes sense to pray to this God who hears and responds to prayer, who knows and wants what is best for all concerned, and who possesses the power to ultimately bring about what is preferable for all concerned.

Whatever else we say, at least this much is evident from Scripture:

1. God needs no information.
2. God needs no power.
3. God need not be convinced to do what is good.

Nevertheless,

1. God invites petitionary prayer.
2. God responds to petitionary prayer.
3. God is depicted as if petitionary prayer sometimes actually influences his action.

In this regard, the questions raised in chapter 1 remain, particularly relative to how it could be that prayer could influence the action of an omniscient, omnipotent, and omnibenevolent God. Would not such a God do what is preferable regardless of whether we pray, particularly when it comes to prayers regarding basic needs and horrendous evils? On the flip side, what about the problem of seemingly unanswered prayers? How are we to balance "the prospect of a divine response to our cries for help against the disappointment of heavenly silence in the face of our suffering?"[92] To address these and other questions, we'll turn next to Jesus's teachings on prayer.

---

92. Crump, *Knocking on Heaven's Door*, 14.

Before proceeding, I invite you to pause and read Hannah's prayer of joyful praise and thanksgiving in 1 Samuel 2, wherein she highlights God's knowledge, power, and good will (benevolence), particularly toward the underprivileged and downtrodden.

3

Your Kingdom Come, Your Will Be Done

The Lord's Prayer in the Midst of Cosmic Conflict

A man brought his demon-afflicted son to Jesus, saying, "I asked your disciples to cast it out, but they could not" (Mark 9:18). Hearing this, Jesus lamented, "You faithless generation, how much longer must I be with you? How much longer must I put up with you? Bring him to me" (9:19). When they brought the boy to Jesus, the evil spirit saw Jesus, and "immediately it convulsed the boy, and he fell on the ground and rolled about, foaming at the mouth" (9:20). The father pleaded with Jesus, "If you are able to do anything, help us! Have compassion on us!" (9:22).

"If you are able!" Jesus replied. "'All things can be done for the one who believes.' Immediately the father of the child cried out, 'I believe; help my unbelief!'" (Mark 9:23–24). Jesus did not tell the father, "Come back when you have more faith." This humble request was enough. Jesus "rebuked the unclean spirit" and cast it out (9:25).

Afterward, Christ's disciples asked why they could not cast out the demon. "This kind can come out only through prayer," Jesus replied (Mark 9:29). What is the meaning of this? Here, Jesus teaches that (at least in some cases) prayer is a requirement for casting out a demon, indicating some rules of engagement in the conflict between Christ's kingdom and the demonic domain of darkness (see chap. 4).

We will return to this strange case in Mark 9 a bit later. First, toward better understanding prayer in the context of this cosmic conflict, this chapter offers a theological reading of the Lord's Prayer, examining Christ's teachings therein about the nature of petitionary prayer relative to God's name, kingdom, will, daily bread, forgiveness, trials, and deliverance from the evil one—all of which are set in the midst of cosmic conflict.

The Lord's Prayer

"Lord, teach us to pray," a disciple asked Jesus (Luke 11:1). In response, Jesus delivered his most famous teaching on prayer, known as the Lord's Prayer.

> Pray, then, in this way:
>
>> Our Father in heaven,
>>> may your name be revered as holy.
>> May your kingdom come.
>> May your will be done
>>> on earth as it is in heaven.
>> Give us today our daily bread.
>> And forgive us our debts,
>>> as we also have forgiven our debtors.
>> And do not bring us to the time of trial,
>>> but rescue us from the evil one. (Matt. 6:9–13)

Our Father, Who Hears and Responds

Jesus first instructs his followers to address God as Father. Although God related to his covenant people as Father even before the incarnation, Christ's ministry opens the way for even closer relationship such that through Christ we can boldly approach the throne of grace (Heb. 4:16).

As I. Howard Marshall puts it, "It is generally agreed that the distinctiveness of Jesus' understanding of prayer is integrally and vitally related to his relationship to God as his Father, a relationship to which he admitted his disciples."[1] At the same time, Crump points out, referring to God as Father

1. Marshall, "Jesus," 127.

in this context involves *honoring* God: "To call God Father is to unconditionally pledge allegiance to his eternal kingship," including the honor due to his name (see, e.g., Mal. 1:6).[2]

This relates closely to the seven petitions that follow, petitions for

1. God's name to be hallowed—that is, for God's name to be made holy (sanctified) or vindicated.
2. God's kingdom to come.
3. God's will to be done.
4. God to provide "our daily bread."
5. God to forgive our sins, as we forgive others.
6. God to not bring us to the time of trial.
7. God to deliver us from "the evil one."

Here and elsewhere, the way Christ instructs his followers to pray indicates that petitionary prayers can actually influence divine action. In Luke's account, the Lord's Prayer is followed by Christ's parable of the friend at midnight (see chap. 5) and then this teaching: "Ask, and it will be given to you; search, and you will find; knock, and the door will be opened for you. For everyone who asks receives, and everyone who searches finds, and for everyone who knocks, the door will be opened" (Luke 11:9–10; see also 11:11–13). Crump comments, "It is very difficult to read the Lord's Prayer—not to mention the rest of Jesus' prayer teaching—as anything but misleading, even deceptive, if God's responses to petition are only 'apparent.'"[3]

This brings to the forefront many questions, such as, Why should we offer petitionary prayers to our loving Father, who already knows what is preferable for all concerned, desires what is preferable for all, and possesses all power to do as he wills? As Jesus teaches (just prior to the Lord's Prayer in Matthew), "Your Father knows what you need before you ask him" (Matt. 6:8). Whatever else prayers might accomplish, then, they do *not* inform God. So how could petitionary prayers influence God's actions?

Christ's teaching in the Lord's Prayer does not answer these questions directly, but it does shed significant light on the framework within which any answer must fit. To see this, in part, we turn to the seven petitions of this prayer.

2. Crump, *Knocking on Heaven's Door*, 100.
3. Crump, *Knocking on Heaven's Door*, 129. Bloesch adds that the Lord's Prayer "is essentially petitionary in nature." Bloesch, *Struggle of Prayer*, 72.

Praying That God's Name Be Vindicated

First, Christ prays to the Father, "May your name be revered as holy," which many translations render, "Hallowed be your name" (Matt. 6:9). As Crump explains, "Praying 'hallowed be your name' asks" for God's name to be sanctified "throughout all the people of the earth" (cf. Ezek. 38:16).[4] This, Andrew Lincoln adds, is to pray "that God's reputation be seen for what it is." The plea "glorify your name" elsewhere in Scripture is "equivalent to 'hallowed be your name,' the first petition of the Lord's Prayer."[5]

This involves more than mere recognition of God's holiness. It is a prayer for God's name to be honored and glorified throughout the world—for God to vindicate his name before all nations (countering the enemy's slander), reminiscent of God's promises, "I will sanctify my great name, which has been profaned among the nations," and "the nations shall know that I am the LORD" (Ezek. 36:23). As Carmen Joy Imes explains, "Yahweh's own reputation is at stake."[6] John Onwuchekwa adds, "To pray 'hallowed be your name' means being concerned more with the advancement of God's reputation in the world than your own. It's praying that God himself would protect his name from being defamed and obscured."[7]

As seen earlier, prayer itself might be defined in terms of calling on the name of the Lord, and Scripture links God's name with his character and reputation. Laszlo Gallusz explains that "God's name denotes his innermost being: the essence of his character and activity."[8] In this world, however, God's name has been dragged through the mud. Accordingly, throughout Scripture, questions about God's character repeatedly arise: Is God truly righteous and loving? If so, why is there so much injustice and evil?

Against such questions, Christ's work of atonement demonstrates God's righteousness and love, vindicating God's name (for the good of all). God "put forward" Christ "as a sacrifice of atonement . . . to demonstrate his righteousness" and "to demonstrate at the present time his own righteousness, so that he is righteous and he justifies the one who has the faith of Jesus" (Rom. 3:25–26). As Crump explains, "Ultimately, God alone is capable of sanctifying his name. . . . In asking the Father to sanctify his name, we make the fulfillment of God's salvific work through

---

4. Crump, *Knocking on Heaven's Door*, 116. So also Bloesch, *Struggle of Prayer*, 72.
5. Lincoln, "God's Name," 160.
6. Imes, *Bearing God's Name*, 123.
7. Onwuchekwa, *Prayer*, 46.
8. Gallusz, *Seven Prayers of Jesus*, 44.

Abraham, Israel, and finally through Christ our deepest, most passionate longing."[9]

This petition for God's name to be sanctified/vindicated closely relates to the two petitions that follow (for God's kingdom to come and for God's will to be done). Many scholars believe that the phrase "on earth as it is in heaven" applies to all three petitions. The vindication of God's name (reputation) hinges on the fulfillment of God's promises, which are inseparable from the coming of God's kingdom and the fulfillment of God's will. These three petitions thus all amount to praying for the same overarching aim. To pray that God's name is made holy or vindicated is to pray that God's kingdom come and God's will be done. In Crump's words, "Just as praying for the kingdom to come is to ask for the sanctification of God's name, so too is it asking for the Father's 'will to be done.'"[10]

God's name cannot be sanctified or vindicated, in full, until evil is eradicated. As long as injustice and evil remain, the question of God's justice will remain—voiced throughout Scripture in many cries: "How long?" (Ps. 13:1). "Shall not the Judge of all the earth do what is just?" (Gen. 18:25). Why, then, does injustice remain? Why do the filth and sewage of sin and evil continue to fill God's creation?

Praying That God's Kingdom Come

This brings us to the second petition: "May your kingdom come" (Matt. 6:10). For this petition to make sense, it must be that (in some sense) the kingdom of God has *not yet* come—that is, God's kingdom has not yet fully arrived. "God's kingdom is still coming."[11]

Yet isn't the whole world *already* God's kingdom? Why is there any need for God's kingdom to "come" in the first place? This makes sense if we remember that this world is fallen, embroiled in the cosmic rebellion against God's rule that began in heaven (more on this later). Adam and Eve's fall (see Gen. 3) effectively gave this world over to the serpent's enemy rule (Luke 4:6; John 12:31; 14:30; 16:11; cf. Gen. 1:28). In Sandra L. Richter's words, "God's

9. Crump, *Knocking on Heaven's Door*, 118. Crump also recognizes (with many other scholars) a "twofold understanding of hallowing the name" that includes some role of humans "as long as the priority of the Father's work remains central" (120). Likewise, see Gallusz, *Seven Prayers of Jesus*, 44–45; cf. Isa. 29:23.

10. Crump, *Knocking on Heaven's Door*, 126; cf. Cullmann, *Prayer in the New Testament*, 50–51; Origen, *Prayer* 26.2 (p. 88).

11. Crump, *Knocking on Heaven's Door*, 300. So also Baelz, *Prayer and Providence*, 80. Wright adds that "the evil empire will be defeated." Wright, *Lord and His Prayer*, 14.

original intent was sabotaged by humanity, stolen by the Enemy."[12] This required another ruler—Christ—to come (foretold in Gen. 3:15) and reclaim
on behalf of humanity the rulership that Adam and Eve forfeited, while also
restoring the fullness of God's rule.

But didn't Christ indicate that God's kingdom was already here (cf. Luke
17:21)? In one sense, God's kingdom already came with Christ's first coming.
In many other ways, however, God's kingdom has not yet come in fullness:
"We do not yet see all things subjected to him" (Heb. 2:8 NASB). Even after
Christ's first coming, "the whole world lies under the power of the evil one"
(1 John 5:19)—the devil, whom Christ called "the ruler of this world" (John
12:31; 14:30; 16:11).[13]

The devil's "domain of darkness" remains, from which Christ rescues his
followers, "transfer[ring] us to the kingdom of His beloved Son" (Col. 1:13
NASB; cf. Acts 26:18). Crump explains: "The life and ministry of Jesus carved
out a beachhead for the kingdom's arrival, and the history of the church
advanced God's offensive against the realm of darkness, but there are many
battles yet to be fought."[14] Thus "we pray between the times."[15]

Scholars have long spoken of this tension regarding God's kingdom as
"already, but not yet" (see, e.g., Heb. 2:8–9).[16] Christians await the return of
Christ—the true King—and the full establishment of his kingdom of perfect
peace and love, in which there is no suffering, injustice, or evil. As Richter puts
it, "Satan knows it is just a matter of time. Yet we still await the kingdom's
consummation, the *not yet*."[17] In the end, the domain of darkness will be uprooted, and the following proclamation will be fully fulfilled: "The kingdom
of the world has become the kingdom of our Lord and of his Messiah, and
he will reign forever and ever" (Rev. 11:15). As Richard Bauckham writes,
"In his earthly witness," via the cross, Christ achieved "the decisive victory
which must now be carried through in the events that lead to the complete
and uncontested realization of God's kingdom."[18]

Further, Bauckham writes, "Revelation 4 portrays God's sovereign rule
in heaven. Revelation 5 onward, however, presents God's sovereign rule as
implemented on earth through the victory of the Lamb and those who follow

12. Richter, *Epic of Eden*, 106.

13. Joachim Jeremias comments, "These petitions are a cry from" a "world which is enslaved
under the rule of evil and in which Christ and Antichrist are locked in conflict." Jeremias,
Lord's Prayer, 22.

14. Crump, *Knocking on Heaven's Door*, 300.

15. Crump, *Knocking on Heaven's Door*, 299.

16. See, e.g., Beale, *New Testament Biblical Theology*; Ladd, *Presence of the Future*.

17. Richter, *Epic of Eden*, 219.

18. Bauckham, "Prayer in the Book of Revelation," 255.

him." Here, "the prayers of the Lamb's people . . . play an important role in the coming of God's kingdom." Bauckham further explains, "The prayers of the saints," represented by the incense in Revelation 5:8, "are for the coming of God's kingdom—indeed, prayers which could be summed up in the words of the Lord's Prayer: 'Your kingdom come, your will be done, on earth as it is in heaven' (Matt. 6:10)."[19] Further, "the offering of the prayers of the saints in [Rev.] 8:3–5 results in the eschatological theophany-and-judgment of the world."[20] Millar adds, "There is no question that God is listening to these prayers, the prayers of the saints. Their prayers for judgment and salvation will be answered."[21] Eventually, the "saints' prayers for the coming of the kingdom are answered. God's kingdom comes when God manifests his holiness in such a way that all evil must perish before him."[22]

Accordingly, "the evil of this world is such that to pray for the coming of God's kingdom is to pray also for God's judgment" against evil and oppression (cf. Ps. 73).[23] And God's final judgment against evil itself is necessary for the vindication of God's name. As Crump puts it, "Ultimately, God's name is sanctified when his kingdom definitively arrives on earth, an arrival that means God judges this wicked world with righteousness and that he completes the salvation of his chosen people."[24]

Ultimately, Bauckham concludes, the "petition in the Lord's Prayer and the church's prayer" for the return of Christ "are equivalent (cf. Rev. 11:15). It is to complete God's purposes for the world—that is, to bring God's rule to its ultimate perfection—that Jesus is coming."[25] As such, "prayer for" Christ's second coming (e.g., Rev. 22:20) "encompasses and completes all other prayers" because it "asks for everything—for all that God purposes for and promises to his whole creation in the end."[26]

Temporarily, God's "rule is not yet fully exercised," for the "world is 'in the power of the evil one.'"[27] The domain of the devil and his minions has not yet been uprooted, but the devil's "time is short" (Rev. 12:12). The petition

---

19. Bauckham, "Prayer in the Book of Revelation," 255.

20. Bauckham, "Prayer in the Book of Revelation," 257. These prayers represented by the incense, Ranko Stefanovic adds, "are evidently the prayers for justice and judgment of the saints." Stefanovic, *Revelation of Jesus Christ*, 292.

21. Millar, *Calling on the Name of the Lord*, 228.

22. Bauckham, "Prayer in the Book of Revelation," 257.

23. Bauckham, "Prayer in the Book of Revelation," 257.

24. Crump, *Knocking on Heaven's Door*, 120.

25. Bauckham, "Prayer in the Book of Revelation," 269.

26. Bauckham, "Prayer in the Book of Revelation," 270.

27. Baelz, *Prayer and Providence*, 116, 117. Nijay K. Gupta likewise notes, "There is a sense in the Gospels that the earth had come under the rulership of Satan *de facto* (cf. John 12:31)." Gupta, *Lord's Prayer*, 82–83.

for God's kingdom to come, then, looks forward to the final eradication of evil. Millar comments, "To pray for the·'kingdom' to come is the ultimate extension of 'calling on the name of Yahweh.'"[28]

Praying That God's Will Be Done

Evil will not be eradicated until God's kingdom comes in fullness, coinciding with God's will being done on earth as it is in heaven. Thus, the petition "May your will be done, on earth as it is in heaven" directly follows the petition for God's kingdom to come (Matt. 6:10). Even as sincerely praying for the coming of God's kingdom entails submitting to Christ's lordship, sincerely praying for the Father's will to be done entails submission to the Father's will.

The petition for God's will to be done on earth as it is in heaven indicates that God's will is *not* always done but that somehow prayer can make a difference. Crump writes, "When Jesus tells us to pray for God's will to be done, he makes it plain that God's will is not being done completely and that his kingdom is not now fully established."[29] Unlike in heaven, God's will is often *not done* on earth. Currently, there is a rupture between the two realms that awaits final restoration such that at the "heart" of this petition "lies a prayer for the appropriate integration of heaven and earth," which "was already accomplished in Jesus himself" but which is not yet fully established on earth.[30]

How could this be? The all-powerful God could make everyone always do precisely what he wants. But does he? Does God always get what he wants? According to Scripture, the answer is no. Many things happen otherwise than God prefers. Indeed, Scripture includes many examples of humans willing otherwise than God desires.

For example, God invited his covenant people to return to him and be saved, but they "were not willing" and "said, 'No'" (Isa. 30:15–16 NASB).[31] They were "a rebellious people, faithless children, children who will not hear the instruction of the LORD" and who "reject" God's word (30:9, 12; cf. 1:2; 30:1; 63:10; Rom. 10:21). Nevertheless, God "longs to be gracious" to them and "waits on high to have compassion" such that "He will certainly be gracious to [them] at the sound of [their] cry; when He hears it, He will answer" (Isa. 30:18–19 NASB).

28. Millar, *Calling on the Name of the Lord*, 173.
29. Crump, *Knocking on Heaven's Door*, 300.
30. Wright, "Lord's Prayer," 142. So also Gallusz, *Seven Prayers of Jesus*, 46.
31. "The Holy One had extended his arms to them with a gentle word of strength (28:12), but they refused." Oswalt, *Isaiah 1–39*, 554.

Likewise, God laments that the people of Israel "are not willing to listen to [him]," for they have "a stubborn heart" (Ezek. 3:7). Indeed, God "called" to his people, but "they would not listen." They "refused to pay attention, and turned a stubborn shoulder and plugged their ears from hearing" and "made their hearts as hard as a diamond" (Zech. 7:11–13 NASB). Elsewhere, in response to repeated rebellion, God laments,

> My people did not listen to my voice;
>> Israel would not submit to me.
> So I gave them over to their stubborn hearts,
>> to follow their own counsels.
> O that my people would listen to me,
>> that Israel would walk in my ways!
> Then I would quickly subdue their enemies
>> and turn my hand against their foes. (Ps. 81:11–14, cf. 78:22;
>> Isa. 65:12; 66:4; Jer. 19:5)

Likewise, Jesus himself cried out, "Jerusalem, Jerusalem, the city that kills the prophets and stones those who are sent to it! How often have I desired [thelō] to gather your children together as a hen gathers her brood under her wings, and you were not willing [thelō]!" (Matt. 23:37; cf. Luke 13:34; John 5:40).[32] Further, Luke 7:30 reports that "the Pharisees and the experts in the law . . . rejected God's purpose [boulē] for themselves" (cf. Mark 7:24).[33]

Here and elsewhere, Scripture repeatedly teaches that humans often rebel against God and reject God's will, demonstrating that they possess what I call consequential freedom—the God-given power to act and bring about events, including actions contrary to what God prefers.[34] As I understand it (and explain in more detail elsewhere), God has committed himself to granting this kind of freedom because such freedom is a necessary prerequisite of love.[35] As Simundson puts it, "It appears that even God . . . is hindered by the stubborn, willful disobedience of human beings."[36]

32. Craig Blomberg comments, "God never imposes His love by overriding human will." Blomberg, *Matthew*, 350.

33. Joseph Fitzmyer writes, "The Pharisees and lawyers thwarted God's design on their behalf" (Fitzmyer, *Luke I–IX*, 670). This assumes "that the *boulē* of God can be hindered." Ritz, "βουλή," 224.

34. Consequential freedom requires that creatures possess freedom to act within some nonarbitrary parameters in a context where relatively predictable effects follow from intentional causes (requiring some regularity that we might call laws of nature or lawlike regularity—i.e., "nomic regularity"). See Peckham, *Divine Attributes*, 169–70; cf. Plantinga, *Where the Conflict Really Lies*, 103.

35. See Peckham, *Theodicy of Love*, 27–54; Peckham, *Love of God*, 89–116; see also Loke, *Evil, Sin, and Christian Theism*, 50–58.

36. Simundson, *Where Is God?*, 71.

Yet Scripture also teaches that God "accomplishes all things according to his counsel and will" (Eph. 1:11).[37] How can both be true? Both can be true if we recognize a distinction between God's *ideal* will and God's *remedial* will. God's ideal will is what God actually prefers, what would take place if everyone always did what God wishes. God's remedial will, conversely, is what God wills after taking into account all other factors, including creatures' free decisions, which often depart from God's ideal will and thus bring about evil. God's remedial will consists of God's plan to counteract (and thus remedy) the evil in the world and eventually restore all things to perfect harmony (his ideal will).[38]

Think of a cooking competition in which chefs are required to use some particular ingredients but are free to add other ingredients to make whatever meal they choose. The resulting meal includes ingredients the chef did not choose. In somewhat similar fashion, because God consistently grants consequential freedom to creatures, God's remedial will includes many "ingredients" of history that God does not want, which result from creatures' bad decisions. God, however, adds his own good decisions and works to bring about the best outcomes that can be brought about without breaking his commitment to the kind of freedom necessary for love.

If Ephesians 1:11 refers to God's remedial will, inclusive of creatures' free decisions contrary to God's ideal will, then it can be true both that God's ideal will is sometimes unfulfilled (see, e.g., Luke 7:30) and that God ultimately "accomplishes all things according to his counsel and will" (Eph. 1:11). Given this understanding, God accomplishes all things according to his remedial will, but many things happen that God does not prefer because creatures often will otherwise than God ideally wills. Thus, in many cases God takes what appears to be a circuitous route to his purposes, working around many unseen factors and impediments resulting from creatures' bad decisions.[39]

---

37. The word translated as "predestined" (*proorizō*) in Eph. 1 (and elsewhere) combines the Greek terms *pro* ("before") and *horizō* ("to decide or mark out boundaries or limits"), which together mean "to decide beforehand." One could decide something beforehand unilaterally (as determinists think God does), or one could decide something beforehand in a way that takes into account the free decisions of others. For a case that Scripture consistently teaches the latter, see Peckham, *Divine Attributes*, 141–74. As A. Chadwick Thornhill explains, "The term simply means to decide beforehand, and does not contain any inherently deterministic value within the term itself." Thornhill, *Chosen People*, 219.

38. God does some things directly, without the input of others (via direct agency/strong actualization), and other things indirectly, in a way "that depends upon the free decisions" and input of others (indirect agency/weak actualization). See Plantinga, *Nature of Necessity*, 173.

39. Yancey writes, "Think of the centuries that passed between the disruption caused by Adam and the reconciliation brought by Jesus: centuries that included Abraham's waiting for

As a Portuguese proverb puts it, "God writes straight, but with crooked lines."[40]

Many years ago, my then one-year-old son needed a test for a life-threatening condition. Of course, even though the test would involve some pain, my wife and I chose to have him tested. I did not want him to experience pain—that was against my ideal will. Had there been any way for me to ascertain his health without causing him any pain, I would have chosen it. But no such avenue was available to me. In a somewhat similar fashion, sometimes a direct avenue to God's purposes is not available even to God, because of the real consequences of creaturely decisions.[41]

Though God is all-powerful, some courses of action are not morally open to him. Any avenues that would involve God acting contrary to his perfectly good character (e.g., requiring him to lie or break a promise) are not morally available to him. He "cannot deny himself" (2 Tim. 2:13), and his promises are unchangeable, for "it is impossible that God would prove false" (Heb. 6:18; cf. Num. 23:19; Ps. 89:34; Titus 1:2; James 1:13). Thus while God is all-powerful, he operates within some parameters (or "rules"); his actions are (morally) limited in accordance with any promises or commitments he has made.

Some things God otherwise prefers to bring about, then, are morally unavailable to him, given his promises or commitments (relative to creaturely freedom granted for the sake of love and otherwise). But what if (in some cases) petitionary prayer might change whether a given avenue is (morally) available to God? Suppose God wants to bring you some good, but God's action to do so would impinge on your free will. In such a case, your prayer for God's will to be done might grant God permission to do so, morally opening up an avenue that was otherwise (morally) unavailable to him (given his commitment to creaturely free will).

This provides one example of how prayer for God's (ideal) will to be done might influence God's action in a way consistent with God's perfect knowledge (omniscience), good will (omnibenevolence), and power (omnipotence). Such prayer would not inform God (consistent with omniscience), influence God to desire some good he did not already desire (consistent with omnibenevolence), or increase God's power (consistent with omnipotence). Instead, such prayer

---

a child, the Israelites' waiting for liberation, the prophets' waiting for Messiah. Biblical history tells a meandering, zigzag tale of doglegs and detours." Yancey, *Prayer*, 238.

40. Quoted in Cullmann, *Salvation in History*, 125.

41. Dietrich Bonhoeffer writes, "We know that God and the devil are locked in combat over the world and that the devil has a word to say even at death. In the face of death we cannot say in a fatalistic way, 'It is God's will'; we must add the opposite: 'It is not God's will.'" Bonhoeffer, *Selected Writings*, 127.

would open up an avenue for divine action that was otherwise not morally available to him. As Marshall writes, if "we freely yield ourselves to God," then "he is able to accomplish his will through us and our prayers. In a very real sense, therefore, the accomplishment of God's will in the world does depend on our prayers."[42]

Yet, as seen earlier, the petition "Your will be done" in the Lord's Prayer corresponds to praying for God's kingdom to come in fullness and God's name to thus be vindicated.[43] Praying for this broad outcome, however, involves many things that are not within the purview of the free will of the one praying. As briefly noted in chapter 1, many proposals have been set forth to account for how prayer might make a difference for things beyond the purview of our free will. However, such proposals struggle to account for prayers regarding basic needs (such as "daily bread") and great evils.

In this regard, Scripture consistently tells of celestial creatures (demons) hard at work in opposition to God's ideal will. They are part of an overarching cosmic conflict that is highlighted in the last petition of the Lord's Prayer. As Simundson puts it, alongside "human behavior contrary to God's will, . . . the Bible also recognizes the presence in the world of satanic forces that counteract God's will."[44] To this we will return. First, however, we turn to the fourth petition.

Praying That God Give Us Our Daily Bread

Some commentators believe that the petition "Give us today our daily bread" (Matt. 6:11) is not requesting earthly needs, such as food, but metaphorically referring to transcendent, eschatological goods and is thus another way of praying for the ultimate coming of God's kingdom.[45] If so, it complements what we've seen regarding the first three petitions.[46]

---

42. Marshall, *Epistles of John*, 245.

43. This prayer effectively "contains all possible petitions; we cannot conceive of a prayer not already contained in it." Weil, *Waiting for God*, 226.

44. Simundson, *Where Is God?*, 81.

45. For example, the Neoplatonist mystic Evagrius Ponticus writes, "You will not be able to pray purely if you are all involved with material affairs and agitated with unremitting concerns. For prayer is the rejection of concerns" (Evagrius, *Praktikos*, 66). Further, "in the writings of Origen, Cyprian, Augustine and other influential church figures, 'daily bread' is viewed as a reference to the Eucharistic bread or the Word of God" (Gallusz, *Seven Prayers of Jesus*, 49). See also Augustine, *Sermon on the Mount* 2.7 (pp. 41–42); Cyprian, *Lord's Prayer* 18 (pp. 46–47); Origen, *Prayer* 27.2 (pp. 92–93).

46. "Almost every Christian commentator down to the present day has understood the focus of the first three petitions to be 'heavenly,' or directed towards godly concerns like making

Many other commentators believe, however, that "on balance a more literal reading of the prayer is to be preferred," which can be understood as praying for daily sustenance.[47] Notably, Psalm 145 juxtaposes recognition that God gives to all "their food in due season . . . , satisfying the desire of every living thing" (vv. 15–16), with recognition that petitionary prayer makes a difference to God, saying,

> The LORD is near to all who call on him,
>   to all who call on him in truth.
> He fulfills the desire of all who fear him;
>   he also hears their cry and saves them. (vv. 18–19)

Perhaps the petition for daily bread could be understood both as prayer for daily sustenance and, as such, implicit prayer for the full coming of God's kingdom, in which there will no longer be any danger of lacking such sustenance.[48] Whether understood this way or not, if this petition is rightly understood as involving a request for daily sustenance here on earth, then it is a petition for basic needs, raising difficult questions relative to the influence aim of petitionary prayer. As David Basinger argues, "With respect to our basic needs [such as food, health, and shelter] it is never justifiable for God to withhold that which he can and would like to give us until petitioned."[49] If Basinger is right, then believing that petitionary prayer might influence God to bring about a basic need he otherwise would not have brought about would be inconsistent with affirming God's perfect goodness.

If God is entirely good and all-powerful, would he not provide basic needs regardless of whether anyone asks him to do so? The Lord's Prayer does not spell out the answer to this conundrum, but understanding that this world is fallen and lies in the power of the evil one (see the final petition) provides a helpful framework. Scarcity of resources for sustenance and other daily sufferings and hardships of life are not what God ideally wills for us but products of alien evil in this world, bondage from which "the whole creation groans" to be freed (Rom. 8:22 NASB; cf. Gen. 3). And this prayer indicates that somehow petitionary prayers can make a difference in our sin-stricken world.

God's name holy, seeking God's kingdom and obeying God's will." Hammerling, "Exegetical History," 93.

47. Millar, *Calling on the Name of the Lord*, 173. So also Fisher, *Prayer in the New Testament*, 76; Gallusz, *Seven Prayers of Jesus*, 48–51.

48. See, e.g., Wright, *Lord and His Prayer*, 27–30.

49. Basinger, "God Does Not Necessarily Respond," 267.

When God's kingdom is finally fully established,

> [God] will wipe every tear from their eyes.
> Death will be no more;
>   mourning and crying and pain will be no more,
> for the first things have passed away. (Rev. 21:4)

For now, however, we live in a corrupted world filled with evil and injustice of all kinds—a world in which God's (ideal) will is often not accomplished and, among other things, people often go hungry and other basic needs go unmet. In this context, Christ instructs his followers to pray for "daily bread." This calls for a framework that can make sense of petitionary prayers aimed at influencing God to bring about things like basic needs, a framework to which we will return in coming chapters.

Praying That God Forgive Us as We Forgive Others

Alongside prayer for "daily bread," Christ instructs his followers to pray, "Forgive us our debts, as we also have forgiven our debtors" (Matt. 6:12). If the former is understood as prayer for daily sustenance, the two petitions together encompass prayer for physical sustenance to keep on living and prayer for spiritual rescue—forgiveness of sins—a requirement for eternal life in God's coming kingdom.

The petition for God to forgive our sins, as we forgive others, indicates again that how we act might affect how God may act toward us.[50] Somehow, whether we ask God to forgive us and whether we forgive others affects God's forgiveness of our sins. To genuinely ask forgiveness involves repenting of any actions that were in keeping with the enemy's selfish kingdom of darkness, which is diametrically opposed to God's kingdom of unselfish love. True repentance includes the desire to turn from selfishness to unselfish love in devotion to others. Thus genuinely praying to be forgiven as we forgive others requires not only that we repent of our own sins but also that we intend to treat others according to the principles of unselfish love. In short, genuinely asking for forgiveness requires allegiance to God's kingdom of unselfish love and, correspondingly, the intention to abandon the devil's (anti-love) kingdom of selfishness.

---

50. Though, Wright points out, "this *isn't* saying that we do this in order to *earn* God's forgiveness. It's a further statement of our loyalty to Jesus and his Kingdom." Wright, *Lord and His Prayer*, 39–40, emphasis original.

Elsewhere Jesus tells a parable in which a servant owes his master a massive debt of ten thousand talents (roughly six billion dollars today), which would take the average day laborer about two hundred thousand years to earn—a debt he could not possibly repay. So, the servant pleaded, "Have patience with me, and I will pay you everything" (Matt. 18:26). In response, the master "felt compassion, and he released him and forgave him the debt" (18:27 NASB). Afterward, this same servant encountered a fellow servant who owed him one hundred denarii (one hundred days' wages) and "seizing him by the throat he said, 'Pay what you owe'" (18:28). That fellow servant pleaded with him as the first servant pleaded with his master, "Have patience with me and I will pay you" (18:29). But the man refused and had him thrown into prison. When the master heard of this, he rebuked the wicked servant and reinstated his massive debt because he refused to show his fellow servant even a fraction of the compassion and forgiveness he had been shown. Jesus explained, "So my heavenly Father will also do to every one of you, if you do not forgive your brother or sister from your heart" (18:35).

Likewise, just after the Lord's Prayer in Matthew, Jesus comments, "If you forgive others their trespasses, your heavenly Father will also forgive you, but if you do not forgive others, neither will your Father forgive your trespasses" (Matt. 6:14–15).[51] Further, Jesus teaches in Mark 11:25, "Whenever you stand praying, forgive, if you have anything against anyone, so that your Father in heaven may also forgive you your trespasses."

These instances provide further examples of petitionary prayers that align with what God already prefers to bring about (cf. 2 Pet. 3:9) but that nevertheless can (at least in some cases) make a difference relative to divine action.

Praying That God Not Bring Us to the Time of Trial

The final two petitions frame this prayer in the context of a struggle with evil. Before counseling his followers to pray for God to "rescue [them] from the evil one," Jesus teaches his followers to pray that God will not lead them into temptation or bring them to the time of trial (Matt. 6:13; cf. 26:41; Mark 14:38; Luke 22:40). The term translated as "temptation" or "trial" (*peirasmos*) might also be translated as "test," referring to something proven by trial.

On the one hand, Scripture teaches that God tempts no one: "No one, when tempted [*peirazō*], should say, 'I am being tempted [*peirazō*] by God,' for God cannot be tempted by evil and he himself tempts [*peirazō*] no one"

---

51. "God will not forgive those whose lives are not changed by the grace that they experience." Marshall, "Jesus," 127.

(James 1:13). On the other hand, in many instances God is said to put people to the test. For example, "By faith Abraham, when put to the test [*peirazō*], offered up Isaac" (Heb. 11:17; cf. Deut. 8:2).

These passages are not contradictory if one understands that the term "tempt" or "test" has different connotations depending on context. God sometimes puts people to the test (to prove them by trial, often by indirect agency) but not in a way aimed at actually causing them to fall.[52] The latter aim is the goal of the devil, whom Scripture identifies as the arch-deceiver and arch-tempter (1 Thess. 3:5; Rev. 12:9; cf. Job 1–2; Matt. 4:1–11; 1 Cor. 7:5). Satan seeks to entrap or ensnare (1 Tim. 3:7; 2 Tim. 2:26; cf. 1 Pet. 5:8), but God always provides a way of escape: "No testing [*peirasmos*] has overtaken you that is not common to everyone. God is faithful, and he will not let you be tested [*peirazō*] beyond your strength, but with the testing [*peirasmos*] he will also provide the way out so that you may be able to endure it" (1 Cor. 10:13; cf. 2 Pet. 2:9).[53]

The Spirit led Jesus into the wilderness to be tempted, but the devil was the one who tempted Jesus. Thus, Justo González writes, "Since it is the Spirit, God, who leads Jesus to the place where he is to be tempted, we may well pray today that this may not happen to us, that God will not lead us into temptation, as we say in the Lord's Prayer. But at the same time it is the devil who then tempts us, and therefore we must also ask God that when we are tested we have God's strength and protection."[54]

In this life we all face temptation, and James encourages, "Blessed is any-one who endures temptation. Such a one has stood the test and will receive the crown of life that the Lord has promised to those who love him" (James 1:12). One can endure temptation, however, only through the power of God available through prayer. In a sense, "all of life is a test—or a series of tests by which our character is both shown and formed."[55] This is so because we live in a fallen world embroiled in a cosmic conflict, wherein the arch-tempter, "your adversary, the devil, prowls around like a roaring lion, seeking someone to devour" (1 Pet. 5:8 NASB). In this context, prayer for God not to bring us to a time of trial asks God to direct our steps away from the ground on which

---

52. "To say 'lead us not into temptation' does not, of course, mean that God himself causes people to be tempted" but asks for "escape from the great tribulation" and that we would not "be led into temptation that we will be unable to bear." Wright, *Lord and His Prayer*, 54–55.

53. Wright comments, "Despite the apostle's firm conviction regarding the sovereignty of God, such 'testings' come from 'the Satan.'" Wright, "Lord's Prayer," 146.

54. González, *Teach Us to Pray*, 133. R. T. France adds that this references the "need for God's help and protection in the face of the devil's desire to lead astray." France, *Gospel of Matthew*, 251.

55. González, *Teach Us to Pray*, 134.

we are most susceptible to the devil's schemes (cf. Eph. 6 [see chaps. 4–5 in this book]; Rev. 3:10). This leads us into the final petition of this prayer.

Praying That God Rescue Us from the Evil One

The last petition, "rescue us from the evil one" (Matt. 6:13), further frames this prayer in the context of struggling with evil, identifying "the evil one" as an antagonist from whom humans need deliverance.[56] First John 5:19 identifies this "evil one" as the devil, teaching that "the whole world lies under the power of the evil one."[57]

Elsewhere, Jesus tells a parable about a landowner "who sowed good seed in his field, but while everybody was asleep an enemy came and sowed weeds among the wheat and then went away" (Matt. 13:24–25). When the pernicious weeds became apparent, the landowner's servants asked, "Master, did you not sow good seed in your field? Where, then, did these weeds come from?" (13:27). Likewise, many ask today, If God created the world good, why is there evil?

"An enemy has done this," the landowner answered. The servants then replied, "Then do you want us to go and gather them?" (Matt. 13:28). In other words, why not eliminate evil immediately? "No," the landowner replied, "for in gathering the weeds you would uproot the wheat along with them. Let both of them grow together until the harvest" (13:29–30). Later, Jesus explains that he is the landowner and the devil is the enemy who sowed the weeds (13:37–39).

In this parable, Jesus sets forth a cosmic conflict framework, depicting evil in this world as the work of God's enemy.[58] Prematurely uprooting evil (the

---

56. Some translations render this "deliver us from evil," but France explains that the translation of *tou ponērou* as "the Evil One" is "perhaps more likely in view of the preceding reference to πειρασμός, an experience which has already been associated with the devil in 4:1, 3. Cf. 13:19, 38 for Matthew's use of ὁ πονηρός for the devil in a similar context. The traditional rendering 'Deliver us from evil' would come to the same thing, but with a less personal understanding of the conflict" (France, *Gospel of Matthew*, 231n14; on the ambiguity of *tou ponērou*, see 193n55). Whether the phrase is rendered "evil" or "the evil one" is, for Gallusz, "of no great importance, since the two concepts show close affinity." Gallusz, *Seven Prayers of Jesus*, 56.

57. Wright adds that this "Evil One [Satan] . . . is a potent force, opposed to God's good creation. . . . But Jesus' victory over evil is also real and powerful." Wright, *Lord and His Prayer*, 53.

58. As W. D. Davies and Dale C. Allison Jr. comment, this manifests "a wider problem, namely, the cosmic struggle between God and Satan" (Davies and Allison, *Matthew 8–18*, 431). Grant R. Osborne adds, "In this world the war between good and evil cannot be avoided, and there is no middle ground. One either belongs to the kingdom or the powers of evil." Osborne, *Matthew*, 533.

weeds) would result in massive collateral damage to the good (the wheat).[59] If evil is to finally be eradicated and collateral damage minimized, the enemy must be allowed to work—temporarily, the wheat and tares must be allowed to grow together.[60]

This cosmic conflict framework appears throughout Scripture.[61] Elsewhere, Jesus repeatedly calls Satan "the ruler of this world" (John 12:31; 14:30; 16:11) and speaks of Satan's "kingdom" (Matt. 12:26), the "domain of darkness" that opposes Christ's kingdom (Col. 1:13 NASB; cf. Acts 26:18). Paul thus urges Christians to put on the armor of God, "to stand against the wiles of the devil, for our struggle is not against blood and flesh but against the rulers, against the authorities, against the cosmic powers of this present darkness, against the spiritual forces of evil in the heavenly places" (Eph. 6:11–12; see also Acts 26:18; Rom. 8:38; 2 Cor. 10:3–5; Eph. 1:19–21; Col. 2:15; 1 Pet. 3:22). In C. S. Lewis's words, "This universe is at war"; it is not "a war between independent powers" but a "rebellion," and "we are living in a part of the universe occupied by the rebel."[62] Kevin Vanhoozer adds, "The world is now under the dominion of the powers of darkness," and, as such, "the world resists and rejects God's authoritative rule."[63]

Yet how could there be such a conflict? No creature could oppose the all-powerful God in terms of sheer power. The conflict must be of another kind. A conflict between God and creatures is possible only if God has committed himself to grant creatures freedom to work within some limits such that his kingdom can be opposed.

Scripture portrays it as a conflict over the devil's slanderous allegations against God's name (character)—an epistemic conflict wherein the devil claims that God is an oppressive, malevolent ruler. Thus the serpent claimed that God was lying to Eve in order to withhold some good from her (see Gen. 3:4). Here and elsewhere, Satan wages a war of disinformation as "the father of lies" (John 8:44) and "the deceiver of the whole world," the arch-slanderer of God's name and "the accuser of our brothers and sisters . . . , who accuses

---

59. John Nolland comments that the tares "are to be removed with as much urgency as is consistent with the protection of all the wheat" (Nolland, *Gospel of Matthew*, 546). Yet, he continues, eventually "what has been sown by Satan is to be rooted out and destroyed" (547).

60. For more on this and cosmic conflict theodicy more broadly, see Peckham, *Theodicy of Love*; cf. Loke, *Evil, Sin, and Christian Theism*, 65–70 ; Faro, *Demystifying Evil*, 119–81.

61. On the cosmic conflict motif throughout Scripture, see Peckham, *Theodicy of Love*, 55–138. See also Arnold, *Powers of Darkness*; Boyd, *God at War*; Cole, *Against the Darkness*; Heiser, *Unseen Realm*; Noll, *Angels of Light*; Page, *Powers of Evil*.

62. Lewis, *Mere Christianity*, 45.

63. Vanhoozer, *Faith Speaking Understanding*, 100.

them day and night before our God" (Rev. 12:9–10; cf. 2 Cor. 11:3).[64] G. K. Beale writes, "After the Fall, the serpent and his agents do on a worldwide scale what [the serpent] began in the garden," putting forth "claims" that "slander the character of God."[65]

Satan's strategy against God's will and kingdom is to slander God's name before the heavenly court (see chap. 4). Paul thus identifies the devil as "the god of this world," who "has blinded the minds of the unbelievers, to keep them from seeing clearly the light of the gospel of the glory of Christ" (2 Cor. 4:4).

Imagine someone alleged that your significant other had been cheating on you repeatedly. Even merely thinking that this report *might* be true would damage your relationship. Unless proven false, trust would be undermined, without which the relationship would eventually suffer irreparable harm. Along somewhat similar lines, the devil's slander against God's name threatens the harmony of the entire universe, which is grounded in a relationship that requires trust. If creatures believe that God might be a tyrant, as Satan alleges, the trust that undergirds love would be broken. Such allegations must be defeated, not for God's sake but for the good of the entire universe.

As long as God grants creatures epistemic freedom (the freedom to believe or disbelieve him), however, such allegations cannot be defeated by sheer power. How much power would a king need to exercise to defeat allegations that he is a tyrant? No display or exercise of power or force, however great, could defeat slanderous allegations against one's character. Indeed, a ruler exercising power to silence accusations would only make the allegations worse.

A conflict over allegations against God's character, then, can be settled not by sheer power but only by a demonstration of God's character that proves the allegations false, which God provides through Christ's work, demonstrating his perfect righteousness and love (see Rom. 3:25–26; 5:8).

This cosmic conflict motif in Scripture can be summarized in three points:

1. Scripture depicts an ongoing conflict between God's kingdom and the demonic realm—the devil and his minions (e.g., Matt. 12:24–29; 13:24–30, 37–39; Eph. 6:11–12; Rev. 12:7–10; cf. Matt. 25:41), celestial creatures who were created perfectly good but rebelled against God's government and thus became fallen angels (2 Pet. 2:4; Jude 6; cf. Col. 1:16–17).

2. Rather than a conflict of sheer power, which would be impossible given God's omnipotence, this is an epistemic conflict over the devil's allegations against God's name (character)—a cosmic courtroom drama in

---

64. The Greek term translated as "devil" (*diabolos*) basically means "slanderer." See Bietenhard, "Satan," 468.

65. Beale, *Book of Revelation*, 656.

which God provides conclusive demonstration to defeat the devil's allegations and eventually eradicate evil (e.g., Job 1–2; Zech. 3:1–3; Matt. 13:27–29; John 8:44; Rom. 3:3–8, 25–26; Heb. 2:14–15; 1 John 3:8; Jude 9; Rev. 12:9–11; 13:4–6; cf. Gen. 3:1–6).

3. In the meantime, the devil, whom Jesus himself identifies as "the ruler of this world" (John 12:31; 14:30; 16:11; cf. 2 Cor. 4:4), exercises temporary rulership in this world, but his domain is quickly approaching its end (Rev. 12:12).[66]

The Lord's Prayer is set in this context of cosmic conflict between the "coming" kingdom of God and the present kingdom/domain of "the evil one," the devil. Temporarily, "the whole world lies under the power of the evil one" (1 John 5:19) such that God's kingdom has not yet come in fullness and God's will is often *not* done in this world, calling God's name (character) into question. This last petition, for God to "rescue us from the evil one" (Matt. 6:13), then, is inextricably linked to the first three petitions for God's name to be sanctified, God's kingdom to come, and God's will to be done on earth as it is in heaven. Since the devil's kingdom continually works against God's will and slanders his name, granting these three petitions requires the defeat of the devil and corresponding demonstration of God's goodness and love—vindicating God's name for the good of the entire universe.

Thus, each of the first three petitions in the Lord's Prayer corresponds to the defeat of Satan and his kingdom through the work of Christ, who "was revealed for this purpose: to destroy the works of the devil" (1 John 3:8; cf. Gen. 3:15), to "destroy the one who has the power of death, that is, the devil" (Heb. 2:14), and "to set us free from the present evil age" (Gal. 1:4; cf. Col. 1:13).

In this regard, Scripture identifies the devil as

1. the slanderer of God's name and the accuser of God and his people in the heavenly court (Rev. 12:10; cf. 13:6; Job 1–2; Zech. 3:1–2; Jude 9).

---

66. Some question the plausibility of cosmic conflict. Yet Alvin Plantinga notes that "plausibility, of course, is in the ear of the hearer, and even in our enlightened times there are plenty of people who think both that there are non-human free creatures and that they are responsible for some of the evil that the world contains" (Plantinga, "Self-Profile," 42). Most people throughout history have believed in supernatural agencies (see Boyd's survey in *God at War*, 18). And a cosmic conflict perspective has been held by the vast majority of Christians throughout the ages and was part of "the common core of patristic theodicy" (Gavrilyuk, "Overview of Patristic Theodicies," 6). Further, Loke rightly emphasizes, "the existence of demons is part of a Christian worldview which is well-supported evidentially with regards to its foundational claims." Loke, *Evil, Sin, and Christian Theism*, 70; cf. Acolatse, *Powers, Principalities, and the Spirit*, 204.

2. the temporary "ruler of this world" (John 12:31; 14:30; 16:11), whose kingdom opposes God's kingdom (cf. Matt. 12:24–29; Luke 4:5–6; Acts 26:18; 2 Cor. 4:4; Eph. 2:2; 1 John 5:19; Rev. 12–13).

3. the deceiver of the whole world from the beginning (Rev. 12:9; Matt. 4:3; cf. John 8:44; Acts 5:3; 2 Cor. 11:3; 1 John 3:8; Rev. 2:10), whose schemes (cf. Eph. 6:11) are ever working against *the will of God*.

In direct contrast, Jesus

1. supremely demonstrated God's perfect righteousness and love via the cross (Rom. 3:25–26; 5:8), defeating the devil's slanderous allegations and vindicating God's name in the heavenly court (Rev. 12:10–11).

2. will finally destroy the kingdom of the devil—who "knows that his time is short" (Rev. 12:12; cf. Rom. 16:20)—establishing God's kingdom over which Christ "will reign forever and ever" (Rev. 11:15).

3. "came into the world, to testify to the truth" (John 18:37), always acting in perfect accordance with the Father's will (cf. 8:29).

At every turn, then, Christ's work undoes the work of the devil against God's name, kingdom, and will—finally delivering the cosmos from the evil one's rule.[67] This does not take place all at once, however. God's kingdom is *already* established through Christ's victory at the cross but *not yet* established in full (cf. Heb. 2:8). The victory comes in two stages. First, via the cross Christ legally defeats Satan's slanderous allegations in the heavenly court, demonstrating God's perfect righteousness and love as both just and justifier (Rom. 3:25–26; 5:8) such that "the accuser of our brothers and sisters" is "thrown down" (Rev. 12:10–11; cf. 1 Cor. 2:6–8; Col. 2:15; 1 Pet. 3:22).[68] Second, Christ will eventually execute final judgment against the domain of darkness and will eradicate evil.

As Beale explains, the "legal defeat of Satan is part of the essence of the inaugurated kingdom that has 'now come about.' The actual execution of the devil and his hordes," however, "comes at the consummation of history (Rev. 18; 19:20–21; 20:10–15)."[69] Accordingly, Adela Yarbro Collins writes that the devil is "defeated

---

67. Brian Han Gregg writes, "The conflict between God and Satan is clearly a central feature of Jesus' teaching and ministry." Gregg, *What Does the Bible Say about Suffering?*, 66.

68. Beale comments that the "death and resurrection of Christ have banished the devil from this privilege formerly granted him by God, because Christ's death" has paid the "penalty" of sin and "vindicated God's character (cf. Rom. 3:25–26)" (Beale, *Book of Revelation*, 659). Stefanovic adds, "This 'casting down' of Satan from heaven suggests his excommunication from the heavenly council." Stefanovic, *Revelation of Jesus Christ*, 396.

69. Beale, *Book of Revelation*, 659.

in heaven, but he [still] reigns on earth."[70] Yet there is good news. Christ's victory is already assured, and the devil "knows that his time is short!" (Rev. 12:12).

Conclusion

"This kind can come out only through prayer" (Mark 9:29). At first glance, these words of Jesus raise more questions than answers. Here, Jesus asserts that the demon afflicting the boy could be cast out only "through prayer."[71] In the Lord's Prayer and many other cases, Jesus likewise indicates that "our petitions can make a real difference to God."[72] But why would prayer make any difference (cf. Matt. 17:14–21)? Was it not already God's will to cast out the demon? How could it be that this demon could be cast out only through prayer? What is going on here?

For this to make sense, there must be far more to the story than initially meets the eye. This is an instance of what I call rules of engagement in the cosmic conflict. At least in some cases, prayer is a requirement for casting out a demon, indicating that there are some "rules" involved in the conflict between Christ's kingdom and the demonic domain of darkness (chap. 4 addresses this further).

This chapter has briefly laid out how the Lord's Prayer is filled with petitions related to God's vindication of his name and ultimate victory over evil, which make sense when one understands the cosmic conflict as an epistemic conflict over the devil's slanderous allegations against God's name. Specifically, the first three petitions of the Lord's Prayer (for God's name to be sanctified/vindicated, for God's kingdom to come, and for God's will to be done) each amount to praying for the same overarching aim: God's complete triumph over evil on the last day. We pray these and other petitions because things are not now as they ought to be. Things have gone terribly wrong in this world, but God has promised that eventually he will set all things right again.

If we understand petitionary prayer against this background of cosmic conflict over God's character—a background that pervades Scripture but that is often foreign to Western ways of thinking—then we may further see a way forward relative to the influence aim problem of petitionary prayer and the problem of seemingly unanswered prayer. Chapter 4 addresses this further, focusing on how petitionary prayer is linked to rules of engagement in the cosmic conflict.

---

70. A. Collins, *Apocalypse*, 141.

71. Some translations (e.g., KJV, NKJV) render this "by prayer and fasting," but the general scholarly consensus is that the phrase "and fasting" is not original to this text (see Metzger, *Text of the New Testament*, 203). Given the limited scope of this book, I leave aside questions about fasting for discussion elsewhere.

72. Crump, *Knocking on Heaven's Door*, 300.

4

Wrestling with God and Angels

Rules of Engagement and the Problem of Petitionary Prayer

Long ago, he swindled his brother, Esau, taking their father's birthright blessing by deceit. Decades later, Jacob would be face to face with his brother again, who likely sought revenge. Afraid for his life and that of his family, Jacob prayed fervently, asking God to deliver him on the basis of his covenant promises (Gen. 32:9–12).

Jacob thought he was alone, but someone was with him. After declaring, "Jacob was left alone," Genesis 32:24 adds, "and a man wrestled with him until daybreak." This "man" is not introduced but breaks into the story seemingly out of nowhere. Genesis says little about this mysterious figure, but the narrative cryptically reveals this was no mere man, for this "man" told him, "You have striven with God and with humans and have prevailed." Afterward, Jacob recognized that he had wrestled with God, saying, "I have seen God face to face, yet my life is preserved" (32:28, 30). Thus, Hosea 12:3–4 declares, Jacob "strove with God. He strove with the angel and prevailed."

Yet how could anyone wrestle with God, let alone "prevail"? While wrestling, Jacob requested a blessing, refusing to let the "man" go unless he received such a blessing. Amazingly, the "man" did bless Jacob. In order for

Jacob to strive with God and yet "prevail" in this way, however, something far more than meets the eye must be going on here. In this and many other instances throughout Scripture (some of which we saw earlier), we see that humans might "wrestle" with God (usually figuratively) and that such wrestling might make a difference to what occurs. How could this be?

This chapter returns to the problems of petitionary prayer introduced in chapter 1, particularly the problem of how human petitions could influence God's action, given that God (as omniscient, omnibenevolent, and omnipotent) already knows what is preferable in any circumstance, already desires what is preferable (all things considered), and already possesses the sheer power to do what is preferable. In what follows—through a close reading of the striking cases related in Daniel 9–10, Revelation 12–13, and Job 1–2, alongside other biblical material that culminates with an examination of Christ's amazing prayers in Gethsemane—we will see how a model that considers both rules of engagement and cosmic conflict appears in Scripture and how it might help answer this and other questions regarding the "workings" of petitionary prayer.

Daniel: Fervently Praying in Exile

Daniel was deeply troubled. He'd received a message from God concerning "a great conflict," and he mourned, fasted, and fervently prayed for understanding for *three full weeks* (Dan. 10:1–2). In exile, under the rule of foreign empires, Daniel was faithful to God through many trials, including refusing the king's decree that all should pray to him and no one else and continuing to pray to the true God just as he always had, even when facing death in a lion's den (6:7–10).

Now, decades later, Daniel fasted and prayed, with no apparent response for three weeks. Have you ever felt as if God is silent in response to your prayers? If so, you are not alone. Even the most faithful of God's servants, like Daniel, have been left with seemingly unanswered prayers—including Jesus himself.

Previously, Daniel had also prayed fervently and waited for God's answer. When Daniel and his three friends faced death unless someone could tell Nebuchadnezzar, the king of Babylon, the contents and meaning of his dream, Daniel and his three friends fervently prayed. God heard their prayers, and "the mystery was revealed to Daniel in a vision of the night" (Dan. 2:19).

Intercessory Prayer in Exile

In Daniel 9, Daniel fervently prays again, offering a stirring intercessory prayer for his people, Israel, with whom he languished in exile. Concerned about whether the exile would end after seventy years, as Jeremiah foretold (Jer. 25:11–12; 29:10), Daniel sought "an answer by prayer and supplication with fasting and sackcloth and ashes." He praises God's covenant-keeping character of love and confessed, "We have sinned and done wrong, acted wickedly and rebelled, turning aside from your commandments and ordinances" (Dan. 9:3–5). After further confessing Israel's "treachery" and their failure to repent and "entreat the favor of the LORD," Daniel proclaims, "The LORD our God is right in all that he has done, for we have disobeyed his voice" (9:6–10, 13–14).

Though a model of faithfulness, Daniel includes himself among the *unfaithful* of God's people, saying again, "We have sinned, we have done wickedly" (Dan. 9:15). He then humbly pleads,

> O Lord, in view of all your righteous acts, let your anger and wrath, we pray, turn away from your city Jerusalem. . . . Our God, listen to the prayer of your servant and to his supplication, and for your own sake, Lord, let your face shine upon your desolated sanctuary. Incline your ear, O my God, and hear. Open your eyes and look at our desolation and the city that bears your name. We do not present our supplication before you on the ground of our righteousness but on the ground of your great mercies. O Lord, hear; O Lord, forgive; O Lord, listen and act and do not delay! For your own sake, O my God, because your city and your people bear your name! (9:16–19)[1]

This model intercessory prayer includes thanksgiving and praise, confession and repentance, and *humble* petition that recognizes one's unworthiness such that any answer is a result not of merit or requirement but of God's freely bestowed mercy, demonstrating his character (name). Therein, Daniel prays specifically on the basis of God's name (character), asking God to hear and act in response. Here, again, Imes notes, "Daniel . . . knows that Yahweh's reputation is at stake."[2]

Then, while Daniel was still "speaking in prayer," the angel Gabriel came to Daniel "in swift flight" and said, "Daniel, I have now come out to give you wisdom and understanding. At the beginning of your supplications a word went out, and I have come to declare it, for you are greatly beloved" (Dan. 9:21–23). Then, in response to Daniel's prayer about the prophesied seventy years of exile, Gabriel delivered an amazing prophecy concerning seventy weeks of years (foretelling the Messiah's coming nearly five hundred years

---

1. Daniel's pleas, "incline your ear" and "open your eyes," are idiomatic expressions calling God to hear and respond.

2. Imes, *Bearing God's Name*, 134.

later). The ultimate solution to Israel's plight, however, would take far longer than seventy years.

Prayer amid the "Great Conflict"

Years later, the story continues with Daniel still distressed over whether the exile would end after seventy years, as Jeremiah foretold, or whether the vision of Daniel 9 meant that the exile would be far longer. Then "a word was revealed to Daniel" that "concerned a great conflict" (Dan. 10:1).

As seen earlier, Daniel mourned, fasted, and fervently prayed for twenty-one days. Then Daniel saw a "man" of great splendor and "heard the sounds of his words" and "fell into a deep sleep" with his "face to the ground" (Dan. 10:4–9 NASB). Then "a hand touched" Daniel and roused him, and a heavenly being said, "Daniel, greatly beloved, . . . I have now been sent to you. . . . Do not fear, Daniel, for from the first day that you set your mind to gain understanding and to humble yourself before your God, your words have been heard, and I have come because of your words. But the prince of the kingdom of Persia opposed me twenty-one days" (10:10–13).

Notice that "from the first day" Daniel began fervently praying, which was three weeks earlier, his "words" were "heard," but a mysterious "prince" of Persia opposed and withstood God's angel for "twenty-one days," until Michael the prince "came to help" (Dan. 10:13; cf. 10:20–11:1). Most biblical scholars believe that this "prince" of Persia was a celestial ruler, an example of the common Old Testament motif of celestial rulers behind earthly rulers (the "gods" of the nations), which the New Testament often refers to in terms of principalities and powers (e.g., Eph. 6:12).[3] Tremper Longman III comments that this is "a clear case of spiritual conflict"; even "though the divine realm heard and began responding immediately to Daniel's prayers three weeks earlier, there was a delay because of a conflict, an obstacle in the form of the 'prince of the Persian kingdom' (v. 13)."[4] Gleason L. Archer likewise

---

3. Timothy G. Gombis comments that this "prince" refers to one of the "archangelic rulers who was given authority over the nation to order its national life and mediate the rule of God over that nation" (Gombis, *Drama of Ephesians*, 37). Many church fathers held this view of demonic rulers behind earthly rulers and applied it to Dan. 10 (see, e.g., Origen, *On First Principles* 3.3.2; Theodoret of Cyrus, *Commentary on Daniel* 10.13; Jerome, *Commentary on Daniel* 10.13, 10.20; John Cassian, *Conferences* 8.13.2 [in Stevenson and Glerup, *Ezekiel, Daniel*, 276–78, 280]; see, likewise, J. Collins, *Daniel*, 374; Goldingay, *Daniel*, 292; Hartman and Di Lella, *Daniel*, 282; Longman, *Daniel*, 250; S. Miller, *Daniel*, 285; Smith-Christopher, "Daniel," 137). Yet, even if one believes that this "prince" is merely a human ruler, Dan. 10 nevertheless portrays God's angel working within apparent parameters that delay him from answering Daniel's prayer.

4. Longman, *Daniel*, 249.

comments, "The powers of evil apparently have the capacity to bring about hindrances and delays, even of the delivery of the answers to believers whose requests God is minded to answer."[5]

But how could an angel sent by God be opposed and withstood for three full weeks by this "prince"? As all-powerful (e.g., Jer. 32:17; Matt. 19:26; Rev. 19:6), God possessed the sheer power to respond to Daniel immediately. Yet Scripture here depicts a genuine conflict between celestial forces of light and darkness. For such a conflict to take place, the enemy must be allotted some genuine power and jurisdiction, which is governed by some rules of engagement known to both sides in the conflict, rules that God does not capriciously remove, change, or contravene.

Commenting on this episode, Philip Yancey concludes that the question "'Why do bad things happen?' gets little systematic treatment in the Bible because Bible writers believed they knew why bad things happen: we live on a planet ruled by powers intent on blocking and perverting the will of God. . . . Of course bad things happen! On a planet ruled by the Evil One we should expect to see violence, deception, disease, and all manner of opposition to the reign of God."[6]

Revelation: Demonic Rulers and Rules of Engagement

Scripture identifies the "gods of the nations," central to so many Old Testament stories, as demons in disguise—celestial "rulers" who stood behind earthly rulers, seeking to usurp worship and destroy God's people.[7] Deuteronomy 32:16–17 identifies the "gods" that the nations worshiped as "demons," saying of Israel's fall into idolatry, "They sacrificed to demons, not God, to deities they had never known" (cf. Ps. 106:37). Likewise, Paul explains, when the gentiles sacrifice to idols, "they sacrifice to demons and

---

5. Archer, "Daniel," 124.

6. Yancey, *Prayer*, 117–18.

7. John Goldingay explains that behind the idols were "so-called deities [that] do indeed exist, but they do not count as God, and they are subject to God's judgment," yet these "supernatural centers of power" can "deliberately oppose Yhwh's purpose" (Goldingay, *Israel's Faith*, 43). Notably, God "executed judgment on" Egypt's "gods" (Num. 33:4; cf. Exod. 12:12; 18:10–11), and many other instances refer to the "gods" of the nations (cf. Exod. 12:12; 15:11; 23:32; Deut. 4:19–20; 6:14; 32:8, 17; Josh. 24:15; Judg. 6:10; 10:6; 11:24; 1 Sam. 5:7; 6:5; 1 Kings 11:5, 33; 18:24; 20:23, 28; 2 Kings 17:29–31; 18:33–35; 19:12–13; 1 Chron. 5:25; 2 Chron. 25:14–15, 20; 28:23; 32:13–17; Ezra 1:2–3; Isa. 36:18–20; 37:12; Jer. 5:19; 46:25; 50:2; 51:44; Zeph. 2:11). Scripture emphasizes, however, that YHWH is utterly superior (1 Chron. 16:25–26; 2 Chron. 2:5–6); there is "none like" YHWH "among the gods" (Ps. 86:8; cf. 77:13; 95:3; 96:4–5; 97:9; 135:5; 2 Chron. 6:14). See Block, *Gods of the Nations*.

not to God" (1 Cor. 10:20; cf. 2 Cor. 6:14–15; Rev. 9:20), and he identifies Satan as "the god of this world," who "has blinded the minds of the un-believers" (2 Cor. 4:4).[8] Elsewhere, Paul refers to these demons who mas-querade as "gods" as "rulers and authorities in the heavenly places" (Eph. 3:10), the "cosmic powers of this present darkness," the "spiritual forces of evil in the heavenly places" (6:12; cf. Rom. 8:38; 1 Cor. 4:9; Col. 2:15; 1 Pet. 1:12).[9]

Another major example of this motif of celestial rulers behind earthly rulers appears in Revelation 12–13, which identifies Satan as the "great dragon," the "ancient serpent" who is the "deceiver of the whole world" (Rev. 12:9) and the "ruler" behind earthly kingdoms that oppose God's rule and oppress God's people through the ages (13:2–5). Specifically, Revelation 13 records a vision of a beast from the sea, representing successive empires that oppose God's kingdom and persecute God's people over the ages; and "the dragon [Satan] gave it his power and his throne and great authority" such that "the whole earth followed the beast" and "worshiped the dragon, for he had given his authority to the beast, and they worshiped the beast" (13:2–4; see also 13:5–7; 17:13–14). As G. K. Beale and many other scholars point out, this sea beast is a composite beast (including parts of the four beasts of Dan. 7), representing the successive oppressive empires of Babylon, Persia, Greece, Rome, and beyond (Rev. 13:1–2; echoing Dan. 7:4–8) such that the "dragon in Revelation 12 was seen as the ultimate force behind the earthly kingdoms of the world" that oppose God's kingdom and persecute his people.[10]

According to these and many other biblical passages, the devil possesses significant *rulership* in this world. While tempting Jesus in the wilderness, Satan declared that rulership of this world "has been given over to me, and I give it to anyone I please" (Luke 4:6; cf. John 19:11). Further, as seen earlier, Jesus himself repeatedly called Satan "the ruler of this world" (John 12:31; 14:30; 16:11), and, according to 1 John 5:19, "the whole world lies under the power of the evil one." Being a mere creature, however, the devil could never oppose the all-powerful God in terms of sheer power. The devil, then, must have been granted some significant power and jurisdiction over this world within some specified limits or rules of engagement, which (given that God has agreed to them) *morally* limit God's action.

---

8. Gordon D. Fee comments that Israel "had rejected God their Rock for beings who were no gods, indeed who were demons" (Deut. 32:17)." Fee, *First Epistle to the Corinthians*, 472.

9. See Arnold, *Powers of Darkness*; Gombis, *Drama of Ephesians*, 36–37; Noll, *Angels of Light*, 81.

10. Beale, *Book of Revelation*, 683.

These rules of engagement may be defined as parameters to which God has committed himself in relationship to creatures, for the good of all, including commitments God has made regarding the extent of rulership and jurisdiction temporarily afforded to the rebels in the cosmic conflict.[11] Such rules of engagement appear in many places throughout Scripture.

Here are just a few New Testament examples:

1. Christ repeatedly identifies Satan as the "ruler of this world" (John 12:31; 14:30; 16:11; cf. 2 Cor. 4:4), indicating that the devil possesses some genuine rulership over this world, which Christ came to reclaim (Heb. 2:14; 1 John 3:8; cf. Eph. 6:11–12).

2. Scripture repeatedly refers to the devil's kingdom or domain of darkness (e.g., Acts 26:18; Col. 1:13; Rev. 12:9–11; cf. Matt. 12:24) and teaches that "the whole world lies under the power of the evil one" (1 John 5:19).

3. Satan claimed, while tempting Christ, that "all the kingdoms of the world" and all "this authority and their glory . . . has been given over to me, and I give it to anyone I please" (Luke 4:5–6; cf. John 19:11).

4. The devil's temptation of Christ was prearranged according to some parameters: the Holy Spirit drove Jesus into the wilderness to fast for forty days and be tempted (Matt. 4:1–2; Luke 4:1–2).[12] Then, after "the devil had finished every test, he departed from him until an opportune time" (Luke 4:13; cf. 22:53; Gen. 3). After the temptations, "suddenly angels came and waited on him" (Matt. 4:11).

5. In Matthew 8:29, when demons encountered Jesus, they shouted, "What have you to do with us, Son of God? Have you come here to torment us before the time?" This indicates a specified time of future judgment as part of some parameters known to both parties.

6. Christ "could do no deed of power" in his hometown (Nazareth), "except that he laid his hands on a few sick people and cured them" (Mark 6:5). Christ's power to work miracles there was restrained "because of their unbelief" (Matt. 13:58; cf. Mark 6:6).

7. In the case of the demon that the disciples could not cast out from a boy, Jesus explained, "This kind can come out only through prayer" (Mark 9:29), thus indicating some "rules" restricting demonic activity, linked to prayer and faith (see Matt. 17:20).

---

11. For more on these "rules of engagement," see Peckham, *Theodicy of Love*, 87–118. See also Faro, *Demystifying Evil*, 158–81; Loke, *Evil, Sin, and Christian Theism*, 193–94.

12. Notably, absent some rules prohibiting it, there would be nothing wrong with Christ turning stones to bread.

8. Shortly before his crucifixion, Jesus told Peter and the other disciples, "Satan has *demanded* to sift all of you like wheat, but I have prayed for you that your own faith may not fail" (Luke 22:31–32; cf. 1 Pet. 5:8; Jude 9).[13]

9. Paul reports that he "wanted to" visit the Thessalonians "again and again—but Satan blocked our way" (1 Thess. 2:18; cf. Rev. 2:10).

10. Revelation 12:12 states that "the devil has come down to" earth "with great wrath because he knows that his time is short!" This indicates not only that Satan has significant power in this world but also that Satan's domain is temporary and limited (cf. the time period of "forty-two months" given in Rev. 13:5).

Such rules of engagement also appear in the strange case of Job, wherein such "rules" are a topic of heavenly court proceedings. Before we turn to Job, however, it must be emphasized that Satan and his demonic minions are mere creatures (Col. 1:16). Their reign is both limited and temporary, the eradication of which is assured through the victory of Christ, who "has rescued us from the power of darkness and transferred us into the kingdom of his beloved Son" (Col. 1:13; cf. Luke 4:6; Gal. 1:4; Eph. 5:5; see also Dan. 2:44–45) and "disarmed the rulers and authorities and made a public example of them, triumphing over them in it" (Col. 2:15; cf. 1 Cor. 2:6–8; 1 Pet. 3:22; 1 John 4:4).[14]

In this conflict, there are not only demonic forces that oppose God's kingdom but hosts of angels who serve the all-powerful God operating behind the scenes. For example, when the prophet Elisha received a report of a great enemy army surrounding the city of Dothan, he replied, "Do not be afraid, for there are more with us than there are with them." He then prayed, "O LORD, please open his eyes that he may see," and then his attendant "saw; the mountain was full of hordes and chariots of fire all around Elisha" (2 Kings 6:16–17). Though otherwise unseen, an angelic host surrounded them, far greater than the forces of darkness arrayed against them.

The cosmic conflict is not a conflict between equals. Not even close. God remains the sovereign, all-powerful one, whose final victory is assured, no matter how dark things might appear.

---

13. The term translated as "demand" (*exaiteō*) "includes the idea that the one making the request has a right to do so." Here, "both God and Satan seem compelled to operate within certain constraints." Gregg, *What Does the Bible Say about Suffering?*, 64.

14. "Although defeated by the cross-resurrection event, the powers are still active (Eph. 6:12; Gal. 4:9)," but "will finally be destroyed at the consummation (1 Cor. 15:24)." Arnold, "Principalities and Powers," 467.

The Strange Case of Job

Crying Out to God in the Midst of Great Suffering

"I cry out to you, and you do not answer me; I stand, and you merely look at me. You have turned cruel to me; with the might of your hand you persecute me" (Job 30:20–21).[15] In the midst of great suffering, Job cried these words to God. In various calamities in quick succession, Job had lost his many oxen, donkeys, sheep, and camels. Worse still, he lost many servants. And, worst of all, a house fell on Job's seven sons and three daughters, killing them (1:13–19). Shortly afterward, Job himself was afflicted with loathsome sores from head to foot (2:7).

At first, Job's three friends—Eliphaz, Bildad, and Zophar—did well, mourning with him in silence for one week (Job 2:11–13). But then they attempted to explain what had occurred, claiming that such calamities must be God's righteous judgment against Job's sins. Their misguided attempts at explanation only multiplied Job's agony. Even if they had been right in their explanations (they were not), their attempted explanations at the time ran contrary to empathy. As Laura W. Ekstrom puts it, philosophical explanations of suffering "are often the last thing a suffering person needs to hear" amid their distress.[16] There is a time and place for such discussion, approached humbly and carefully.[17] But that time is not when someone is in the throes of loss and agony. Perhaps this is (in part) why God did not immediately reply to Job's queries. Maybe Job wouldn't have been prepared to receive God's replies earlier. I do not know, but if God himself was slow to speak (for whatever reasons), it seems to me that we should be far slower to speak in such circumstances—remaining silent relative to explanations and instead grieving with those who grieve (see chap. 6).

Angered by their false claims, God told Job's friends, "My servant Job shall pray for you, and I will accept his prayer not to deal with you according to your folly, for you have not spoken of me what is right" (Job 42:8). Job's friends did not know what they were talking about. Contrary to the theology of retribution voiced by Job's friends, suffering is *not* a sign of unfaithfulness.[18] Throughout Scripture, many wicked persons prosper, while

---

15. On complaining to God in prayer, see Crisp, "Prayer as Complaint."

16. Ekstrom, "Christian Theodicy," 266. See also Wolterstorff, *Lament for a Son*, 34.

17. As Ante Jerončić explains, in many cases an "answer" to suffering cannot "be existentially absorbed" and is thus unhelpful. Yet "acknowledging the structural limitation of 'answers' does not mean demonizing them or rendering them useless; it simply means allocating them their proper role, be it apologetic or otherwise," while rejecting the "unhelpful dichotomy" of "abstract versus practical theodicy." Jerončić, "Eye of Charity," 50.

18. "As the story of Job makes especially clear, in biblical context the pain and suffering that comes our way may have its origin in the fallen freedom of created beings and need not be interpreted as divine judgment or punishment." Westphal, "Prayer as the Posture," 23–24.

many righteous persons suffer undeservedly (see, e.g., Eccles. 7:15; 8:14; Jer. 5:28; 12:1; Luke 13:1–5)—Jesus himself being the ultimate example. If you have suffered undeservedly, you are not alone. Because God loves us so, even as a loving mother compassionately suffers when her children suffer, God suffers with us whenever we suffer (cf. Isa. 49:15; 63:9), while also working to eradicate suffering once and for all.[19]

Job's prayers seemed to go unheard and unanswered, and Job interpreted God's silence as divine cruelty (Job 30:21; cf. 3:1; 9:24).[20] Yet God did not abandon Job. God was not silent in heaven and eventually answered Job from out of a whirlwind:

> Who is this that darkens counsel by words without knowledge? . . .
> Where were you when I laid the foundation of the earth?
>   Tell me, if you have understanding. . . .
> Have the gates of death been revealed to you,
>   or have you seen the gates of deep darkness?
> Have you comprehended the expanse of the earth?
>   Declare, if you know all this. (38:2, 4, 17–18; cf. 11:7; 38:4, 33; 40:2, 8)

"I have uttered what I did not understand," Job replied, "things too wonderful for me that I did not know," and "[I] repent in dust and ashes" (Job 42:3, 6; cf. 40:3–5). Like Job, we should recognize how little we know about the things of God, whose thoughts and ways are far higher than ours (Isa. 55:8–9; cf. Rom. 11:33–34). As C. S. Lewis puts it, human "conjectures as to why God does what He does are probably of no more value than my dog's ideas of what I am up to when I sit and read."[21]

Perhaps you've also cried out in prayer or with groanings too deep for words and were met with apparent silence. If so, be assured that God is not absent. God is active, even when we do not see what he is doing behind the scenes in this cosmic conflict. In Job's case, far more was going on than met the eye.

Rules of Engagement in the Heavenly Court

"Now there was a day when the sons of God came to present themselves before the LORD, and Satan also came among them" (Job 1:6 NASB; cf. 2:1). This is one of many heavenly council scenes in Scripture, in which a council

---

19. See Peckham, *Theodicy of Love*, 125–33.
20. Gustavo Gutiérrez comments, "God's love becomes difficult to understand for one living a life of unmerited affliction," often leading to "radical questioning of God." Gutiérrez, *On Job*, 13.
21. Lewis, *Reflections on the Psalms*, 115.

of heavenly beings "discusses and makes decisions about earthly events more broadly (see, e.g., 1 Kings 22:19–22; Ps. 82; Isa. 6:1–13; Zech. 3:1–7; Dan. 7:9–14)."[22]

Before this heavenly court, God asked Satan, "From where do you come?" Satan answered, "From roaming about on the earth and walking around on it" (Job 1:7 NASB). This same dialogue is repeated in Job 2:2, indicating that this is procedural dialogue in which Satan claims the right to be present as earth's ruler.

"Have you considered my servant Job?" God asks further. "There is no one like him on the earth, a blameless and upright man who fears God and turns away from evil" (Job 1:8). God's words here reveal a preexisting dispute, in which God raises Job as an example of faithfulness over and against Satan's charges.

In response, Satan alleges that Job does not "fear God for nothing" but serves God only because God has blessed him and "made a fence around him" and all he has. Satan then suggests that Job would curse God if met with calamity (Job 1:9–11 NASB; cf. 2:5). As Eric Ortlund notes, "When Satan cannot find any fault in Job's integrity, he manages to turn Job's integrity itself into a problem."[23] Satan acts in accordance with Revelation's description of him as "the accuser of our brothers and sisters . . . , who accuses them day and night before our God" (Rev. 12:10; cf. Zech. 3:1–2).

In this case, Satan directed his charges not only against Job but also against God, directly contradicting God's judgment of Job as blameless, upright, and God-fearing (Job 1:8; cf. 2:3; Rev. 12:10). As Lindsay Wilson comments, this "is a questioning not just of Job's motives but also of God's rule. The accuser is saying to God that Job does not deserve all his blessings, and thus God is not ruling the world with justice."[24] This, Victor P. Hamilton adds, is "patently slanderous."[25]

Satan further argued that the "fence" around Job prevented him from proving God's judgment of Job false. This highlights some boundaries or limits

---

22. Goldingay, *Israel's Faith*, 45. "Several passages in the OT" appear "to assume that God governs the world through a council of the heavenly host" while also upholding "monotheistic belief" (Hartley, *Job*, 71). This heavenly council or court is often referred to as the divine council or divine assembly. See Heiser, "Divine Council," 10; Mullen, "Divine Assembly," 214; cf. Ortlund, *Piercing Leviathan*, 13.

23. Ortlund, *Piercing Leviathan*, 15.

24. Wilson, *Job*, 34. Frances Andersen adds, "God's character and Job's are both slighted" (Andersen, *Job*, 89). Likewise, drawing on John Walton, Ortlund comments, "There is an important sense in which God and his policies for creation stand accused, with Job as the unwitting key witness for the defense" (Ortlund, *Piercing Leviathan*, 14). See Walton, "Job 1," 340; cf. Alden, *Job*, 55.

25. Hamilton, "Satan," 985.

(rules of engagement) in place that Satan could not cross and sought to modify before the heavenly council. In response, God agreed to modify the limits on Satan's power (the "fence"), allowing Satan to put his claims to the test, though still within limits. Afterward, Satan brought numerous horrible calamities, but Job refused to curse God and "did not sin with his lips" (Job 2:10; cf. 1:20–22), thus falsifying Satan's allegations (1:20–22; 2:9–10).

Although some blame God for allowing Satan to harm Job, Frances Andersen argues that God had "good reason" to handle Satan's allegations before the heavenly court as he did—"namely to disprove the Satan's slander" of God's character and judgment.[26] Wilson adds, "If God is treating Job as righteous when he is not, then God is not acting fairly. Much is at stake."[27]

It is crucial to remember that these are not private dialogues between God and Satan but take place in open heavenly court proceedings—a "cosmic covenant lawsuit" involving allegations Satan brought against God's justice regarding Job.[28] To be effective, God's answer to Satan's allegations must take into account the way the case is viewed by those in the heavenly council. If Satan were not allowed to make his case, his allegations would remain open in the heavenly court (and beyond), casting significant doubt on the justice and transparency of God's character and government, with widespread ramifications for creatures everywhere.[29] As John Hartley comments, "The main function of this assembly here is to provide an open forum in which Yahweh permits the testing of Job. That is, the plan to test Job was not hatched in a secret meeting between Yahweh and the *satan*. Rather it was decided openly before the heavenly assembly. In this setting Yahweh's motivation, based on his complete confidence in Job, was fully known and thus it was above question."[30]

This case reveals numerous things about the cosmic conflict. First, contrary to the theology of Job's friends, bad things happen to "good" people (cf. Eccles. 7:15; 8:14; Jer. 5:28; 12:1; Luke 13:1–5). Through it all, Job did not give up on praying, and in the end God set forth Job as one who is righteous and whose prayers are efficacious, telling Job's "friends," "My servant Job shall pray for you, for I will accept his prayer not to deal with you according to your folly" (Job 42:8). Second, it is not God but Satan who afflicts Job (see 2:7; cf. 1:12). Third, Satan possesses power to work in this world but only

26. Andersen, *Job*, 95.
27. Wilson, *Job*, 32.
28. Indeed, "several studies contend that the entire book of Job may be regarded as a cosmic covenant lawsuit." Davidson, "Divine Covenant Lawsuit Motif," 79.
29. See Peckham, *Divine Attributes*, 196.
30. Hartley, *Job*, 72; cf. Wilson, *Job*, 34.

within limits or rules of engagement (the "fence") set in proceedings of the heavenly council.

Understanding the Rules of Engagement Framework

This concept of rules of engagement might seem strange or foreign at first. But, upon closer inspection, you might find that you already believe the basic principles involved. Do you believe that God makes promises? Of course— Scripture includes many examples of divine promises. Do you believe that God always keeps his promises? As we have seen, Scripture teaches that God's promises cannot be broken (Heb. 6:18; see also 2 Tim. 2:13; Titus 1:2). If so, God's action is limited according to whatever promises he has made. If you recognize this much, you already believe in the core principles involved in the rules of engagement, which simply affirm that God has made certain promises or commitments within the cosmic conflict and, therefore, is morally bound to act within the parameters of those commitments.[31]

Put differently, given that God never lies (Titus 1:2) or breaks his promises (Heb. 6:18), any commitment God makes is (morally) binding on God's future action. God remains omnipotent, but any commitment he makes morally limits his future action. Insofar as God has committed to some rules of engagement, then, (morally) God cannot intervene to prevent Satan or others from doing what they wish within those "rules" or "parameters." These "rules" do not limit God's sheer power, but they *morally* limit the ways God exercises his power. Further, God remains sovereign even while committing himself to such rules, and the adversary is restricted to operate only within those specified boundaries, which is good news.[32]

From our very limited creaturely perspective, we typically can neither see nor adequately account for the rules of engagement (and many other factors) that operate within the cosmic conflict. Some avenues we think God should

---

31. Alister McGrath notes, "If God is omnipotent, he must be at liberty to set that omnipotence aside, and voluntarily to impose certain restrictions upon his course of action—to put it dramatically, but effectively, he must be free to have his hands tied behind his back" (McGrath, *Mystery of the Cross*, 123, quoted in Crump, *Knocking on Heaven's Door*, 293; cf. Davis, *Logic and the Nature of God*, 70–73). Joshua Rasmussen highlights that God operates "along lines of pre-established order—rules of engagement with other sentient beings. The purpose of the rules is to maintain orderly arenas" (Rasmussen, "Great Story Theodicy," 239). There are "consistent rules that cannot be broken at the characters' whims" (227). See also the earlier discussion of "nomic regularity" in chap. 3, note 34.

32. Bloesch notes, "Petition for the protection of the angels of God also has biblical warrant (cf. Gen. 24:7; Num. 20:16; Pss. 34:7; 91:11, 12; 1 Kings 19:5–7; Isa. 63:9; Matt. 2:19, 20; 4:6, 11; Luke 4:10, 11; Acts 5:19; 27:23, 24)." Bloesch, *Struggle of Prayer*, 86.

take might result in far worse outcomes. Some other courses that God otherwise prefers might not be available to him within the parameters of the rules of engagement. Indeed, when God does not intervene to prevent some horrible event or bring about some great good, for God to do so might have: (1) been against the rules of engagement, (2) negated the kind of consequential freedom necessary for the flourishing of love relationship, and/or (3) resulted in less flourishing of love or far greater evil.

Why would God agree to such "rules" in the first place? I do not claim to know. But if left unaddressed, the devil's allegations against God's government would unravel the very harmony of love in the universe. For the good of all, then, it is crucial that God defeat such allegations. And perhaps the most preferable way to permanently defeat Satan's allegations while maintaining the consequential freedom necessary for love was to allow an open hearing and demonstration—requiring some rules of engagement by which both parties in the conflict abide.

As noted earlier, even as a king cannot prove by sheer power that he is just, so the devil's slanderous allegations could be defeated not by force but only by some fair and open demonstration that would prove the allegations false, once and for all (see 1 Cor. 4:9; cf. 6:2–3; Matt. 13:29). For a finite creature such as Satan, however, to make any case against the all-powerful God, he must be granted some power and authority to operate within some consistent parameters, which God promises not to arbitrarily change or contravene. Since such rules are not set unilaterally by God but result from heavenly court proceedings in which God takes into account the way the case is viewed by those in the heavenly council, they might be far from ideal. Yet, in light of all the factors, they might nevertheless be the best available to God in order to permanently settle the conflict and inoculate the universe from evil ever arising again, with the least collateral damage for all concerned (Rev. 21:3–4; cf. Nah. 1:9).

"Selective" Miracles, Prayer, and the Rules of Engagement

Scripture repeatedly portrays God working miracles, including miracles that meet basic needs or stop great evils.[33] This raises what some call the problem of selective miracles.[34] If God could work such miracles in some cases, why does

---

33. For a case that "special divine action in the world [that causes] a miracle" is compatible with science and that God works within some "laws of nature," or lawlike regularity, see Plantinga, *Where the Conflict Really Lies*, 91–125. See, further, Abraham, *Divine Agency and Divine Action*; Brümmer, *What Are We Doing When We Pray?*, 69–73.

34. This problem arises "if God sometimes voluntarily acts miraculously but not at other times." Oord, *Uncontrolling Love*, 192.

God not do so in other, similar cases? Given a rules of engagement framework (with many unseen factors), in one situation God might have the moral license to work a miracle, whereas in another situation (that might look identical to us) the rules of engagement (and/or other unseen factors) might be such that working a particular miracle might not be morally available to God. If so, many avenues God otherwise wishes to take might not be (morally) available to him or might be delayed (cf. Dan. 10).

This framework likewise sheds light on the problem of seemingly unanswered prayers, to which we will return in the next chapter. For now, suffice it to say that, in some cases, it might be that God otherwise prefers to grant a given prayer request, but for God to do so might be against the rules of engagement. For such cases, however, what if the rules of engagement are set up in a way that petitionary prayer might open up avenues to God that otherwise were not morally available to him? Perhaps, in some cases, petitionary prayer might grant God moral license to do what he already wanted to do but (in the absence of prayer) was morally restricted from doing so by the rules of engagement.

Perhaps the rules of engagement include something like "trigger clauses" common in legal contracts, wherein some provision of the contract is "triggered" or activated when some other condition is met or factor is in place. For example, legal contracts regarding the sale of property commonly include a "trigger clause" stating that the property sale agreement is conditional upon an inspection, or the buyer acquiring financing, or some similar conditions. Something like this kind of if-then legal framework appears in Scripture itself, particularly in the covenants God makes with his people and thus in accord with God's modus operandi throughout Scripture as a covenant-making and covenant-keeping God. Against this background, perhaps the rules of engagement establish that, at least in some cases, petitionary prayer "triggers" a clause in the rules of engagement such that God can morally bring about some good he already wanted to bring about but was morally prevented from doing so by the rules of engagement, absent such prayer.

If the rules of engagement in the cosmic conflict are dynamically related to other factors, including some human actions (such as prayer) that might "trigger" provisions in the rules of engagement, then whether God can (morally) bring about a particular good might depend (at least in part) on whether humans have petitioned God to do so. In other words, the rules of engagement might be set up such that some things temporarily fall within the jurisdiction of the demonic realm, but the limits of this jurisdiction might be dynamically related to how humans relate to God. If so, petitionary prayer may grant God additional permission or open up avenues for God that were not previously (morally) available to him within the rules of engagement.

Such rules of engagement might be in the background when God lays out the covenantal parameters of his blessings toward Israel, especially when God declares in 2 Chronicles 7:14, "If my people who are called by my name humble themselves, pray, seek my face, and turn from their wicked ways, then I will hear from heaven and will forgive their sin and heal their land" (cf. Dan. 9:13). Perhaps the demonic realm has more jurisdiction to antagonize Israel (directly or through surrounding nations) if the people have removed themselves from proper covenant relationship with God. Yet if God's people would sufficiently humble themselves and pray, then provisions in the rules of engagement would be triggered such that God could bring about goods for their sake that otherwise would not have been morally permissible within the rules of engagement.

Further, recall the case of the demon-afflicted boy in Mark 9. When the disciples asked why they were unable to cast the demon out, Jesus replied, "This kind can come out only through prayer" (Mark 9:29). Here, Jesus explicitly declared that prayer makes a difference relative to whether some kinds of unclean spirits can be cast out. This seems to indicate that there are some parameters—some rules of engagement—within which such demons operate and that such parameters may be affected by petitionary prayer. At least in some cases, then, prayer can make a difference relative to the extent of the jurisdiction of the demonic realm.

Other biblical passages also indicate that God's action might be affected by the presence or absence of factors such as faith and prayer. As seen earlier, the unbelief of those in Jesus's hometown of Nazareth limited his miracle-working there. Specifically, Jesus "could do no deed of power there, except that he laid his hands on a few sick people and cured them," and this was "because of their unbelief" (Mark 6:5; Matt. 13:58; cf. Matt. 17:20). Conversely, Jesus repeatedly links faith to answered prayer, teaching (for example), "Whatever you ask for in prayer with faith, you will receive" (Matt. 21:22; cf. Mark 11:22–24). To these teachings of Christ we will return later.

Many other instances in Scripture indicate that human actions might affect the parameters in which Satan and his cohorts are permitted to operate. For example, James teaches, "Submit yourselves therefore to God. Resist the devil, and he will flee from you" (James 4:7; cf. Matt. 6:10–13). Likewise, Paul urges, "Do not give the devil an opportunity" (Eph. 4:27 NASB). Later in Ephesians, Paul instructs further, "Put on the whole armor of God, so that you may be able to stand against the wiles of the devil, for our struggle is not against blood and flesh but against the rulers, against the authorities, against the cosmic powers of this present darkness, against the spiritual forces of evil in the heavenly places" (6:11–12; cf. Dan. 10). Then, a few verses later, Paul adds, "With all prayer and petition pray at all times in the Spirit," and "be on the alert with all perseverance and petition for all the saints" (Eph. 6:16, 18 NASB95; cf. 6:19–20).

Jesus himself offers prayer aimed at counteracting the devil's influence. For instance, after warning Peter, "Satan has demanded [permission] to sift all of you like wheat," Jesus adds, "But I have prayed for you that your own faith may not fail" (Luke 22:31–32). These passages indicate that, at least in some cases, the way humans relate to God—via prayer and otherwise—makes a difference regarding what the devil and his minions are permitted to do.[35]

This all fits well within a cosmic conflict framework wherein God has committed himself to rules of engagement in the cosmic conflict such that (in some cases) God is morally prevented from bringing about some good or goods that he is aware of, otherwise would like to bring about, and possesses the sheer power to bring about, unless he is petitioned to do so by an appropriate party or parties.

Given this understanding, prayer aimed at influencing God's action would be consistent with God's omniscience, omnibenevolence, and omnipotence (resolving the influence aim problem). Petitionary prayer does not inform God of our desires or needs, persuade God to bring about some good he already did not prefer, and/or increase God's power to bring about that good, but it might grant God increased jurisdiction to intervene in ways that otherwise would not be morally available to him within the rules of engagement. That is, petitionary prayer might provide God moral jurisdiction within the rules of engagement for God to bring about some good and thus might influence whether God brings about that good in a way that is entirely consistent with divine omniscience, omnipotence, and omnibenevolence.

Yet since there are many unseen factors, we should not assume that when God does not bring about the outcome we desire, it must be due to lack of enough prayer or faith. "Most of the bitterness of unanswered prayer," Harkness writes, "comes from the assumption that God will juggle his universe to give us what we plead for if we plead long enough."[36] In some cases, though, what we pray for might be wrong, because of our motivation or the overall outcomes that would accompany it—all things considered (James 4:2–3; cf.

---

35. This view, however, is significantly different from what Tiessen calls the "church dominion" model (see Tiessen, *Providence and Prayer*, 119–31). This rules of engagement framework agrees that the world has been given over to enemy rule but denies that God will not act in the absence of prayer; God is always acting somehow even in the absence of prayer.

36. Harkness, *Prayer*, 38.

Rom. 8:26; 1 John 5:14–15). Further, perhaps some things we pray for would contravene God's commitments to free will (and the nomic regularity required for consequential freedom) or the rules of engagement more broadly, regardless of how much and how faithfully believers pray (cf. Matt. 26:39; Luke 22:32).[37] That is, in some cases, other factors might be such that, no matter how much and how faithfully God's people pray, the rules of engagement would nevertheless morally prevent God from bringing about some good he otherwise would prefer to bring about (see chap. 5).

In brief, God might be morally prevented from bringing about some good that God knows of, prefers (in and of itself), and possesses the sheer power to bring about if (1) doing so would result in less flourishing of love or greater evil on the whole, (2) doing so would contravene the consequential freedom God has committed to granting creatures for the sake of love, and/or (3) doing so would conflict with the rules of engagement, even after petitionary prayer is offered faithfully by an appropriate party or parties.

"If It Is Possible": Jesus's Prayer in Gethsemane

Jesus was greatly "distressed and agitated" (Mark 14:33). As the cross drew near, Jesus withdrew to pray, as he often did (see Luke 22:39). This time, however, he was "deeply grieved, even to death" (Matt. 26:38). He instructed his disciples to pray that they "may not come into the time of trial" (Luke 22:40). Then he moved a little way off, "fell on His face and prayed, saying, 'My Father, if it is possible, let this cup pass from Me; yet not as I will, but as You will'" (Matt. 26:39 NASB; cf. Mark 14:35).

If it is possible? These words are both puzzling and illuminating. How could anything *not* be possible for God? According to Mark's account, Jesus also prayed, "Abba, Father, for you all things are possible" (Mark 14:36). Taken together, Jesus's words entail that, in some sense, *all things* are possible for God, while in another sense, even for God some outcomes *might not be possible*—such as those that would require God to break his promises or otherwise act contrary to his perfect nature. Given "conditions prevailing" at a given time, Baelz writes that perhaps it is "not possible for God to grant my request. To the retort that all things are possible for God, I should have to reply that, although there might be some sense in which this was true, there

---

37. Highlighting the way God has ordered the world with "remarkable regularity," which we often "describe as the 'laws of nature,'" Harkness notes that "this ordered dependability can be explored and used by human wills, but as far as we can observe, it is not set aside upon request." Harkness, *Prayer*, 38.

is another sense in which it is not true. God's being and purposes together rule out certain things which, when considered abstractly, might be thought possible."[38]

Here, Christ prayed specifically to be spared from the suffering and death before him, "if it were possible" (Mark 14:35). In isolation, it was indeed possible for Christ to avoid the cross if he so chose, but it was not possible insofar as God was to keep his commitment to save sinners while remaining perfectly just (see Rom. 3:25–26). Christ's words "if it is possible," then, indicate that some avenues are not available to God in keeping with his commitments and goals. In this case, God could not bring about his greater desire of saving humans apart from Jesus enduring the cross *for us*.

Accordingly, Christ not only prayed, "If it is possible, let this cup pass"; he also added, "Yet not as I will, but as You will" (Matt. 26:39 NASB). Taken together, these two petitions mean that Christ prayed, "If it is possible" *in keeping with* God's (remedial) will. Thus in Luke's account Jesus prays, "Father, if you are willing, remove this cup from me, yet not my will but yours be done" (Luke 22:42).

Later in Gethsemane, Christ prayed again, *two more times*, "My Father, if this cannot pass unless I drink it, your will be done" (Matt. 26:42, 44). This phrase, "your will be done," is the same phrase Christ instructed his followers to pray in the Lord's Prayer (Matt. 6:10). Here, in the midst of the greatest crisis, Christ models what he taught in the Lord's Prayer. Those who would follow Christ's teaching and practice, then, should also pray, "Your will be done," understanding God's "will" to correspond to the most preferable way forward that is *possible*, given all factors—seen and unseen. This is consistent with wrestling and striving with God in prayer, as Jesus himself does here.[39]

This way of praying, however, sometimes lends itself to misunderstandings of God's will and character. Suppose a young girl hears people praying for the healing of her mother, who is deathly ill with what has been diagnosed as terminal cancer: "Father, if it is your will, please heal this woman, yet not our will, but yours be done." Upon hearing this, the young girl wonders to herself, "Why would it *not* be God's will to heal mommy? Does God want my mommy to suffer and die? Doesn't God love me and my mommy and want what is good for us?" It is not difficult to see how such a prayer, though theologically sound, could lead to severe cognitive dissonance.[40]

---

38. Baelz, *Prayer and Providence*, 115.

39. Jesus here "exemplifies the man of prayer striving with God. . . . He surrendered to the will of his Father only after striving to change this will" (Bloesch, *Struggle of Prayer*, 77). So also Wright, "Lord's Prayer," 133.

40. On the problem of evil more generally, see Peckham, *Theodicy of Love*.

Here, understanding the distinction between what God *ideally* wills and what he *remedially* wills is crucial (see chap. 3). God's ideal will (in isolation) is that no evil ever occur and no one ever suffer or die, from cancer or otherwise—God takes "no pleasure in the death of anyone" (Ezek. 18:32). God is working to restore the entire cosmos to this ideal, but for now we live in a *fallen* world in which many things occur that God does not (ideally) will. God's *remedial* will, on the other hand, is what God "wills" after taking into account all other factors—including the evil decisions of creatures and the many unseen factors in the cosmic conflict, which thus includes many things that God does not want but that are not up to God.

Given God's commitment to creaturely freedom and the rules of engagement (among other factors), some avenues are not (morally) available to God. God's remedial will consists of whatever course of action is preferable, *all things considered,* including the free will decisions of creatures (and the context of nonarbitrary parameters required for consequential freedom),[41] the rules of engagement in the cosmic conflict, and all the future effects of a given course. With this understanding, we can pray for someone to be spared from death with the confidence that such a prayer is in accordance with God's *ideal* will, while also recognizing that his *remedial* will might take another (far from ideal) course due to many other factors that are not strictly up to God, many of which may be unseen from our perspective.[42]

Given that God takes "no pleasure in the death of anyone" (Ezek. 18:32), when Christ prays in Gethsemane, it follows that the Father did not sadistically take pleasure in (or ideally desire) the crucifixion of the Son. God "does not *willingly* afflict or grieve anyone" (Lam. 3:33). Yet in the wider context of the plan of salvation, Christ's death on the cross was part of God's remedial will (see, e.g., Isa. 53:10–11) because it was the *only way* available to God whereby he could defeat the devil's allegations and redeem the world from bondage to the evil one without compromising love and justice (cf. Rom. 3:25–26; 5:8; Heb. 2:14; 1 John 3:8).[43]

Christ's death was the only way for the petitions of the Lord's Prayer to ultimately be fulfilled. Specifically, it was the only way for God's name to be sanctified/vindicated, for God's kingdom to come, and for God's will to be done, on earth as it is in heaven. It was the only way to remove the breach

---

41. On the nonarbitrary limits required for consequential freedom, see the earlier discussion of nomic regularity in chap. 3, note 34.

42. On God's "will" and divine providence, see Peckham, *Divine Attributes*, 163–73.

43. Stephen G. Post explains that divine love "takes on the form of self-sacrifice out of necessity rather than preference due to the tolerance of human freedom" (Post, *Theory of Agape*, 33). See, further, Peckham, *Love of God*, 117–46.

of corruption that leaves some lacking daily sustenance ("give us our daily bread"), the only way (morally) for God to provide forgiveness of sins ("forgive us our sins"), the only way to put an end to trials and temptations, and the only way to ultimately "deliver" the entire cosmos "from the evil one," in whose "power" the "whole world lies" temporarily (Matt. 6:9–13; 1 John 5:19).

Only by the demonstration of God's perfect righteousness and love via the cross could the devil's slanderous allegations be utterly defeated and God's name be vindicated once and for all, for the good of all concerned, ensuring the future security and bliss of the entire cosmos. Thus Jesus prayed elsewhere, "Now my soul is troubled. And what should I say: 'Father, save me from this hour'? No, it is for this reason that I have come to this hour. Father, glorify your name" (John 12:27–28).[44] Christ possessed the sheer power to deliver himself from the cross, but he chose to give himself willingly for us (John 10:18; cf. Heb. 12:2) to demonstrate God's perfect righteousness and love (Rom. 3:25–26; 5:8), thus vindicating God's name and restoring trust and thereby defeating the devil to redeem and reclaim the cosmos.

As the world stands now, however, God's "rule is not yet fully exercised" for the "world is 'in the power of the evil one.'"[45] The fullness of God's kingdom is "not yet." Given this understanding of the cosmic conflict, it seems to me we should also pray not only that God's "will be done" but also that "if it is possible, let this cup pass," thereby explicitly recognizing that some avenues are not (morally) available to God. Here, the phrase "if it is possible" (in word or sentiment) would mean if it is possible in keeping with what is both *available* and *preferable*, given everything God knows about all the other factors involved, seen and unseen—if it is possible in keeping with God's remedial will. In this way, we might pray for God to answer our prayers in the most preferable way possible, which might not align with what we have in mind. While praying this way, one could consistently and confidently affirm that, in isolation, God ideally wants to heal every suffering person, but in many cases that avenue might not be available or preferable due to factors in the cosmic conflict that might be invisible to us.

However one might pray, this cosmic conflict framework recognizes that far more factors are involved relative to God's action (and apparent inaction) than we could fathom. Among other things, Christ's teaching and example demonstrate that one can consistently pray to God for his intervention while at the same time affirming that God knows what is most preferable in any situation, truly wants to bring about what is most preferable in every situation,

44. "Jesus is asking his Father to glorify his name (calling on the name of Yahweh), by enacting his plans." Millar, *Calling on the Name of the Lord*, 188.

45. Baelz, *Prayer and Providence*, 116, 117.

and is always entirely good and loving. Accordingly, we might fervently pray for divine intervention, even perhaps crying out that we feel forsaken (cf. Matt. 27:46), while nevertheless trusting in God's constant, unwavering goodness, justice, and love (cf. Ps. 22; Dan. 3:17–18).

Conclusion

He wrestled with God and prevailed—Jacob, the "God-wrestler."[46] As Bloesch highlights, "True prayer involves not simply pleading with God but also wrestling with God in the darkness. . . . It means refusing to let go of God without a blessing; as Jacob wrestled with the angel of God (Gen. 32:24–30)."[47]

Yet, how can anyone wrestle with God and prevail? Bloesch explains further, "Our striving with God is made possible only because God first encounters us and seeks to make us instruments of the divine will and purpose (cf. Isa. 65:1; Rev. 3:20). We are able to wrestle with God because God chooses to wrestle with us. God also wrestles with the powers of darkness that are bent on enslaving mankind."[48] Kyle Strobel and John Coe write, "We cannot merely affirm that God is God and God will do what he wants. That might seem like a faithful response, but it isn't how the psalmists prayed, and it isn't how Jesus prayed. We have to struggle with God in prayer."[49]

The very possibility and importance of wrestling with God is clearly seen against the backdrop of rules of engagement in the cosmic conflict introduced in this chapter. In the words of Tony Evans, "prayer" might provide "earthly permission for heavenly interference."[50] But what, then, about seemingly unanswered prayers? To this question, we now turn.

---

46. Yancey, *Prayer*, 98.
47. Bloesch, *Struggle of Prayer*, 76.
48. Bloesch, *Struggle of Prayer*, 77.
49. Strobel and Coe, *Where Prayer Becomes Real*, 175.
50. Evans, *Victory in Spiritual Warfare*, 137.

5

Our Struggle Is Not against Flesh and Blood

The Problem of Seemingly Unanswered Prayer

Peter had faithfully preached the gospel. His reward? Imprisonment. By all appearances, the situation was hopeless. But, "while Peter was kept in prison, the church prayed fervently for him" (Acts 12:5). Peter was asleep, bound in chains, surrounded by two guards, with more by the door keeping watch. Then, "suddenly an angel of the Lord appeared, and a light shone in the cell. He tapped Peter on the side and woke him, saying, 'Get up quickly.' And the chains fell off his wrists" (12:7). Then, Peter followed the angel out of prison. An amazing answer to prayer.

Yet earlier in this same chapter, "King Herod laid violent hands upon some who belonged to the church. He had James, the brother of John, killed with the sword" (Acts 12:1–2). Surely James and others also prayed for his situation. Why was one apostle delivered and the other left to die?

This and many other cases like it highlight the problem of seemingly unanswered prayer. Focusing on this problem and related questions about why *persistence* in prayer might matter, this chapter begins with a discussion of Paul's teachings regarding spiritual warfare in Ephesians 6, which emphasizes petitionary prayer in the midst of the cosmic conflict (Eph. 6:18). Then, the chapter considers numerous crucial teachings of Jesus relative to petitionary prayer, before concluding with an examination of numerous factors identified in Scripture as playing a role in the effectiveness of petitionary prayer and how this sheds significant light on the problem of seemingly unanswered prayer.

Armored Prayer: Struggling against the Cosmic Rulers with the Armor of God and Persevering Prayer

"Put on the whole armor of God, so that you may be able to stand against the wiles of the devil, for our struggle is not against blood and flesh but against the rulers, against the authorities, against the cosmic powers of this present darkness, against the spiritual forces of evil in the heavenly places" (Eph. 6:11–12).[1] The "rulers" and "authorities" Paul mentions in this passage are plainly not humans: they are not enemies of "blood and flesh" but "cosmic powers" and demonic "spiritual forces of evil" associated with the devil (cf. Rev. 12:7). As Gombis puts it, "We are not the only actors on the stage. The drama of Ephesians involves the powers and authorities who are cosmic rulers responsible for large-scale patterns of injustice, oppression, exploitation, and idolatry."[2] In this context of cosmic conflict, Paul calls for fervent petitionary prayer: "With all prayer and petition pray at all times in the Spirit, and with this in view, be on the alert with all perseverance and petition for all the saints, and pray on my behalf" (Eph. 6:18–19 NASB95; cf. Rom. 15:30).[3]

Earlier in Ephesians, Paul likewise speaks of "the rulers and authorities in the heavenly places" (Eph. 3:10) and warns of "following the ruler [or "prince"] of the power of the air, the spirit that is now at work among those who are disobedient" (2:2; cf. 4:27). Similarly, Paul elsewhere identifies Satan as "the god of this world," who "has blinded the minds of the unbelievers" (2 Cor. 4:4; cf. John 12:31; 14:30; 16:11). This spiritual warfare, then, is not like earthly warfare among "blood and flesh" but a conflict of a different

---

1. Some interpret biblical references to Satan, demons, principalities, and powers as referring to human systems of power or world systems with inner spirituality. See Wink, *Walter Wink: Collected Readings*. I believe, however, that the biblical data decidedly characterizes these powers as personal agents that also have systematic impact. See the convincing case for the reality, personhood, and systemic impact of evil celestial agencies in Arnold, *Powers of Darkness*, 194–205; cf. Noll, *Angels of Light*, 119; and Page, *Powers of Evil*, 240.

2. Gombis, *Drama of Ephesians*, 58. These "cosmic rulers," he explains, "continue to exercise great influence in our world today" (24).

3. Prayer in the midst of cosmic conflict has a long history in the Christian tradition. For example, Gabrielle Thomas notes that, for the Cappadocians, "prayer is an incontrovertible means for the baptized to equip themselves in resisting the spiritual powers of darkness; namely the devil and demons." Thomas, "Cappadocians," 289.

kind—a primarily epistemic conflict wherein the devil is "the deceiver of the whole world" (Rev. 12:9), who relentlessly wages a war of disinformation.[4] Thus Paul writes, "We do not wage war according to human standards, for the weapons of our warfare are not merely human, but they have divine power to destroy strongholds. We destroy arguments and every proud obstacle raised up against the knowledge of God, and we take every thought captive to obey Christ" (2 Cor. 10:3–5).

Thus Paul instructs Christians how to prepare for spiritual warfare, to "put on the whole armor of God" to "stand against the wiles of the devil" in "our struggle" against these "cosmic powers" and "spiritual forces of evil" (Eph. 6:11–12; cf. 6:13). Unsurprisingly, this armor is suited for an *epistemic* conflict. Paul first instructs, "Fasten the belt of truth around your waist" (6:14 NRSV), directly emphasizing the epistemic nature of this spiritual warfare against the "father of lies" (John 8:44), whose modus operandi is continual deception and slandering of God's name (cf. Gen. 3; Job 1–2). Paul elsewhere warns of those who "will fall away from the faith, paying attention to deceitful spirits and teachings of demons" (1 Tim. 4:1 NASB; cf. Rev. 16:13–14). And, earlier in Ephesians, Paul warned against lies and unbridled anger so as to "not give the devil an opportunity" or additional foothold in this conflict (Eph. 4:27 NASB). Here and elsewhere, Scripture makes clear that the truth matters far more than we often realize. Accordingly, Christ came into this world "to testify to the truth" and thereby "destroy the works of the devil" (John 18:37; 1 John 3:8; cf. Heb. 2:14) and called his disciples to bear witness to the truth (John 15:27; cf. 18:37).

Second, Paul instructs, "Put on the breastplate of righteousness" (Eph. 6:14), highlighting the importance of goodness and justice, which are intrinsic to God's nature and character (e.g., Deut. 32:4; 1 John 1:5) and stand at the center of the cosmic conflict (cf. Ps. 89:14). Next, Paul calls believers to "lace up your sandals in preparation for the gospel of peace," which sets forth the truth in opposition to the devil's lies (Eph. 6:15). Finally, Paul instructs Christ followers, "Take the shield of faith, with which you will be able to quench all the flaming arrows of the evil one. Take the helmet of salvation and the sword of the Spirit, which is the word of God" (6:16–17). Here, Paul emphasizes the importance of faith, which functions as a shield against the devil's arrows designed to undermine faith in God by deception and slander. Paul likewise highlights salvation (cf. Rom. 13:11–12), which comes only *by*

---

4. Diane Langberg comments that Satan "is the father of lies. He is the Deceiver. Nothing he says can be trusted. . . . He would have us follow him in his attempt to supplant the Almighty. He will say anything, use anything, and twist anything to achieve his end." Langberg, *Suffering and the Heart of God*, 36.

faith, and the "word of God," again emphasizing the importance of the truth in this epistemic conflict.

Just after this, Paul urges Christians to persevere in fervent prayer: "With all prayer and petition pray at all times in the Spirit, and with this in view, be on the alert with all perseverance and petition for all the saints, and pray on my behalf" (Eph. 6:18–19 NASB95). In all this, Paul urges Christians to be prepared to stand against cosmic evil with the armor of God and perseverance in prayer. In one phrase: Paul calls Christians to *armored* prayer.[5] As Millar comments, "Paul's global instruction in Ephesians 6 to pray 'at all times in the Spirit, with all prayer and supplication' encompasses all of the previous statements concerning the 'armour of God,'" urging continual prayer in this "raging spiritual conflict."[6] Crump adds, "Prayer itself is not the field of combat but one of the weapons we carry against the enemy (Eph. 6:18)."[7] Trevor Laurence comments, "The demonic powers scheme for the devastation of Christ's church," and Christ's followers "must therefore wage war against the devil's hordes in prayer."[8]

Paul specifically highlights "perseverance" in petitionary prayer, indicating that persevering in petitions offered for others (intercessory prayers) may make a significant difference in this spiritual conflict. Paul elsewhere writes to the church at Corinth, mentioning how "you also join in helping us by your prayers, so that many will give thanks on our behalf for the blessing granted us through the prayers of many" (2 Cor. 1:11). As we will see shortly, Christ's teachings also highlight perseverance in prayer.

But why should *persevering* in prayer make a difference relative to God's action in a way a single prayer might not? The issues surrounding this question closely relate to the problem of seemingly unanswered prayer.

Patient Persistence and Seemingly Unanswered Prayer

Ask, Seek, Knock

"Ask, and it will be given you; search, and you will find; knock, and the door will be opened for you. For everyone who asks receives, and everyone who searches finds, and for everyone who knocks, the door will be opened" (Luke

---

5. I am wary, however, of some approaches to spiritual warfare that attempt claims regarding the precise, inner workings of the spiritual realm, which go far beyond what Scripture reveals. For a balanced discussion of spiritual warfare, see Arnold, *3 Crucial Questions about Spiritual Warfare*; cf. Beilby and Eddy, *Understanding Spiritual Warfare*.

6. Millar, *Calling on the Name of the Lord*, 213, 214.

7. Crump, *Knocking on Heaven's Door*, 251; cf. Bloesch, *Struggle of Prayer*, 133.

8. Laurence, *Cursing with God*, 265.

11:9–10; cf. Matt. 7:7–8).[9] Jesus directly teaches to pray petitions with the expectation that such prayers *will be answered*. Baelz observes that this "suggests that God may act in some specific way in answer to [human] prayer," causing "something to happen in the world which might otherwise not have happened."[10] Simundson adds, "Your prayers make a difference. God hears and responds."[11]

Does this mean, however, that all requests will be granted? Elsewhere, Jesus taught his disciples, "Whatever you ask for in prayer, believe that you have received it, and it will be yours" (Mark 11:24). In isolation, this might be taken to mean that, if we believe, *every* request we make of God will be granted. However, in light of the rest of Scripture, this cannot be Christ's meaning. Indeed, Christ's own petition "let this cup pass" was not granted.

What are we to make of Christ's teaching that "everyone who asks receives" (Luke 11:10)? Just after this, Jesus teaches, "Is there anyone among you who, if your child asked for a fish, would give a snake instead of a fish? Or if the child asked for an egg, would give a scorpion? If you, then, who are evil, know how to give good gifts to your children, how much more will the heavenly Father give the Holy Spirit to those who ask him!" (Luke 11:11–13; cf. Matt. 7:10–11). In context, Christ's promise is not that we will *always* receive what we ask for or that things will always go well for us but that God hears our prayers and will give only good gifts to his children.

The Friend at Midnight

Just before this teaching in Luke (and just after the Lord's Prayer), Jesus told a parable about someone going to a friend at midnight, asking, "Friend, lend me three loaves of bread, for a friend of mine has arrived, and I have nothing to set before him." From his home, the friend answers, "Do not bother me; the door has already been locked, and my children are with me in bed; I cannot get up and give you anything." Jesus explains the meaning of this parable thus: "I tell you, even though he will not get up and give him anything out of friendship, at least because of his persistence he will get up and give him whatever he needs" (Luke 11:5–8).

This is sometimes interpreted as teaching that our prayers will be answered if we pray with enough persistence.[12] But, Crump points out, in the parable the

---

9. Fisher comments, "What is proposed here is a sort of divine-human partnership." Fisher, *Prayer in the New Testament*, 77.

10. Baelz, *Prayer and Providence*, 58.

11. Simundson, *Where Is God?*, 60.

12. Simundson comments, "The friend is so stubbornly persistent that the man finally gives in. . . . This suggests that we should be unrelenting in making our wishes known to God." Simundson, *Where Is God?*, 60.

man asks only once.[13] Further, the translation "because of his persistence" is highly questionable. Lexical analysis strongly suggests the term translated as "persistence" (*anaideia*) here should be translated as "shamelessness."[14] Some believe that the "shamelessness" (*anaideia*) in this story refers to the sleeping householder reticent to help, while others believe the "shamelessness" refers to the one asking for help. Marshall explains, "After much dispute, it now seems most probable that the word '*anaideia*' refers to the shameless behavior of the man knocking at the door at midnight, despite all social propriety."[15]

What is the point of this parable? As many commentators note, rather than representing God, the reticent friend stands as a contrastive example (in an argument from lesser to greater—a *qal wahomer* argument). If even one who is reticent to help and considers such a request bothersome will help in the end, how much more can we count on God to respond to our prayers? As Crump notes, "The sleeping householder is not like God; he is precisely unlike God. If the householder fails to respond out of friendship alone (Outrageous! Impossible!), how much more may God be counted on to respond promptly out of unfailing love and devotion."[16]

This perfectly aligns with Jesus's teaching a few verses later: "If you, then, who are evil, know how to give good gifts to your children, how much more will the heavenly Father give the Holy Spirit to those who ask him!" (Luke 11:13). Accordingly, Marshall understands this parable's lesson to be that Christ's followers "must not shrink from asking—perhaps from disbelief that God will answer—but must come to God with confidence."[17] Likewise, Crump sees a "twofold lesson" here: "(1) God is always graciously disposed to hear every request; and (2) we are free to approach at any time without hesitation."[18] Green further highlights "the notion that God engages in eschatological redemption in order that he might restore honor to his name."[19]

---

13. Crump, *Knocking on Heaven's Door*, 72. I. Howard Marshall likewise adds, "The parable itself says nothing about persistence, but rather it deals with the unreasonableness of the request" (Marshall, *Gospel of Luke*, 465). Further, "There is nothing in Luke 11:5–8 that suggests that importunity, or continued and intense effort, is required for prayers to be heard by God." Marshall, "Jesus," 122.

14. Joel Green explains, "'Persistence' is not a viable option" to translate *anaideia*, which is "an abstract noun formed from the negation of αἰδώς (via αἰδός, 'shame, self-respect, what causes shame or scandal')" and here refers to shamelessness (J. Green, *Gospel of Luke*, 448n46). See, also, Crump, *Knocking on Heaven's Door*, 67.

15. Marshall, "Jesus," 121.

16. Crump, *Knocking on Heaven's Door*, 70. Fisher adds, "It is universally recognized that this is a parable by way of contrast." Fisher, *Prayer in the New Testament*, 140.

17. Marshall, "Jesus," 121.

18. Crump, *Knocking on Heaven's Door*, 72.

19. J. Green, *Gospel of Luke*, 449.

The Persistent Widow and the Unjust Judge Revisited

Christ does teach about the importance of persistent prayer elsewhere, however, telling a parable about a persistent widow and an unjust judge, who "neither feared God nor had respect for people" (Luke 18:2). The widow kept going to the judge, pleading, "Grant me justice against my accuser" (18:3). "For a while he refused; but later he said to himself, 'Though I have no fear of God and no respect for anyone, yet because this widow keeps bothering me, I will grant her justice, so that she may not wear me out by continually coming'" (18:4–5).

Here, again, this unjust judge who has no concern for others *cannot* represent God—who is perfectly good, just, and loving (e.g., Deut. 32:4; Ps. 89:14; 92:15; 145:7; 1 John 1:5). This judge is another contrastive example (in another *qal wahomer* argument). If even an unjust judge with no regard for others will nevertheless respond to the widow's persistent pleas for justice, how much more can God be counted on to answer our prayers for justice (cf. Matt. 7:7–11)? Thus Jesus explains, "Will not God grant justice to his chosen ones who cry to him day and night? Will he delay long in helping them? I tell you, he will quickly grant justice to them" (Luke 18:7–8). Yet one might ask, Why does it often seem like prayers for justice go unanswered? We will return to this question later. For now, suffice it to say that this parable "suggests that the really important factor in prayer is the character of God as the One who wants to do good for his people and to accomplish his own purpose, which will also be for their good."[20]

In this regard, some strongly reject the view that this parable teaches something like this: if only one persevered more in prayer, God would grant one's request. Many commentators argue that repetition is not valuable to God and thus downplay the importance of persistence in prayer. For my part, I agree that *merely* repeating a prayer does not by itself add value or motivate God to respond, but I disagree with any corresponding move to downplay the importance of persistent prayer.[21]

Whatever else we say about the meaning of this parable of the unjust judge and the persistent widow, Luke himself states that this is a parable about continual, persevering prayer—"a parable about their need to pray always and not to lose heart" (Luke 18:1).[22] Millar comments, "The point? Keep calling

---

20. Marshall, "Jesus," 122–23.

21. For his part, Crump concludes, "Persistent prayer is an essential component of the Christian life. . . . Yet, is there a biblical basis for the formula long-term repetition + sufficient fervency = positive response? No." Crump, *Knocking on Heaven's Door*, 75.

22. Green comments, "Read against the horizon of 17:22–37, Jesus' teaching here is particularly oriented toward the necessity of tenacious, hopeful faith in the midst of present ordeal." J. Green, *Gospel of Luke*, 637; cf. Sir. 35:15–25.

out to God, asking him to do exactly what he has promised," knowing that the perfectly good God "will readily and swiftly give justice to his people in due time."[23] Jesus himself modeled fervent, persevering prayer (sometimes praying all night; Luke 6:12) and taught his followers to also persevere in prayer—an emphasis echoed elsewhere in Scripture (see the later discussion in this chapter).

Yet, again, why would persistence in prayer matter relative to God's action? Any view that persistent prayer is more effective at moving God, as if God needs to be convinced to give good gifts—and repetition does the trick— contradicts the wider teachings of Scripture regarding God's character (e.g., Luke 11:13). The parable's emphasis on the "need to pray always and not to lose heart" (18:1), then, should not be taken to mean that asking God for something repeatedly somehow counts more toward inclining or persuading God to grant a request. But why, then, would we "need to pray always and not . . . lose heart" (18:1)?

As seen (in part) earlier, sometimes an answer to our prayer might be delayed by other factors, such as when God's angel was opposed by the prince of the kingdom of Persia for three weeks (Dan. 10). Since many unseen factors operate in this cosmic conflict (during the "already, but not yet" of God's kingdom), persevering in faith and prayer without losing heart is paramount (cf. Gal. 6:9). Jesus himself warned, "In this world you will have trouble. But *take heart*! I have overcome the world" (John 16:33 NIV). We currently live in enemy territory. And, for now, as Crump comments, "suffering remains the norm for God's people."[24] Our "adversary, the devil, prowls around like a roaring lion, seeking someone to devour" (1 Pet. 5:8 NASB; cf. Job 1–2), and "the whole world" temporarily "lies under the power of the evil one" (1 John 5:19). Accordingly, Lincoln notes, "Protection from the evil one and being kept in God's name will not necessarily mean protection from hostility, persecution, or even violent death for the sake of Jesus' name."[25] But we can nevertheless *take heart*, for Christ has "overcome the world." As Psalm 30:5 promises, "Weeping may linger for the night, but joy comes with the morning."

God may have an answer to our prayers on the way, but (whether due to the rules of engagement or otherwise) it might not reach us if we "lose heart" and cease praying in the meantime. Further, persevering in prayer, even when things might *seem* hopeless, serves as a testament of faith in God—a sign of allegiance to the true king, even in the midst of this domain of darkness. In this regard, consider again Christ's explanation of this parable: "Will not

23. Millar, *Calling on the Name of the Lord*, 184.
24. Crump, *Knocking on Heaven's Door*, 302.
25. Lincoln, "God's Name," 172.

God grant justice to his chosen ones who cry to him day and night? Will he delay long in helping them? I tell you, he will quickly grant justice to them" (Luke 18:7–8). Here, Crump comments, Jesus "encourag[es] God's people to remember that while their prayers may appear to be in vain, they wait because of God's timing, not because of God's neglect. The heavenly judge hears every petition immediately, and he always rules justly; sometimes, however, the timing remains mysteriously his own, leaving petitioners waiting and wondering."[26] Yet God's "eventual response" is assured because God is "motivated by a two-pronged passion: the honor of his name and the love of his people."[27]

The rules of engagement in the cosmic conflict may shed light on God's "mysterious timing." In some cases, an apparent delay might be due to unseen factors in the cosmic conflict (or relative to God's commitments more broadly). The avenue God otherwise prefers might not be available to him such that what God wishes to bring about—for the good of all concerned—might require a more difficult path (as it was in Christ's prayer in Gethsemane). Or what God wishes to bring about might only be delayed due to the rules of engagement (as in the case of Dan. 10) or other unseen factors.

In such cases, persistence in prayer might make a difference. Suppose God's answer to a prayer is delayed, but the answer is on the way (as in the case of Dan. 10) in response to petitionary prayers that opened up avenues for God to intervene in ways that otherwise were not (morally) available to him. If, in the meantime, one gives up or loses heart, those avenues opened up by prayer might not remain (morally) available to God. In such a case, perseverance in prayer could make a significant difference regarding God's action—not by persuading God to act in ways he did not already want to act, but by opening up avenues for God to bring about the good he already wanted to bring about.

Yet, in some cases, one might pray persistently without any apparent answer. Some have gone to the grave without any apparent answer to their prayer requests. This brings us back to the question of why some prayers seem to go unanswered. This question is particularly troubling in light of the many biblical promises—especially those of Christ—that God will answer our prayers. We now turn to this question.

If You Ask Anything "in My Name"

In his Farewell Discourse (John 14–17), Jesus proclaimed, "I will do whatever you ask in my name, so that the Father may be glorified in the Son. If in my

26. Crump, *Knocking on Heaven's Door*, 84.
27. Crump, *Knocking on Heaven's Door*, 86.

name you ask me for anything, I will do it" (John 14:13–14). Does this mean that Christ will give us anything we ask for? Here and elsewhere, a condition is specified: *if* one asks in his name.

Later, Christ promised further, "If you abide in me and my words abide in you, ask for whatever you wish, and it will be done for you" (John 15:7). A few verses later, Jesus adds, "The Father will give you whatever you ask him in my name" (15:16). In the following chapter, Jesus elaborates, "If you ask anything of the Father in my name, he will give it to you. Until now you have not asked for anything in my name. Ask and you will receive, so that your joy may be complete" (16:23–24; cf. 16:26).

Regarding these texts, Lincoln comments, "The magnificent promises about the efficacy of prayer in the Farewell Discourse mention six times that the presupposition or condition of such prayer is that it is in Jesus' name (cf. 'in my name' in 14:13, 14; 15:16; 16:23, 24, 26; see also 'abide in me' in 15:7). Just as Jesus has come and has done his works in the Father's name, acting as the Father's fully authorized representative (cf., e.g., 5:43; 10:25), so the praying of believers is in Jesus' name and to be carried out by his fully authorized human representatives (cf. 17:18; 20:21b)."[28]

Yet what counts as praying "in his name"? Can one merely state the name "Jesus" (like a magic spell) and expect to receive whatever one requests? Certainly not. Some itinerant exorcists found this out in Ephesus when they attempted to cast out an evil spirit in "the name of the Lord Jesus" (Acts 19:13).[29]

As Millar explains, "'Praying in the name of Jesus' is the New Testament equivalent of 'calling on the name of the Lord,'" and "in both cases prayer is construed as asking God to do what he has promised."[30] As seen earlier, throughout Scripture, God's name is linked to his reputation and honor (glory). And, as briefly explained in chapter 3, asking in God's name corresponds to asking according to God's overarching will for his kingdom in a way that abides in Christ (cf. 1 John 3:22; 5:14)—that is, asking for that which aligns with God's character and that which will glorify God's name (cf. John 12:27–28) and vindicate his character before the world, legally defeating the enemy's slanderous allegations in the cosmic conflict (cf. John 12:31).[31]

This sheds significant light on other teachings of Jesus, such as these promises: "Whatever you ask for in prayer, believe that you have received it, and it will

28. Lincoln, "God's Name," 176.

29. Fisher, *Prayer in the New Testament*, 110.

30. Millar, *Calling on the Name of the Lord*, 179. Likewise, see J. Green, "Persevering Together," 188.

31. Lincoln observes how Jesus notes that the voice from heaven was "an accommodation for the crowd, signaling that the crucial moment of the cosmic trial is at hand (cf. v. 31)." Lincoln, "God's Name," 158.

be yours" (Mark 11:24); "Whatever you ask for in prayer with faith, you will receive" (Matt. 21:22; cf. 21:21); and "Ask, and it will be given to you; search, and you will find; knock, and the door will be opened for you" (Luke 11:9). Insofar as one is committed to canonical reading (as I am), these passages must be understood in a way that is consistent with the conditions Christ lays out in the passages in John quoted earlier—that requests be in his name, in accord with God's character and overarching will in the cosmic conflict. This condition of being aligned with God's will is explicitly stated in 1 John 5:14: "If we ask anything according to his will, he hears us" (more on this later in this chapter; cf. 1 John 3:22). As such, Christ's promises in Mark 11:24 and elsewhere cannot mean that Christ promises to grant *every* request asked of him in faith.

Indeed, in the preceding chapter in Mark, Jesus directly denied the request of James and John, who asked, "We want you to do for us whatever we ask of you. . . . Appoint us to sit, one at your right hand and one at your left, in your glory" (Mark 10:35–37). Notice that Jesus's declaration regarding "whatever you ask" in Mark 11:24 echoes their words "whatever we ask," but Jesus *denies* their request, saying, "You do not know what you are asking" and "to sit at my right hand or at my left is not mine to appoint, but it is for those for whom it has been prepared" (10:38, 40).

Even requests made in faith, then, might be denied if they are out of step with God's overarching will and, in this way, not "in his name." Like James and John, we often do not know what we are asking, for there are many factors and ramifications we cannot see. This is one reason, among many, that we need the intercession of the Holy Spirit (see chap. 6), "for we do not know how to pray as we ought, but that very Spirit intercedes with groanings too deep for words" (Rom. 8:26).

Notably, Jesus's own prayer request in Gethsemane—"let this cup pass"—was not granted. Indeed, Katherine Sonderegger notes, "This is the great example of prayer unanswered, or answered only in the coinage of silence."[32] Crump adds, "Contrary to much popular opinion, Jesus never describes faith as a means to guarantee that we will always get exactly what we request in prayer. We are invited to have faith enough to look for miracles, but the overarching consideration is always God's plan, as Jesus's own prayers in the Garden of Gethsemane dramatically demonstrate. Ask in faith, but then trust in God's wisdom and goodness to do what is best."[33]

Taking any of Christ's sayings as blanket promises that he will grant *everything* one asks of him in faith would entail that Christ would grant even evil

32. Sonderegger, "Act of Prayer," 151.
33. Crump, *Knocking on Heaven's Door*, 72. Crump reminds us that "God always remains free to say no to any request that conflicts with his plan" (58–59).

requests and requests that would result in massive harm (not to mention impossible requests), as long as one asks in faith. But this is manifestly absurd.
As we have seen, God does only what is good and righteous (cf. Deut. 32:4)
and cannot deny himself or break his promises (2 Tim. 2:13; Heb. 6:18–19).
The promise, then, is not that God will give us everything we ask for (even
when our requests are misguided) but, better, that God will "give *good* things
to those who ask him" (Matt. 7:11).[34]

Thus whether a given prayer request might be granted by God always
depends on whether one's request is in keeping with God's goodness, promises, commitments, and will. In short, whether a request might be granted is
contingent on whether it accords with God's *name* (i.e., God's character of
perfect goodness and love) and thus whether it aligns with God's good will for
all concerned, which takes into account all factors—including many unseen
factors in the cosmic conflict (cf. 1 John 3:21–22; 5:14–15).[35]

As Lincoln explains, "'Whatever you ask' does not mean whatever is on
your wish list, but, in effect, whatever you ask in line with Jesus' prayer"
in John 17, "because what is in line with Jesus' prayer represents his name,
what he stands for, and what his mission in the world entails. This ex-
planatory qualification is not intended to rationalize unanswered prayer
but to encourage prayer that is in line with the will of God, as revealed in
Christ, and that can therefore confidently expect to be answered (cf. 1 John
3:21–22)."[36] Lincoln goes on: "Prayer, then, is one of the primary means
for cooperation in God's mission in the world. And requests supporting
the essentials of Jesus' prayer will be answered because they conform to
God's purposes for this world in the making known of the divine name
through Jesus."[37]

Yet because there are many factors of which we are unaware, "neither
faith, persistence, nor passion can guarantee us anything" with respect to
precisely how God will respond to our prayer requests here and now.[38] There
are a host of factors involved, seen and unseen, to some of which we now
turn.

---

34. Here, we must remember that answers to prayers may come not in the form of material
blessing but in the form of unspeakably wonderful spiritual blessings, which might comfort
and sustain us in the midst of material hardship in the domain of darkness in which we now
dwell, during the "already, but not yet" of God's kingdom.

35. Philip Yancey comments, "The assurance of answered prayers, still sweeping in its scope,
comes with conditions. Am I abiding in Christ [John 15:7]? Am I making requests according to
his will [1 John 5:14]? Am I obeying his commands [1 John 3:22]?" Yancey, *Prayer*, 235.

36. Lincoln, "God's Name," 176.

37. Lincoln, "God's Name," 177.

38. Crump, *Knocking on Heaven's Door*, 73.

Praying by the Rules: The Art of Prayer in the Midst of Spiritual Warfare

Against the background of cosmic conflict, Scripture repeatedly links human dispositions and actions to the potential effectiveness of prayer. For example, Peter instructs husbands, "Show consideration for your wives in your life together, paying honor to the woman . . . so that nothing may hinder your prayers" (1 Pet. 3:7; cf. 3:12; Eph. 4:26–27). Prayers, then, might be hindered by human dispositions and acts.

Further, numerous passages of Scripture indicate that the effectiveness of petitionary prayer is (at least partially) dependent on factors such as abiding in right relationship with God, repentance, faith, good and unselfish motives, perseverance, and humbly praying in submission to and alignment with God's will.[39] Each of these will be discussed in what follows.

Even given recognition of such factors, however, we should not think of prayer in terms of "special content, particular technique, or the quality of a person's spirituality," but should always remember that "it is talk with the living God," according to his "name."[40] Petitionary prayer does not work like a magic formula or an algorithm or a vending machine.[41] Many factors affect whether a petition might be granted—seen and unseen—not least of which is God's sovereign will.

Whatever else we say about the factors below, we must first recognize that God's initiative makes prayer possible in the first place (cf. 1 Chron. 29:19; Zeph. 3:9). As Millar puts it, "Despite the profound break in our relationship with Yahweh he continues to speak to his creatures, and makes it possible for us to respond to him. We can call on Yahweh, but only because he has called on us."[42] Indeed, "We can cry out to him to come through on his promises only because he has already made his promises. In this sense all biblical prayer is covenantal—all prayer is gospel driven."[43] Here, relationship is key and thus praying in Christ's name and abiding in him (John 15:7) go hand in hand.

---

39. Compare these to the six factors Crump identifies in the General Letters and Revelation: (1) failure to ask, (2) selfishness, (3) foolish prayer, (4) disobedience or misalignment with God's will, (5) broken relationship(s), (6) subject to God's sovereign timing. Crump, *Knocking on Heaven's Door*, 276–77.

40. Seitz, "Prayer in the Old Testament," 5–6.

41. "Prayer is not magic, and there is no blanket promise, no faith formula, to guarantee God's granting any and every petition if only the one praying will believe." Crump, *Knocking on Heaven's Door*, 38; cf. Simundson, *Where Is God?*, 62.

42. Millar, *Calling on the Name of the Lord*, 29.

43. Millar, *Calling on the Name of the Lord*, 29.

Righteous and Repentant Prayer: Praying with Obedience and Contrition

"The prayer of the righteous is powerful and effective" (James 5:16). Here, James links prayer's power and effectiveness with "righteousness." James then cites Elijah as an example: "He prayed fervently that it might not rain, and for three years and six months it did not rain on the earth. Then he prayed again, and the heaven gave rain, and the earth yielded its harvest" (James 5:17–18).

Many other passages also link righteousness with effective petitionary prayer. Psalm 66:18–19 states,

> If I had cherished iniquity in my heart,
>   the Lord would not have listened.
> But truly God has listened;
>   he has heard the words of my prayer. (cf. Ps. 51; John 9:31)

Likewise, Proverbs 15:29 teaches: "The LORD is far from the wicked, but he hears the prayer of the righteous." Conversely, "when one will not listen to the law, even one's prayers are an abomination" (Prov. 28:9; cf. Isa. 55:6–7; Jer. 7:16; 15:1).

After urging husbands to treat their wives well "so that nothing may hinder your prayers," Peter adds, "The eyes of the Lord are on the righteous, and his ears are open to their prayer. But the face of the Lord is against those who do evil" (1 Pet. 3:7, 12; cf. Ps. 33:13–17; Isa. 59:2; Mal. 2:13–17).[44] Here, Peter quotes from Psalm 34, which goes on to state,

> When the righteous cry for help, the LORD hears,
>   and rescues them from all their troubles.
> The LORD is near to the brokenhearted
>   and saves the crushed in spirit. (Ps. 34:17–18)

Conversely, God himself declares to oppressors,

> When you stretch our your hands,
>   I will hide my eyes from you;
> even though you make many prayers,
>   I will not listen;
>   your hands are full of blood. (Isa. 1:15)

---

44. John Wesley writes, "That your prayer may have its full weight with God, see that ye be in charity with all men. . . . Nor can you expect to receive any blessings from God while you have not charity towards your neighbour." Wesley, *Wesley's Standard Sermons*, 529.

Seitz comments that this is because "a generation has so turned away from God that he has withdrawn to protect his own name and holy covenant."[45] Bloesch notes, "the Bible indicates that sometimes God refuses to hear prayers, but there is always an overriding reason."[46]

Are only the prayers of the "righteous" answered? If so, what hope can we sinners have? God's words in the next verses hold the key:

> Wash yourselves; make yourselves clean;
>> remove your evil deeds
>> from before my eyes;
> cease to do evil;
>> learn to do good;
> seek justice;
>> rescue the oppressed;
> defend the orphan;
>> plead for the widow. (Isa. 1:16–17; cf. Mic. 6:8)

Forgiveness and cleansing are possible for the truly repentant, those willing to turn and do justice (Isa. 1:18–19; cf. 1 John 1:9). Scripture is filled with God's responses to repentant prayers (e.g., Ps. 51; cf. Ps. 66:18)—even those of horrendously wicked people like King Manasseh.[47] As God himself declared, "If my people who are called by my name humble themselves, pray, seek my face, and turn from their wicked ways, then I will hear from heaven and will forgive their sin and heal their land" (2 Chron. 7:14).

Given our sinfulness (cf. Rom. 3:23), "righteous" prayer requires repentance (see, e.g., 2 Chron. 7:14).[48] It is necessarily humble and contrite—bathed in confession and sincerely fervent rather than pretentious. In one parable, Christ contrasts the proud prayer of a Pharisee and the humble prayer of a tax collector, noting that the latter "went down to his home justified rather than the other, for all who exalt themselves will be humbled, but all who humble themselves will be exalted" (Luke 18:14; cf. Matt. 6:1–8; Mark 12:40).

---

45. Seitz, "Prayer in the Old Testament," 17.

46. Bloesch, *Struggle of Prayer*, 45. Millar adds that, after much rebellion in the history of Israel, times came when "God's people are no longer calling on the name of Yahweh, and Yahweh is no longer listening to his people. However, a day is envisaged when the people will pray, and Yahweh will be delighted to answer." Millar, *Calling on the Name of the Lord*, 104; cf. Zech. 7:12–14; 8:20–23; 10:6.

47. Millar writes, "Such is Yahweh's grace in hearing and answering our prayers that even Manasseh's prayers were heard, although he was probably the worst king that either Judah or Israel ever had." Millar, *Calling on the Name of the Lord*, 135; see also 2 Chron. 33:10–19.

48. For more on prayers of confession and repentance, see P. Miller, *They Cried to the Lord*, 244–61.

Accordingly, just before declaring that "the prayer of the righteous is powerful and effective," James instructs, "Confess your sins to one another and pray for one another, so that you may be healed" (James 5:16). Even our best offerings are soiled and are acceptable to God only through Christ's mediation (1 Pet. 2:5; cf. Rom. 8:26–27). Whatever blessings God brings, then, are never merited but always freely bestowed grace.[49] And God often delivers people despite their unrighteousness (see, e.g., Ps. 106:7–8).

Though failing to be in right relationship with God (e.g., failure to abide in Christ; John 15:7) might hinder petitionary prayers (e.g., Isa. 1:15; 1 Pet. 3:7), and though "the prayer of the righteous is powerful and effective" (James 5:16), even the prayer requests of the "righteous" might not be granted. The "righteous" often suffer and pray prayers that seem to go unanswered, even as the wicked prosper (see, e.g., Eccles. 8:14). As we have seen, Job suffered undeservedly, John the Baptist was beheaded, Paul suffered with a "thorn in his flesh," despite his petitions, and Jesus's own request in Gethsemane—"let this cup pass"—was not granted. It is not true, then, that when one's prayer request is not granted, it *must* be because of unrighteousness. Indeed, sometimes the most faithful suffer the most and endure a dark night of the soul.

James himself cites "the prophets who spoke in the name of the Lord" as "an example of suffering and patience," including Job (James 5:10–11). Likewise, shortly after teaching that God's "ears are open to" the "prayer" of the righteous, Peter makes it clear that the righteous often "suffer for doing what is right" and that "Christ also suffered" for us (1 Pet. 3:12, 14, 18). Sometimes the unrighteous prosper. And sometimes the "righteous" suffer and their prayers seemingly go unanswered (cf. Heb. 11:35–40). Many other factors are also involved.

Faithful Prayer: Praying with Faith in God

James also links faith with the effectiveness of prayer: "If any of you is lacking in wisdom, ask God, who gives to all generously and ungrudgingly, and it will be given you. But ask in faith, never doubting, for the one who doubts is like a wave of the sea, driven and tossed by the wind. For the doubter, being double-minded and unstable in every way, must not expect to receive anything from the Lord" (James 1:5–7).[50]

49. Yet God's grace can be rejected and forfeited. Scripture consistently teaches that God's blessings are *foreconditional*—that is, freely given prior to any conditions but not apart from conditions relative to their continuance. They are not merited or earned but given freely by God in his grace; yet they can be forfeited. Even as a child can forfeit unmerited privileges, humans can do so relative to God. See Peckham, *Love of God*, 147–90.

50. The "doubt" James warns against is doubting God's goodness and faithfulness and his ability to keep his promises, but James does not endorse a kind of presumption that assumes

Later, James writes, "The prayer of faith will save the sick, and the Lord will raise them up, and anyone who has committed sins will be forgiven" (James 5:15; cf. 5:13–14). Yet James does not specify the types of maladies (physical, mental, and/or spiritual) in view or the timing in which such requests might be granted.[51] In isolation, James might be interpreted as teaching that "the prayer of faith" will bring healing of one's malady right away. However, while Scripture includes cases of immediate healing, faith does not guarantee immediate healing (e.g., the case of the "thorn" in Paul's side), and nothing in this passage indicates such a guarantee.

Instead, James might be interpreted as meaning that, whether or not one's malady is healed here and now, the prayer of faith will bring deliverance in the end (at least relative to salvation).[52] Scripture promises that, at least in the end, "the Lord will raise" up the faithful and "anyone who has committed sins will be forgiven" (James 5:15), for "everyone who calls on the name of the Lord shall be saved" (Rom. 10:13; cf. Joel 2:32; Acts 2:21).

Whatever one concludes about James's precise meaning, here James directly links effective prayer with faith.[53] Likewise, after giving a blind man sight in response to his plea, Jesus declared, "Your faith has saved you" (NRSVue) or "Your faith has made you well" (NASB) (Luke 18:42; cf. Matt. 8:10, 13). Elsewhere Jesus declared, "If you have faith and do not doubt," then "even if you say to this mountain, 'Be lifted up and thrown into the sea,' it will be done. Whatever you ask for in prayer with faith, you will receive" (Matt. 21:21–22; cf. Mark 11:22–24). These and many other passages set forth some significant links between faith and effective prayer.

This raises two distinct, but related, questions:

1. Is there a one-to-one correlation between granted petitions and faith (simpliciter)?
2. Is there a correlation between granted requests and *the amount of faith*— as if little faith is ineffective but *more* faith does *more* to influence divine action?

God will give one *anything* one asks for, nor does this rule out questions the faithful might ask about what they are experiencing. Recall, again, Jesus's own cries on the cross, "My God, my God, why have you forsaken me?" (Matt. 27:46).

51. J. Ramsey Michaels is representative of many scholars who believe that the ambiguity is intentional: here "healing and forgiveness are virtually unchangeable (cf. Mark 2:9)." Michaels, "Finding Yourself an Intercessor," 239; cf. Crump, *Knocking on Heaven's Door*, 264–65.

52. Michaels suggests, "If all prayer is eschatological, then in an eschatological sense, at least, all prayer will be answered." Michaels, "Finding Yourself an Intercessor," 239.

53. Biblical scholars make robust arguments on many sides of this question of precisely what James is teaching, which I will not try to settle here.

Relative to the first question, as seen earlier in this chapter, while Jesus teaches that "whatever you ask for in prayer with faith, you will receive" (Matt. 21:21–22; cf. Mark 11:22–24), other teachings of Jesus (and Scripture more broadly) add conditions such as praying in God's name and according to his will. As Hendriksen explains, "Such praying and asking must, of course, be in harmony with the characteristics of true prayer which Jesus reveals elsewhere" and "in line with all of scriptural teaching."[54] Hendriksen thus concludes that Christ's teaching means that "no task *in harmony with God's will* is impossible to be performed by those who believe and do not doubt."[55] Accordingly, I understand Jesus's words in Matthew 21 as a call to believe that God can do even the seemingly impossible and thus to pray in faith that God will grant our requests, *if* such requests are in God's name and aligned with his (remedial) will. At the same time, we should also remember that God sometimes works miracles even in cases of little or no faith (cf. Mark 9:24–26; Luke 1:13, 20).[56]

Faith is an important factor, but it is only one factor relative to whether a request is granted or not. Our understanding of the relation between faith and effective prayer must be properly qualified and nuanced in accordance with all that Scripture teaches regarding the link between the two. As we have seen, Scripture demonstrably teaches that there is some significant correlation, but the results of the correlation are unpredictable (perhaps due to unseen factors such as the rules of engagement).

Relative to the second question, we saw earlier that Jesus "did not do many deeds of power" in his hometown of Nazareth "because of their unbelief" (Matt. 13:58). Indeed, Jesus "could do no miracle there except that He laid his hands on a few sick people and healed them," being "amazed at their unbelief" (Mark 6:5–6 NASB). Yet we have also already seen that God sometimes works miracles even when those involved possess little (or no) faith—such as when Jesus told the father of a demon-afflicted boy, "All things can be done for the one who believes," and the man cried out to Jesus, "I believe; help my unbelief!" (Mark 9:23–24).[57] Christ did not say, "Come back to me when you have more faith." He delivered the boy.

54. Hendriksen, *Exposition of the Gospel*, 461.

55. Hendriksen, *Exposition of the Gospel*, 459, emphasis added.

56. Consider those who claimed to "prophesy" and "cast out demons" and "do many mighty works in [Christ's] name" but of whom Jesus will say in the end, "I never knew you" (Matt. 7:22–23).

57. Crump contends that the boy's father was issuing "more than the tentative query of a man with faltering faith"; the father's request was "at least in part, a test . . . bait in a cynical trap set to discredit Jesus" (Crump, *Knocking on Heaven's Door*, 48). I am not convinced, however, that there is sufficient evidence to support this reading.

Even here, though, prior to casting out the demon, Jesus lamented, "You faithless and perverse generation, how much longer must I be with you?" (Matt. 17:17). Afterward, Jesus explained that the disciples could not cast the demon out "because of [their] little faith" or (in some versions) "unbelief," and said, "If you have faith the size of a mustard seed, you will say to this mountain, 'Move from here to there,' and it will move, and nothing will be impossible for you" (Matt. 17:20; cf. Mark 9:29; Luke 17:5–6).[58]

These passages teach both that (1) lack of faith can hinder God's response to one's requests and that (2) even faith the size of a mustard seed can move a mountain. It cannot be, then, that a large amount of faith is always required for God to grant one's request.

Some thus downplay any link between strength of faith and whether a request is granted. In this regard, Crump rightly highlights that strongly believing that God will bring something about is no guarantee it will occur.[59] Because so many unseen factors are involved, absent divine revelation we do not know what God will do in a given situation. Recall that those praying for Peter's release from prison were greatly surprised when he showed up (Acts 12:5, 12–17); they fervently prayed without knowing what God would do or not do. Likewise, when faced with death in a fiery furnace, the three Hebrew youths expressed faith that God was able to deliver them yet also declared that even "if [he did] not," they would "not serve" the Babylonian "gods" (Dan. 3:18).[60] The kind of faith that might rightly be deemed "strong," then, is not *presumptuous* faith that claims certainty about what God will do (the sin of presumption was at issue when the devil tempted Jesus to throw himself from the top of the temple to put God to the test; Matt. 4:6–7) but *appropriate* faith that God will keep his promises (even if fulfillment seems delayed), do what is preferable for all concerned, and make all things right in the end.[61]

---

58. Some contend that the "mountain" here is the temple mount and this should be read of the destruction of the temple. See, e.g., Garland, *Mark*, 441; cf. Crump, *Knocking on Heaven's Door*, 31. Others contend that the saying is more general. I will not weigh in on this debate here, but however the reference to the "mountain" is understood, the text makes a connection to faith.

59. Crump, *Knocking on Heaven's Door*, 72. Crump states, "The New Testament offers no predictable relationship between faith and miracle . . . ; neither is there any quantitative correlation between measures of faith, fervency, or persistence and the likelihood of miraculous answers to prayer" (302–3).

60. Goldingay comments, "The three have no doubt that he can and will rescue them: [Dan. 3:17] makes this explicit" (Goldingay, *Daniel*, 71). Yet the three also note the possibility that he might not.

61. "Petitionary prayer must be offered in faith, but it may not presume upon God. For this reason it is usually expressed in conditional form: God is asked to grant something—but only on condition that he wants to grant what is asked." Brümmer, *What Are We Doing When We Pray?*, 6.

Whatever else we might say, Christ's own ungranted request in Gethsemane demonstrates that great faith does not guarantee that one's request will be granted here and now. Ungranted requests, then, do not necessarily indicate that those praying lacked sufficient faith. Conversely, while lack of faith can impede prayers, the case of the demon-afflicted boy in Mark 9 (and others) demonstrates that less faith does not exclude the possibility that one's request will be granted. It does not follow, however, that the strength of faith of those praying *never* makes any difference. It could be that (in some cases, for all we know) the rules of engagement are such that more faith unlocks more avenues for God to work. I do not claim to know, but whatever one concludes, the passages surveyed above (and numerous others) demonstrably set forth some significant correlation between faith and effective prayer.

Unselfish Prayer: Praying with the Right Motivations

Unselfish love is also linked to the effectiveness of prayer. Peter writes, "Be serious and discipline yourselves for the sake of your prayers. Above all, maintain constant love for one another" (1 Pet. 4:7–8). Likewise, James teaches, "You do not have because you do not ask" (James 4:2). Not asking can make a difference. As Millar puts it, "The course of salvation history it seems is potentially threatened by the failure of God's people to cry to him so that he might work out his agenda."[62]

Further, James goes on: "You ask and do not receive, because you ask with the wrong motives, so that you may spend what you request on your pleasures" (James 4:3 NASB). Selfish motives, then, might impede one's prayers. Here, it must be noted that praying for oneself is not necessarily selfish. If it were, we would have to conclude Jesus was selfish when he prayed, "Let this cup pass from me" (Matt. 26:39), which is absurd (cf. John 15:13). Instead, we need to distinguish between proper self-care, which is a good thing (God commands us, for instance, to rest; Exod. 34:21; cf. 20:8–11), and selfishness, which places oneself above others. God cares for us more than we do and wants us to take care of ourselves, as long as we are not doing so at the expense of or while neglecting others. Prayers that are self-absorbed or that place one's own desires and concerns above those of others, however, are selfish. In contrast, Paul exhorts, "Be devoted to one another in brotherly love; give preference to one another in honor, not lagging behind in diligence, fervent in spirit, serving the Lord" (Rom. 12:10–11 NASB; cf. Phil. 2:3–4).

---

62. Millar, *Calling on the Name of the Lord*, 46.

Unsurprisingly, prayers in Scripture are frequently prayers for the good of others—intercessory prayers, with many focusing on the fulfillment of God's mission to save the world.[63] For example, Paul instructs the Colossians, "Devote yourselves to prayer, keeping alert in it with thanksgiving. At the same time, pray for us as well, that God will open to us a door for the word, that we may declare the mystery of Christ, for which I am in prison, so that I may reveal it clearly, as I should" (Col. 4:2–4; cf. 2 Cor. 1:11; 2 Thess. 3:1–2).

Elsewhere, Paul frequently encouraged intercessory prayer, as in 1 Timothy: "I urge that supplications, prayers, intercessions, and thanksgivings be made for everyone, for kings and all who are in high positions" and for everyone else, for God "desires everyone to be saved and to come to the knowledge of the truth" (1 Tim. 2:1–2, 4). James likewise instructs, "Confess your sins to one another and pray for one another, so that you may be healed" (James 5:16; cf. 5:14–15). Here, the call is to pray for others not only in isolation but in community.

Paul himself continually modeled intercessory prayer. For instance, he assured Timothy, "I remember you constantly in my prayers night and day" (2 Tim. 1:3). Further, Paul wrote to the Colossians, "I want you to know how greatly I strive for you and for those in Laodicea and for all who have not seen me face to face" (Col. 2:1) and told them that Epaphras also "is always striving in his prayers on your behalf, so that you may stand mature and fully assured in everything that God wills" (4:12).

Many ask how such prayers for others could make any difference. However, given an understanding of the rules of engagement, such prayers might grant God the (moral) right to do more in the lives of others than the rules of engagement would otherwise permit. Accordingly, as seen earlier, Paul exhorts Christians to prepare for spiritual warfare and to "keep alert and always persevere in supplication for all the saints" and for him also (Eph. 6:18–19). Crump comments that "intercessory prayer genuinely assists in the spiritual success of fellow believers."[64]

However, as fallen humans we are naturally inclined to pray with selfish motivations. We thus need to pray for the disposition of unselfish love itself—for God to bring our desires into alignment with his will. As Bloesch comments, "The 'give me' prayer should always be subordinated to the 'make me' prayer" (cf. Luke 15:12, 19 NASB).[65] Here, we desperately need the intercessory ministries of Christ and the Holy Spirit, mediating on our behalf (see chap. 6).

63. "Paul's prayers of petition . . . are focused primarily on the spiritual welfare of his readers." Longenecker, "Prayer in the Pauline Letters," 225.
64. Crump, *Knocking on Heaven's Door*, 219.
65. Bloesch, *Struggle of Prayer*, 76.

Thankfully, "the Spirit helps us in our weakness, for we do not know how to pray as we ought, but that very Spirit intercedes with groanings too deep for words," and "the Spirit intercedes for the saints according to the will of God" (Rom. 8:26–27).

Persevering Prayer: Praying Continually with Hope and Gratitude

Scripture also urges Christians to gratefully "persevere in prayer" (Rom. 12:12), to "pray without ceasing [and] give thanks in all circumstances" (1 Thess. 5:17–18; cf. Col. 4:2; 1 Thess. 3:10). Further, Paul exhorts, "Do not be anxious about anything, but in everything by prayer and supplication *with thanksgiving* let your requests be made known to God" (Phil. 4:6).[66] Does Paul mean for us to suppress our worries? No. As Craig Keener explains, "Paul's alternative to worry is not the anxious attempt to suppress it but rather acknowledging the needs to God and entrusting them to him."[67]

For Paul and others in Scripture, petition and thanksgiving go together.[68] As Bloesch explains, "Even when prayer takes the form of praise and adoration the petitionary element will nonetheless be present," and petition "needs always to be informed by the motivation to extol and magnify the name of God and to give thanks for his great goodness toward us."[69] Thus the psalmist wrote,

> I love the LORD because he has heard
>   my voice and my supplications.
> Because he inclined his ear to me,
>   therefore I will call on him as long as I live. (Ps. 116:1–2; cf. 118:21)

Praying continually plays a crucial role in keeping believers in right relationship with God and providing other therapeutic benefits. Yet given the busyness of life, it is easy to neglect prayer. In this regard, Origen of Alexandria wrote, "It is shameful that you sometimes eat twice a day, even eat three times a day, and all of you eat at least once, but, when it comes to the soul, you do not give it its appropriate nourishment. Prayer is the nourishment of the soul."[70]

---

66. John Wesley writes, "If your eye is not steadily fixed on Him who has borne all your sins, Satan will again bring you under that fear of death in which you were once subject to bondage." Wesley, *How to Pray*, 40.

67. Keener, *Mind of the Spirit*, 223.

68. Stephen Farris writes, "At the heart of both hymns and prayers is recognition of who God is and what God has done." Farris, "Canticles of Luke's Infancy Narrative," 93.

69. Bloesch, *Struggle of Prayer*, 71.

70. Origen, *Homilies on the Psalms*, 54.

Petitionary prayer and the therapeutic benefit of bringing our cares to God stand side by side.

Beyond therapeutic benefits, however, numerous biblical passages indicate persistence in prayer can make a difference relative to divine action and otherwise in the cosmic conflict. And, likewise, Joel Green adds, "In the face of diabolic opposition, faithful perseverance comes through prayer."[71] For example, as we saw earlier, in the context of spiritual warfare Paul exhorts Christians, "With all prayer and petition pray at all times in the Spirit, and with this in view, be on the alert with all perseverance and petition for all the saints, and pray on my behalf" (Eph. 6:18–19 NASB95; cf. Matt. 6:13; 1 Pet. 5:8). As John Bunyan puts it, "Pray often, for prayer is a shield to the soul, a sacrifice to God, and a scourge for Satan."[72]

Why might persistence make a difference, though? It is not that God does not want to help us unless we pray fervently and persistently enough but that (as noted earlier) in some cases the rules of engagement might temporarily prevent God (morally) from bringing about goods (for us and others for whom we pray) that he already wants to bring about. In such cases, continuing to pray might eventually open up avenues within the rules of engagement that would not otherwise open up in the absence of prayer.[73]

Perhaps the timing is not right for God to grant a request initially, but conditions would be right later on (relative to the rules of engagement or otherwise), *if* one does not *lose hope and give up* in the meantime. In a case of seemingly unanswered prayer, God's answer might not be "no" but "not yet." Given this context, persevering prayer involves patience to wait on God's timing. As the psalmist attests, "I waited patiently for the LORD; he inclined to me and heard my cry" (Ps. 40:1). The danger is not that God will neglect our prayers but that we will lose heart and fail to persevere in prayer. Here, again, we see the importance of abiding in Christ (John 15:7).

As Crump explains, "Jesus taught his disciples how to pray for the victorious establishment of a kingdom that has yet to vanquish all opposition; the battle still rages, and the praying disciple waits for the Father's promised outcome. . . . Christ's decisive victory is won [at the cross] and guarantees the final victory of God, but that celebration is still future."[74] We must, then, not give up hope. The most fervent prayer is not the most emotional—emotions

71. J. Green, "Persevering Together," 198.
72. Bunyan, *Complete Works*, 80.
73. Baelz observes, "Because of the tension between the 'already' and the 'not yet' a deliberate persistence in prayer is as important as a heart-felt but transient desire to pray." Baelz, *Prayer and Providence*, 102.
74. Crump, *Knocking on Heaven's Door*, 250.

come and go—but of the deepest persistence and commitment to God's will, kingdom, and the sanctification (or vindication) of God's name. Your requests may not be granted as you'd like here and now, but the sincere, fervent prayers of faith, offered in love and hope through Christ, are always heard by God, who will make all things right in the end (see chap. 6).

I discussed many other such passages earlier in this chapter and will not repeat that discussion here. Alongside those, however, notice that Jesus was upset when his disciples failed to persevere in prayer with him in Gethsemane, lamenting, "You men could not keep watch with Me for one hour? Keep watching and praying, so that you do not come into temptation; the spirit is willing, but the flesh is weak" (Matt. 26:40–41 NASB). Here, persevering in prayer is linked with the ability to withstand temptation. It is no coincidence that Jesus modeled persistent prayer—sometimes praying all night (Luke 6:12). Further, Yancey comments, "Jesus taught a model prayer, the Lord's Prayer, but otherwise gave few rules. His teaching reduces down to three general principles: Keep it honest, keep it simple, and keep it up."[75]

Coupled with the previous two factors (of faithful and unselfish prayer), we see here the importance of praying in accordance with the virtues that Paul highlights in 1 Corinthians 13:13: faith, hope, and love. Yet even if one prays humbly and repentantly (in right relationship with God) with *deep* faith, love, and hope, one's prayers might nevertheless not be in accordance with the will of God, a discussion to which we now turn.

Submissive Prayer: Praying in Accordance with God's Will

Righteousness, repentance, faith, unselfishness, and perseverance with gratitude do not *guarantee* that a particular request will be granted here and now. Whether one's request is granted depends significantly on whether it obeys God's commands and is aligned with God's *will*. Thus, John writes, "We receive from him whatever we ask, because we obey his commandments and do what pleases him" (1 John 3:22). Further, "If we ask anything according to his will, he hears us. And if we know that he hears us in whatever we ask, we know that we have obtained the requests made of him" (5:14–15).

Recall here the distinction between God's ideal and remedial will. In this fallen world, God's ideal will is often unfulfilled. Yet prayer for God's will to be done might open up avenues for God to bring about outcomes closer to his ideal will than might otherwise be available to him (morally).

75. Yancey, *Prayer*, 191.

Yet some outcomes might not be in accordance with God's remedial will no matter how much or how fervently people pray.[76] Many unseen factors are involved such that God may ideally want to bring about a particular outcome in and of itself (e.g., healing a loved one of cancer), but doing so might contravene his commitments (e.g., to creaturely free will or to the rules of engagement) or result in worse outcomes—all things considered. Accordingly, only prayer requests in accordance with God's remedial will, which takes into account all factors (including many unseen factors), are guaranteed to be granted. While our requests are often bound up with relatively immediate desires, God always takes the long view.

As seen earlier, to pray according to God's will corresponds to praying in God's name (reputation)—in accord with God's character and overarching will in the cosmic conflict (cf. John 14:13–14; 15:16; 16:23; 1 John 5:14–15). Many prayers conclude with a phrase like "in Jesus's name we pray" or "in your name we pray." However, to genuinely pray *in Jesus's name* entails that we are intending to pray in accordance with God's character (name) and overarching will, recognizing that our will might be out of step with what is preferable—all things considered. Understood this way, saying "in Jesus's name we pray" can be a shorthand way of praying for God's will to be done— with recognition that even for God some things are not possible, for some otherwise preferable avenues might not be (morally) available to him. Thus we might pray like Christ did in Gethsemane, yielding our requests to God's overarching will in accordance with his name: "My Father, if it is possible, let this cup pass from Me; yet not as I will, but as You will" (Matt. 26:39 NASB).

Jesus's request to avoid the cross was not granted, but his prayer was nevertheless *answered*—"not as I will, but as You will." As Hebrews 5:7 teaches, "In the days of his flesh, Jesus offered up prayers and supplications, with loud cries and tears, to the one who was able to save him from death, and he was heard because of his reverent submission." While the very idea of "submissive" prayer strikes our selfish hearts as objectionable, this is the way Jesus himself prayed (Matt. 26:39) and instructed his followers to pray—"Your will be done" (Matt. 6:10). Here, again, we should not only bring to God our desires but pray that God will bring our desires into alignment with his will, recognizing that "we do not always know or desire what is best for us."[77]

To truly pray "your kingdom come" and "your will be done" *and mean it* is to pray for God's (overarching) will to come to pass even if that is out of

76. Crump explains that if someone asks, "'Why are some of my prayers answered affirmatively, while others seem to be ignored?' John replies, 'Because some are in accord with God's will, while others are not' [1 John 5:14–15]." Crump, *Knocking on Heaven's Door*, 168.

77. Bloesch, *Struggle of Prayer*, 91.

step with what we think we want. If we knew all that God knows and were properly motivated by unselfish love, we would will what he wills. Thus, submitting our wills to his will, in prayer and otherwise, is to submit ourselves to what is best for us and for all concerned—what we would desire if only we knew what God knows and loved as God loves.[78]

We do not know what tomorrow will bring, but we can nonetheless pray with confidence insofar as we trust God's will—knowing that God is perfectly good, all-powerful, all-knowing, and wise. This accords with what I understand James to be teaching when he wrote, "Come now, you who say, 'Today or tomorrow we will go to such and such a city, and spend a year there and engage in business and make a profit.' Yet you do not know what your life will be like tomorrow. . . . Instead, you ought to say, 'If the Lord wills, we will live and also do this or that'" (James 4:13–15 NASB; cf. Heb. 6:3).

God has promised to redeem all things. And although we do not know just when God will bring his promises to fruition, since God never breaks his promises, we can be assured they will indeed come to pass, at least in the world to come.

Conclusion: Revisiting the Problem of Seemingly Unanswered Prayer

While recognizing that other factors are involved (including unseen factors), we have now considered a number of factors that Scripture links to the effectiveness of petitionary prayer—some "rules" of prayer, as it were. These include

1. praying in right relationship with God (obedient and repentant with mediation of Christ);
2. praying with deep (but not presumptuous) faith;
3. praying with unselfish motivations (in accordance with love);
4. persevering in prayer with hope and gratitude, even in the midst of darkness, when it seems that prayers are unheard; and
5. praying in accordance with (and submission to) God's will.

In short, Scripture calls believers to pray humbly and repentantly, with *deep* faith, unselfish love, persevering hope, and in accordance with God's will—all of which are linked to the effectiveness of petitionary prayer.

---

78. Tim Keller advises that we pray to "God with the confidence that he is going to give you what you would have asked for if you knew everything he knows"—and, I would add, unselfishly desire what is good for all concerned. Keller, *Prayer*, 229.

With these factors on the table, we can more directly revisit the problem of seemingly unanswered prayers: Why are some prayer requests not granted?

We have seen significant links between effective prayer and both "righteousness" and "faith." Unrepentant wickedness raises "barriers" between humans and God (Isa. 59:2) that might impede God's action in response to prayer or cut off avenues of divine action. Likewise, in some cases lack of faith might impede divine action.

In *some* cases, then, a prayer request might not be granted because of (1) unrepentant unrighteousness or (2) lack of faith. Additionally, we saw another link between effective prayer and praying with unselfish motivations—prayers motivated by unselfish love. One might pray in right relationship with God, with humble and deep faith, and yet one's prayer might not be granted because one prays "wrongly" (James 4:3), with *selfish* motivations. One's prayer requests, then, might not be granted due to (3) selfish motivations.

However, as seen earlier, in some cases prayer requests are not granted (at least here and now) even when all three of these factors are in place. One might be in right relationship with God (through repentance and Christ's mediation) and pray with "deep" faith, with the proper unselfish motivations, and yet one's requests might nevertheless be ungranted. Why might this be the case?

To any prayer request, there are three possible lines of response: yes, no, or not yet. Understood this way, not all requests are granted, but all prayers are answered—in some sense.[79] The request might be granted here and now (yes); not granted, even in the future (no); or granted later but not now (not yet). In cases where the answer is not an immediate yes (when the request is not granted here and now), it might not be immediately clear whether the answer is no or not yet.

Thus even requests that are later granted might *seem* like unanswered prayers for a long time. In Hannah's case, her request was eventually granted. For some time, however, it seemed that God did not hear her. The answer to her request was not no; the answer was not yet, and eventually yes. Since we live in the context of the "already, but not yet" of God's kingdom in the midst of cosmic conflict (see chaps. 3–4), it should not be surprising that the answer to many good requests is not yet.

Hannah's case (and many others like it) highlights the importance of another factor: persevering in prayer. In some cases, a prayer request might not be granted because the timing of the request was not right (the answer is not yet due to other unseen factors, such as the rules of engagement), but one

---

79. Simundson notes, "Even if the answer to our prayer seems to be no, we may find other benefits that have come to us or others, demonstrating that God indeed has heard and answered our prayer." Simundson, *Where Is God?*, 63.

gave up on God or broke with God before the appropriate time came, failing to persevere to the "end." That is, in some cases, a prayer request might not be granted because (4) one gives up on God, loses all hope, or otherwise fails to persevere in prayer.

We have seen that the need to persevere in prayer makes sense in the context of a cosmic conflict with rules of engagement. In some cases, God's answer might be delayed due to the rules of engagement (as when the prince of Persia opposed God's angel in Dan. 10) but is on the way and will come in the future if hope is not lost. Yet if one gives up or loses heart in the meantime, an avenue that might be opened through petitionary prayer might close.

Many others have prayed along the lines of Hannah's prayer, however, and the answer nevertheless turned out to be no. In such cases, is it safe to assume that the requests were not granted because those praying were (1) mired in unrepentant wickedness, (2) did not have enough faith, (3) were offering selfish prayers, or (4) did not persevere long or fervently enough?

No. Instead, it might be that all the above factors were properly in place, but the request was not in accordance with God's will. That is, the prayer request might not be granted, at least here and now, because (5) the request is not in accordance with God's will. Some requests might just not be good for us or others—whether now or down the road—perhaps in ways we cannot see. We should always pause and remember how little we know about precisely what the overarching, long-term consequences of a given course might be.

But what about prayers for obviously good outcomes (at least in themselves), such as prayers for basic needs—for example, praying to receive food so that one does not starve? Wouldn't the perfectly good and loving God certainly "want" or "will" these things? Why might some such prayers for obviously good things (in and of themselves) sometimes not be in accordance with God's will?

Here, we need to briefly recall the distinction between God's ideal will and remedial will. In and of themselves, prayers for entirely good outcomes (such as for basic needs that one lacks through no fault of one's own) would be in accordance with God's ideal will but might not be in accordance with God's remedial will, which takes into account all other factors—including those that are not up to God, such as creatures' bad decisions and that which falls within the temporary jurisdiction of the domain of darkness (due to the rules of engagement).

Even a prayer request offered in right relationship with God, in deep faith, with sufficiently unselfish motivations, and with persevering hope might be out of step with God's will in three possible ways. For God to grant that request might

1. result in worse outcomes (on the whole), with less flourishing of goodness and love, all things considered (including *all* unseen factors);
2. contravene creaturely free will of the kind necessary for the flourishing of love (to which God has committed himself); or
3. require God to break his commitments relative to the rules of engagement in the cosmic conflict (or any other of his promises/commitments), even given "righteous" and repentant, faithful, unselfish, and persistent petitionary prayer.

God's promises are guaranteed. Accordingly, anything prayed in accordance with God's (remedial) will (and, thus, his name) is guaranteed to be answered affirmatively, *eventually*, even if the answer now is not yet (see John 14:13–14; 15:16; 16:23; 1 John 5:14–15). For now, even good outcomes that we pray for in all the right ways (in accordance with all known "rules" and factors) might nevertheless be out of step with God's (remedial) will because they might undermine the creaturely freedom necessary for love, go against the rules of engagement or other divine promises/commitments, or lead to worse outcomes on the whole (e.g., Christ's request "let this cup pass").

Given this, we would do well to pray in accordance with Jesus's prayer in Gethsemane, which matches the concerns and instructions of the Lord's Prayer: "My Father, if it is possible, let this cup pass from Me; yet not as I will, but as You will" (Matt. 26:39 NASB).

We might simply ask for God to respond to our prayers in the most preferable way possible, recognizing that what we have in mind might not be it.

While we can be sure that God's promises will come about eventually, we are often not in a position to know precisely what God's (remedial) will is in a given situation here and now, but we can nevertheless have confidence in God's eschatological promises. In the end,

> [God] will wipe away every tear from their eyes.
> Death will be no more;
> mourning and crying and pain will be no more,
> for the first things have passed away. (Rev. 21:4; cf. Rom. 8:18)

To this eschatological hope, even when God seems hidden and the world is filled with unjust suffering and other injustices, we turn in the final chapter.

6

Praying When God
Seems Hidden

*Fervent Prayer and Lament
as We Await God's Final Answer*

Why? It seemed to make no sense. John the Baptist had faithfully followed God's call. His birth was an answer to prayer. He was chosen to prepare the way for the Messiah. Jesus even said of him, "Among those born of women no one is greater than John" (Luke 7:28). Yet John found himself languishing in prison, with many questions regarding why he was left to suffer (cf. Matt. 11:2–3). Despite his faithfulness, he was not delivered from prison. He was beheaded. Evil and injustice seemed to triumph.

Did God not hear John's cries? This, and other cases like it, relates to what is often called the problem of divine hiddenness. Why would the perfectly good and all-powerful God sometimes seem to be silent and hidden, particularly in the midst of distress?

This final chapter draws together some implications of a cosmic conflict approach to petitionary prayer relative to apparent divine hiddenness, especially in the face of injustice. In doing so, this chapter highlights the biblical pattern of lament in the face of injustice—including God's own profound concern for justice, the corresponding call not only to fervently pray for God's will to be done on earth but to intentionally and persistently act in practical, loving ways to relieve suffering and foster justice, alongside assurance of God's final victory and eschatological solution and the ongoing intercession of the Son and the Holy Spirit for us in the meantime.

When God Seems Silent and Hidden: The Case of Elijah

"What are you doing here, Elijah?" God asked (1 Kings 19:9). Not long before, Elijah had been part of an amazing victory, but now he was hiding from the wrath of King Ahab and Queen Jezebel.

After years of terrible drought, God had sent Elijah to Ahab to challenge the hundreds of prophets of the false god Baal to a showdown on Mount Carmel. Both sides would prepare a sacrificial bull placed on wood "but put no fire to it." Each would "call on the name" of their God, and "the god who answers by fire is indeed God" (1 Kings 18:23–24).

The prophets of Baal "called on the name of Baal" all day, even ritually cutting themselves, but they received no answer (1 Kings 18:26–29). After this, Elijah repaired the altar of the Lord and had twelve large jars of water poured on the slaughtered bull and the wood, drenching the altar and everything on and around it (18:30–35).

Then, Elijah prayed. "O LORD, God of Abraham, Isaac, and Israel, let it be known this day that you are God in Israel, that I am your servant, and that I have done all these things at your bidding. Answer me, O LORD, answer me, so that this people may know that you, O LORD, are God and that you have turned their hearts back" (1 Kings 18:36–37). As Millar explains, this "is at root a prayer for God to act to vindicate himself and keep his commitments"—to vindicate his name against the false gods of the nations.[1]

In response to Elijah's prayer, "the fire of the LORD fell and consumed the burnt offering, the wood, the stones, and the dust and even licked up the water that was in the trench. When all the people saw it, they fell on their faces and said, 'The LORD indeed is God; the LORD indeed is God'" (1 Kings 18:38–39). Then the drought ended with "a heavy rain" (18:45; cf. James 5:16–18).

Elijah had seen these and many other amazing miracles in answer to his prayers—including God resurrecting a boy in response to his prayer (1 Kings 17:17–22; cf. 17:6, 14–16). Yet now Elijah was withering in hiding, praying instead that God would take his life (19:4)!

Fortunately, God did not answer this prayer the way Elijah asked. Instead, God sent an angel and provided food and instructed him to go to Mount Horeb. There God asked him, "What are you doing here, Elijah?" (1 Kings

---

1. Millar, *Calling on the Name of the Lord*, 63.

19:9). Elijah responded with a list of complaints (19:10). When things get tough, it is all too easy to forget the "mountaintop" experiences.

It often seems that evil triumphs. In the past and present, even while Jesus walked the earth, the friends of God (such as John) often suffered and faced horrible deaths. It sometimes seems that there is no hope. But, if the promises of Scripture are to be believed, the triumph of evil is only temporary. Yet how are we to face the times of darkness, when all seems lost?

The "Problem" of Divine Hiddenness

The well-known atheist scientist Richard Dawkins was once asked what he'd say if he met God after he died. His reply: "Which God are you, and why did you take such great pains to conceal yourself and to hide away from us?"[2]

Scripture describes many striking encounters between God and humans, yet Scripture also refers to the apparent hiddenness of God. For example, Job cried out,

> Why do You hide Your face
> And consider me Your enemy? (Job 13:24 NASB)

Similarly, the psalmist asks,

> Why do You stand far away, Lord?
> Why do You hide Yourself in times of trouble? (Ps. 10:1 NASB; cf.
>   44:23–24; Isa. 45:15)

Further, Christ himself cried out on the cross, "My God, my God, why have you forsaken me?" (Mark 15:34).

C. S. Lewis described his experience, while grieving his wife's death thus: "Where is God? . . . Go to him when your need is desperate, when all other help is vain, and what do you find? A door slammed in your face, and a sound of bolting and double bolting on the inside. After that, silence. You may as well turn away. . . . Why is He so present a commander in our time of prosperity and so very absent a help in time of trouble?"[3]

Many have cried out to God in distress and were left feeling as if God is absent. But if a perfectly loving God exists, would not such a God respond to the cries of suffering people, if only to let them know he is there with them?

---

2. CNN, "Dawkins." Dawkins's reply follows the atheist philosopher Bertrand Russell, quoted in Angell, "Comment," 29.
3. Lewis, *Grief Observed*, 4–5.

J. L. Schellenberg argues that any good parent would respond to the cries of their distressed young child if they could.[4] Accordingly, he argues along the following lines: A perfectly loving God would make himself known to everyone capable of knowing him who does not resist. Yet some nonresistant people, who apparently are capable of knowing God, nevertheless do not believe that God exists. Therefore, Schellenberg concludes, no perfectly loving God exists.

Possible Answers to the Problem of Divine Hiddenness

Toward answering the problem of divine hiddenness, some contend that God is not hidden at all, but all might know God at least through general revelation in nature. As Psalm 19:1–2 puts it,

> The heavens tell of the glory of God;
> And their expanse declares the work of His hands.
> Day to day pours forth speech,
> And night to night reveals knowledge. (NASB; cf. 14:1; Rom. 1:20)[5]

Further, perhaps God shows himself and answers our prayers in ways one might not recognize—especially if one refuses to seek him. As Blaise Pascal put it, "Willing to appear openly to those who seek Him with all their heart, and to be hidden from those who flee from Him with all their heart, [God] so regulates the knowledge of Himself that He has given signs of Himself, visible to those who seek Him, and not to those who seek Him not. There is enough light for those who only desire to see, and enough obscurity for those who have a contrary disposition" (cf. John 7:17).[6]

Others suggest that Schellenberg might hold incorrect assumptions about the nature and activity of a perfectly loving God, and thus his expectations of how God would or should make himself known are correspondingly incorrect.[7]

Alternatively, some grant that a perfectly loving God would want to reveal himself to humans and (absent impediments) would act to do so for at least those nonresistant persons capable of knowing him (if there are any such

---

4. Schellenberg, "Divine Hiddenness," 62; cf. Schellenberg, *Hiddenness Argument*.

5. Some claim that there are no *inculpable* nonbelievers. See, e.g., Spiegel, *Making of an Atheist*, 11.

6. Pascal, *Pensées*, 118.

7. See, e.g., Meister, "Evil and the Hiddenness of God," 149; Rea, "Divine Hiddenness, Divine Silence," 161–64; Rea, "Hiddenness and Transcendence."

persons). However, perhaps some good reason(s) or impediments prevent God from making himself known more robustly, especially in a world embroiled in a cosmic conflict. Perhaps, for some individuals, God revealing himself more overtly would negatively impact them or have other "deleterious" consequences.[8] Or perhaps God doing so would be out of step with the requirements of creaturely freedom or other divine commitments.[9]

A Cosmic Conflict Reply to Divine Hiddenness

What if there is more to the story—a cosmic conflict framework in which our world is fallen and temporarily a part of "enemy territory"?[10] As Millar notes, prayer itself seems to presuppose some distance between God and us: "It is almost self-evident that prayer is necessary only in a fallen world," in which there is a "profound break in our relationship with Yahweh." But God "continues to speak to his creatures, and makes it possible for us to respond to him."[11]

Genesis presents the fall of humankind as a breaking point, such that (temporarily) God could no longer dwell with his people with the degree of intimacy he originally intended. In this regard, Scripture consistently highlights that sin has severely ruptured the God-human relationship, resulting in a kind of divine hiddenness. As Isaiah 59:2 declares,

> Your wrongdoings have caused a separation between you and your
> God,
> And your sins have *hidden* His face from you so that He does not hear.
> (NASB)

Indeed, the apparent "hiddenness" of God is precisely what we might expect in the context of a primarily epistemic cosmic conflict with rules of engagement, in which we are dwelling in "enemy territory." Beyond the separation from the fuller divine presence caused by sin in this world (Isa. 59:2; cf. Gen. 3; Deut. 31:16–17), the rules of engagement might further limit

8. Perhaps those "who do not believe in God . . . are, for one reason or another, not ready to believe that God exists or put their trust in him. So God hides." Meister, "Evil and the Hiddenness of God," 144; cf. Reibsamen, "Divine Goodness," 140.

9. See, further, A. Green and Stump, *Hidden Divinity and Religious Belief*; Rea, *Evil and the Hiddenness of God*.

10. Here, I make no attempt to provide a full answer to the broader problem of divine hiddenness (that would require a book of its own). I wish to simply propose that a rules of engagement model might help with this problem.

11. Millar, *Calling on the Name of the Lord*, 29.

the circumstances in which God is (morally) permitted to reveal himself to humans, without thereby taking an unfair advantage in this (primarily epistemic) conflict. Perhaps God wishes to make himself known to humans more directly, but some factors in the cosmic conflict (morally) prevent him from doing so.

Imagine an extremely wealthy miser who "steadfastly refuses to give away a penny to help the poor."[12] Everyone thinks he is selfish and greedy. After he dies, however, his will instructs that all his money be given to the church with instructions to deliver it to the poor. We find out further that he had made a promise to his dying father never to give any money to the poor as long as he lived and would not reveal that promise during his lifetime. "The final will and testament of the supposed miser totally alters our reading of his life and character."[13] In some ways, this modern parable (of William Abraham) matches Jesus's parable of the wheat and the tares (Matt. 13:24–30), adding a glimpse of a scenario in which one might be (temporarily) unable to bring about goods that one wants to bring about, because doing so would result in some unacceptable loss(es) in other ways.

In this regard, this cosmic conflict framework suggests that when God *seems* to be hidden and does not *seemingly* respond to our prayers, for God to respond more overtly—or "show himself"—might be against the rules of engagement or otherwise lead to greatly undesirable results. God might otherwise prefer to make himself known more fully, especially to those suffering, but perhaps doing so would (1) undermine the extent of consequential freedom necessary for love relationship, (2) go against the rules of engagement, or (3) otherwise lead to worse results in the long run, for all concerned. Relative to this third possibility, sometimes God does not answer our prayers in the way we request—and might appear to be silent—because God doing so would not be good for us and/or for others concerned. If we could see the end from the beginning, we might frequently find reason to pray, "Thank you, God, for not giving me what I asked for."

Some years ago, I came down with a severe case of the flu, due to which I quarantined myself from my then five-year old son to prevent him from catching this severe illness. My son asked to play with me every day, and I greatly wanted to be with him in answer to his many requests. He did not quite understand why we could not be together in the way he wanted (and I also wanted), but it was for his best good that I be temporarily removed from him in order to protect him from something far worse. In a somewhat similar

12. Abraham, "Revelation Reaffirmed," 208.
13. Abraham, "Revelation Reaffirmed," 208.

fashion, perhaps in *some* cases God is restricted (morally) from even making his presence known or acting in ways he would otherwise prefer.

Here, we must remember that prayer is only *one* factor of many. In one case, God might strikingly reveal himself to people who call on him, while in another case that might seem identical to us, it might be against the rules or otherwise undesirable for God to overtly reveal himself. As noted earlier in this book, two cases might seem nearly identical to us (such as that of Peter, who was saved, and James, who suffered death, in Acts 12), but unseen factors might be such that God has the moral right to intervene in one circumstance but not the other—or otherwise knows that intervening in one case to prevent the "evil" would lead to far worse outcomes on the whole.

For every factor we see, there might be myriads of factors we do not see (particularly when considering the long view). When one encounters apparent hiddenness or silence in response to one's prayers, it does not follow that prayers do not "work" or make any difference—there may be far more to the story.[14] Imagine that I put gasoline in a car designed to run on gasoline, but then the car does not run. Does that mean that gasoline does not work as fuel? Should I take this as an indication that gasoline plays no part in the effective operation of the car? Of course not. In such a scenario, it is not that the gasoline does not "work" but that there are many other possible reasons the car does not run.

When we cannot make sense of what is happening around us—when our questions about God and his goodness grow and seem unanswerable in the face of suffering and grief, coupled with apparent silence and hiddenness—we would do well to remember that there is far more to the story than meets the eye.

God's providence always takes into account what is good for all concerned in the long run. Here, we must not only think in terms of what seems best to us in the short term but must keep the long view in mind, recognizing that much of what that includes is unknowable to us here and now. We do not know just what the future holds. What we can be sure of with respect to the future is limited to that which God has promised (more on God's eschatological promises later). Thus we are left with the long view of faith, coupled with the fact that we cannot see very far down the road. Here, and elsewhere, we desperately need God's word as a lamp unto our feet (Ps. 119:105) as we walk an otherwise dark path—being "always confident" in God and his promises even as we "walk by faith, not by sight" (2 Cor. 5:6–7).

14. Baelz comments, "A hidden God he may be, an absent God never." Baelz, *Prayer and Providence*, 60.

Praying for Justice and Lamenting Injustice

Yet even if a cosmic conflict framework helps us understand why God might seem hidden or silent in some cases, even in the midst of deep suffering or existential angst, we are nevertheless left with how we are to deal with such situations. How are we to pray in the dark, when God seems hidden?[15]

Let us look to Christ. On the cross, Jesus provided an example demonstrating that lament is not sinful. He cried out, "My God, my God, why have you forsaken me?" (Mark 15:34). Christ's lament, however, was not one of hopelessness. The very words he cried out were from Psalm 22:1, a psalm that *ends* in triumph. In the next verse, the psalmist states, "My God, I cry out by day, but You do not answer; And by night, but I have no rest" (22:2 NASB). Later, however, the psalm turns to petition for deliverance (22:19–21), then exhortation to praise God, for "he did not hide his face from me but heard when I cried to him" (22:24), and "future generations will be told about the Lord" and will "proclaim his deliverance to a people yet unborn, saying that he has done it" (22:30–31; cf. 1 Pet. 3:14, 17–18).

As in this psalm, what began in near despair at the cross would end in triumph at the resurrection. Christ was not spared from the cross, but he rose again, defeating death itself. The Father had not forsaken him. By outward appearances, it seemed that he had and evil would triumph. But what looked like evil's greatest triumph was actually evil's greatest defeat. Through the cross, evil itself would be dealt the death blow: Christ died "so that through death He might destroy the one who has the power of death, that is, the devil" (Heb. 2:14 NASB).

Scripture is filled with faithful servants crying out to God in lament over evil and injustice—including many psalms of lament (communal and individual), the most common type of psalm.[16] Here, I will mention only a few examples, but I encourage you to dive deeply into these and others in the book of Psalms, the prayer book of Scripture.

Psalm 6:1–10 offers a stirring prayer for healing:

> Lord, do not rebuke me in Your anger,
> Nor discipline me in Your wrath.
> Be gracious to me, Lord, for I am frail;
> Heal me, Lord, for my bones are horrified.
> And my soul is greatly horrified;
> But You, Lord—how long?

---

15. On lament in prayer, see Timpe, "Toward an Account of Lamenting Well."

16. See, further, Brueggemann, *Praying the Psalms*; Waltke, Houston, and Moore, *Psalms as Christian Lament*.

> Return, LORD, rescue my soul;
> Save me because of Your mercy.
> For there is no mention of You in death;
> In Sheol, who will praise You?
>
> I am weary with my sighing;
> Every night I make my bed swim,
> I flood my couch with my tears.
> My eye has wasted away with grief;
> It has grown old because of all my enemies.
>
> Leave me, all you who practice injustice,
> For the LORD has heard the sound of my weeping.
> The LORD has heard my pleading,
> The LORD receives my prayer.
> All my enemies will be put to shame and greatly horrified;
> They shall turn back, they will suddenly be put to shame. (NASB; cf.
>   Hab. 1:1–4, 13)

A few chapters later, Psalm 10:1–2 offers a prayer for deliverance:

> Why do You stand far away, LORD?
> Why do You hide Yourself in times of trouble?
> In arrogance the wicked hotly pursue the needy;
> Let them be caught in the plots which they have devised. (NASB; cf.
>   88:14; Isa. 63:15)

After lamenting that the wicked prosper with seeming impunity (10:3–11), the prayer continues,

> Arise, LORD; God, lift up Your hand.
> Do not forget the humble.
> Why has the wicked treated God disrespectfully?
> He has said to himself, "You will not require an account."
> You have seen it, for You have looked at harm and provocation to take
>   it into Your hand.
> The unfortunate commits himself to You;
> You have been the helper of the orphan.
> Break the arm of the wicked and the evildoer,
> Seek out his wickedness until You find none.
>
> The LORD is King forever and ever;
> Nations have perished from His land.
> LORD, You have heard the desire of the humble;

You will strengthen their heart, You will make Your ear attentive
To vindicate the orphan and the oppressed,
So that mankind, which is of the earth, will no longer cause terror.
   (10:12–18 NASB)

Scripture includes many such imprecations against evildoers, calling for
God to bring justice.[17] Trevor Laurence makes a strong case that such biblical "imprecations" should be understood as "kingdom-protecting, enemy-
expelling petition[s]," noting specifically that Scripture teaches that "Satan
and the demonic forces of the kingdom of darkness" are "engaged in violent
battle against the temple-kingdom of God."[18] In this regard, Gombis notes,
"one of the main strategies of the [cosmic] powers is to make injustice, oppression, idolatry and exploitation seem normal and inevitable—business
as usual."[19] Against this, all who would truly follow Christ must stand and
"resist participating in broader systems of injustice and exploitation and pray
for wisdom to forge creative pathways of renewal that are redemptive and
life-giving and represent a return to *shalom*."[20]

Yet even as we rightly call for and work toward justice, we should remember that God also seeks to save those same evildoers. We can pray both
for justice to be done and for God to bring evildoers to repentance, even as
Saul of Tarsus—the arch-persecutor of Christians—came to faith. If we cry
only for justice but not mercy for those willing to repent, then we condemn
ourselves and fail to follow Christ's command, "Love your enemies and pray
for those who persecute you" (Matt. 5:44). Yet we should be careful not to
overemphasize forgiveness and mercy at the expense of justice. As Dorena
Williamson emphasizes, we need to listen to calls both for "radical forgiveness" and for "justice"—consonant with God's character of compassionate
mercy and justice (cf. Exod. 34:6–7; Ps. 85:10).[21]

---

17. Carmen Joy Imes comments, "If we believe that God is just—that YHWH does not
leave the guilty unpunished—then to pray the imprecatory psalms is to call upon God to act
in accordance with God's own character. It is to call upon God to put an *end* to violence. The
Psalms offer language for occasions when evil has gone unchecked and we desire for God to
step in and *do* something." Imes, "Ethics of Vengeful Prayer."

18. Laurence, *Cursing with God*, 265, 264.

19. Gombis, *Drama of Ephesians*, 54.

20. Gombis, *Drama of Ephesians*, 56.

21. Williamson writes this in a moving piece on the juxtaposition of a Black person's forgiveness of his brother's murderer going viral, while the victim's mother's cries for justice went
largely overlooked. She writes: "When a black person extends radical forgiveness, we see the
grace of the gospel. But when we ignore a black person's call for justice, we cheapen that grace.
Both are acting like the God we serve; we need to listen to both." Williamson, "Botham Jean's
Brother's Offer of Forgiveness."

Psalm 44 offers a communal lament and prayer for help. After recounting God's past deeds for his covenant people and lamenting his apparent inaction in the midst of suffering in the present, this psalm concludes,

> Rouse yourself! Why do you sleep, O Lord?
>> Awake, do not cast us off forever!
> Why do you hide your face?
>> Why do you forget our affliction and oppression?
> For we sink down to the dust;
>> our bodies cling to the ground.
> Rise up, come to our help.
>> Redeem us for the sake of your steadfast love. (44:23–26)

Here and elsewhere, Scripture is filled with the cry, "How long, O Lord?" (see, e.g., Ps. 77:7–10; 94:3–7; Rev. 6:9–11).[22] Psalm 130 adds,

> Out of the depths I cry to you, O LORD.
>> Lord, hear my voice!
> Let your ears be attentive
>> to the voice of my supplications! . . .
> I wait for the LORD; my soul waits,
>> and in his word I hope. (130:1–2, 5)

These are but a few biblical examples of believers pouring their heart out to God in lament, with many even questioning God (see, e.g., Moses in Exod. 5:22–23; Elijah in 1 Kings 17:17–22; Lamentations). These examples (and many others) demonstrate that it is okay to bring to God our true feelings—to ask questions of God, even hard questions, humbly and in the right spirit. You can be honest with God. He already knows what is in your heart. If you are ashamed of what is in your heart, do not hide it from God, but ask him to change your heart.

As Diane Langberg explains, many "mistakenly believe their grief and questions and anger are ungodly," but such "feelings" are "mirrored in the Scriptures and not condemned," which might encourage us "to lament the evil and suffering" in this world.[23] In this regard, Tish Harrison Warren writes, "The amount of pain shouldered by even the seemingly happiest among us is enough to leave me reeling."[24] Indeed, she adds, we all suffer with "muted

---

22. Bauckham notes that there is a "pattern of delay" in God's response to eliminating injustice, but the prayers will be answered in the end. Bauckham, "Prayer in the Book of Revelation," 264–65.

23. Langberg, *Suffering and the Heart of God*, 246.

24. Warren, *Prayer in the Night*, 40.

sorrow" that we bear. And even though the world often signals that there is no time to stop and grieve—to lament and pray—we must learn or relearn to grieve and to pray our laments and sorrows (individually and collectively), even if such prayers are not answered in the way we'd like.[25] As Soong-Chan Rah explains, "The practice of lament must be purposely reintroduced to the church," and "we should begin to embrace those who lament."[26] For believers, praying in lament is not something to be ashamed of; it is itself an act of faith. As Langberg writes, when a believer prays in lament, "faith is being demonstrated by someone in extreme pain because they are talking to God about that pain and the questions it raises."[27]

Sometimes, all we can muster is to cry out to God in grief and anger. He knows it better than we do.[28] He understands. In Langberg's words, "We must not forget that we serve a God who weeps."[29] He will not turn away anyone who sincerely cries to him, whether in anger or sadness or near despair. God can handle our emotions, even when we cannot. In such times, I often pray the words that the man with the demon-afflicted son spoke to Jesus: Lord, "I believe; help my unbelief!" (Mark 9:24). When we feel as if all is lost, as if there is no hope, we might pray like Jehoshaphat prayed when surrounded by a "great horde," which Judah was "powerless" against: "We do not know what to do, but our eyes are on you" (2 Chron. 20:12).

Prayer as Protest against the Forces of Darkness

Not only is praying in the midst of darkness an act of faith, but to pray in lament of injustice—asking for God's deliverance—is also to resist and protest the enemy's rule and the systemic evil of his domain of darkness in this cosmic conflict, or what Justo González calls the "empire of evil."[30]

Prayers for justice ring hollow, however, if we fail to do anything to bring justice and peace to those around us. Pray, yes. But also act in love.[31] As Baelz

---

25. Warren, *Prayer in the Night*, 40.

26. Rah, *Prophetic Lament*, 198–99. On the "need to get closer to the poorest and abandoned in the world" and how we are "to pray with the unwanted in the world," see Carvalhaes, "Praying with the Unwanted People," 688.

27. Langberg, *Suffering and the Heart of God*, 190.

28. W. Bingham Hunter writes, "On some days we may find prayer impossible. Pain, anguish and grief can become so consuming that there is nothing left over to pray with." Hunter, *God Who Hears*, 85.

29. Langberg, *Suffering and the Heart of God*, 62.

30. González, *Mañana*, 93.

31. See, e.g., Mooney, "Becoming What We Pray," 55.

puts it, "Prayer is no substitute for work."[32] In his Sermon on the Mount (Matt. 5–7), Christ instructs us to pray and also teaches us how we ought to *act* in love to others (cf. 25:31–45). This is particularly significant if we remember that, in light of the cosmic conflict, God might face moral restrictions that prevent him from intervening to eliminate evils in some cases, but some such evils are within our power to mitigate or prevent, if we are willing to act.

God himself rebukes his people when they make outward shows of devotion while neglecting to care for the poor and oppressed, saying that their "hands are full of blood" and he "cannot endure solemn assemblies with iniquity." Further, even if they "make many prayers," God declares that he "will hide [his] eyes" from those who fail to turn from injustice and evil deeds to instead "seek justice; rescue the oppressed; defend the orphan; [and] plead for the widow" (Isa. 1:13–17). Sincere, heartfelt prayer must be accompanied with repentance and love for others. As Proverbs 21:13 teaches, "One who shuts his ear to the outcry of the poor will also call out himself, and not be answered" (NASB; cf. Prov. 14:31; James 2:5–8, 13). As Bloesch notes, if we "pray in the biblical way," we "become more sensitive to the crying needs of the world, both spiritual and material, and [be] moved to alleviate these needs."[33]

In Scripture, justice and love are inseparable. Love without justice is crippled, and justice without love is heartless and cold. The God of the Bible is "a God of justice" (Isa. 30:18); he "love[s] justice" (Ps. 37:28; Isa. 61:8) and hates injustice. Scripture repeatedly describes God's profound concern for the downtrodden and oppressed, calling his people to act. For example, God declares, "Dispense true justice and practice kindness and compassion each to his brother; and do not oppress the widow or the orphan, the stranger [foreigner] or the poor; and do not devise evil in your hearts against one another" (Zech. 7:9–10 NASB; see also Ps. 9:9; Isa. 10:1–3; Mic. 6:8; Matt. 23:23; Luke 11:42).

To follow these and other teachings, we are not to pretend everything is okay but to recognize the realities of suffering in the world—weep with those who weep—while also possessing an undergirding and overarching confidence and hope in the better future that is to come. As Scripture assures us, "The sufferings of this present time are not worth comparing with the glory about to be revealed to us" (Rom. 8:18). One day God will finally "wipe every tear" from our eyes, and there will no longer be any death or mourning or crying or pain, for the former things will have passed away (Rev. 21:4). God will fulfill

---

32. Baelz, *Prayer and Providence*, 102.
33. Bloesch, *Struggle of Prayer*, 143.

his promises in the end. The dragon's empire will be utterly eradicated and replaced by the Lamb's kingdom of unselfish love—the first shall be last and the last shall be first.

In the midst of deep distress, we might likewise remember Job, John the Baptist, and others who suffered undeservedly. No lack of divine concern or favor left John in prison. John was greatly beloved. Jesus himself—the perfect, beloved Son—died on the cross as an innocent victim. The apparent silence or hiddenness of God in some situations, then, cannot rightly be taken as an indication of lack of God's favor.

At times we might nevertheless be tempted to think that God has forgotten us. In this regard, Isaiah reports the doubts of God's people, saying, "The LORD has forsaken me; my Lord has forgotten me." But in response God declares,

> Can a woman forget her nursing child
>   or show no compassion for the child of her womb?
> Even these might forget,
>   yet I will not forget you.
> See, I have inscribed you on the palms of my hands;
>   your walls are continually before me. (49:14–16)

Even when God seems absent, he is with his people, wherever we may go (Ps. 139:7–12). Trust in him, and he will "never leave you or forsake you" (Heb. 13:5). God will bring justice in the end and deliverance from all suffering and injustice. In the meantime, let us not lose hope or faith. When we feel like our faith is not enough, we may simply pray to the Lord, "I believe; help my unbelief!" (Mark 9:24). God will hear even the smallest cry of those who call on his name.

God's answers to your prayers might not bring immediate deliverance from what you face right now but will bring ultimate deliverance in the end. In the meantime, know that God loves you more than you could imagine and wants deliverance and justice for you (and everyone else) even more than you do—exponentially more.

The psalmist Asaph was deeply troubled by the oppression, injustice, and evil around him and struggled with his own suffering, despite his faithfulness. He lamented,

> Surely in vain I have kept my heart pure
> And washed my hands in innocence;
> For I have been stricken all day long,
> And punished every morning. (Ps. 73:13–14 NASB)

Meanwhile, the wicked prospered, oppressing others and blaspheming God, while "always at ease, they increase in riches" (73:12; cf. 73:3–11). When he "thought of understanding this, it was troublesome" to him (73:16 NASB). But then, Asaph declares, "I went into the sanctuary of God; then I perceived their end" (73:17).

Asaph found the solution in the sanctuary of God, from which God will eventually bring judgment in favor of the faithful, many of whom are downtrodden and victims of oppression in this domain of darkness.[34] In the end, God will bring justice, vindicate his name, and deliver all who call on his name. In the meantime, as discussed further in the next section, Christ ministers in the heavenly sanctuary even now, interceding for all who call on the name of the Lord.

The Ultimate Intercessors: The Son and the Holy Spirit

Deliverance is coming. Christ will finally eradicate the devil's domain. In the meantime, Christ himself prays and intercedes for us. Via the cross, Christ demonstrated God's righteousness and love and thus defeated the enemy's slanderous allegations against God's character (Rom. 3:25–26; 5:8; Rev. 12:10–11). Afterward, he arose and ascended, taking "His seat at the right hand of the throne of the Majesty in the heavens, a minister in the sanctuary and in the true tabernacle, which the Lord set up, not man" (Heb. 8:1–2 NASB).[35] Even now, as our cosmic royal priest "he always lives to make intercession for" all "who approach God through him" and "is able for all time to save those who approach God through him" (Heb. 7:25–26; cf. Rom. 8:34).[36]

In this regard, Revelation 4–5 sets forth an amazing scene in heaven in which, Richard Bauckham explains, "the prophet John is taken up into the heavenly sanctuary or throne room of God."[37] There, John sees (among other things) a scroll sealed with seven seals. "The ability to take and open the scroll would represent the right to rule," but no one was found worthy to open the

---

34. See Davidson, *Song for the Sanctuary.*

35. Crump writes, "The idea that God's throne is located in an eternal heavenly temple has its roots in the Old Testament (Hab. 2:20; Ps. 18:6; Testament of Levi 3.4–6; 5.1; 18.6) and is consistent with the idea of human prayer rising to heaven like incense from the altar (Ps. 141:2; Rev. 5:8; 8:3)" (*Knocking on Heaven's Door*, 270). See, further, Moffitt, *Atonement and the Logic of Resurrection.*

36. Bloesch notes, "Our prayers have no worthiness or efficacy apart from his atoning sacrifice and redemptive mediation" (*Struggle of Prayer*, 37). Likewise, Crump, *Knocking on Heaven's Door*, 53.

37. Bauckham, "Prayer in the Book of Revelation," 253.

scroll and break its seals—no one was found worthy to rule over this world and deliver it from the enemy's demonic rule.[38] Without such a one, all would be lost. Seeing this, John was overtaken with grief and wept bitterly (Rev. 5:1–4). But, then, an elder told John, "Do not weep. See, the Lion of the tribe of Judah, the Root of David, has conquered, so that he can open the scroll and its seven seals" (5:5; cf. 12:10–11). After his victory on the cross, then, Christ (the Lamb who was slain; 5:6) was found worthy to open the scroll—to reclaim the rule forfeited by the first Adam.

Then, "the four living creatures and the twenty-four elders" around God's throne "fell before the Lamb, each holding a harp and golden bowls full of incense, which are the prayers of the saints" (Rev. 5:8; cf. 8:3–5). Here, we find the prayers of God's people symbolized by the incense in the heavenly sanctuary, corresponding to the incense that was burnt on the altar of incense in the earthly sanctuary and wafted into the Most Holy Place, effectively carrying the prayers of God's people before God's throne. "The incense, ascending in smoke from the altar, was understood to symbolize the prayers of the people or symbolically to carry these prayers into God's presence."[39] Bauckham suggests, "Set in the context of chapter 5, it is natural to suppose that 'the prayers of the saints' of verse 8 are for the coming of God's kingdom—indeed, prayers which could be summed up in the words of the Lord's Prayer: 'Your kingdom come, your will be done, on earth as it is in heaven' (Matt. 6:10)."[40] Further, "the offering of the prayers of the saints in 8:3–5 results in the eschatological theophany-and-judgment of the world," bringing justice to the oppressed.[41]

Christ's victory at the cross opened the way so that, though him—our "great high priest"—all believers can "approach the throne of grace [God's very throne] with boldness, so that we may receive mercy and find grace to help in time of need" (Heb. 4:14, 16). In the heavenly sanctuary, Christ continues the intercessory ministry he modeled on earth (and more). In his high priestly prayer in John 17, Jesus prayed for his followers at the time and all "who believe in me through their word" (John 17:20). *All* who believe in Jesus, then, are included in this prayer. Further, in that prayer, Jesus emphasized his mission of glorifying the Father and making his "name known" (17:4, 6). Among other things, he prayed "for the Father's name to be glorified, for believers being kept in that name, for the protection of Jesus' followers from

---

38. Stefanovic, *Revelation of Jesus Christ*, 205.

39. Bauckham, "Prayer in the Book of Revelation," 254; cf. Millar, *Calling on the Name of the Lord*, 228.

40. Bauckham, "Prayer in the Book of Revelation," 255.

41. Bauckham, "Prayer in the Book of Revelation," 257.

the evil one, for their being set apart in truth, and for their mission of love and unity in the world."[42]

Before this prayer, Jesus assured believers that they could confidently come to the Father in prayer (John 16:26–27). Through the mediation of Christ—the ultimate intercessor—believers can boldly approach God's throne (Heb. 4:14–16). In the heavenly sanctuary, Christ functions as our "advocate with the Father," presenting himself as "the atoning sacrifice for our sins" and "also for the sins of the whole world" (1 John 2:1–2). Whatever hardships or sufferings you may encounter, as a believer you can be assured Christ prays *for you*. You are also called to pray, with assurance that your prayers ascend to God in heaven, symbolized in the sanctuary through the altar of incense (cf. Rev. 5:8).

Christ's function as our "advocate with the Father" is not to persuade or convince the Father to forgive or favor us. The Father already desires only our good, for "the Father himself loves" us (John 16:27). Rather, Christ is our advocate and intercessor before the heavenly council to defeat the allegations of the devil, "the accuser of our brothers and sisters . . . , who accuses them day and night before our God" (Rev. 12:10). Christ's interceding ministry is necessary to make a way for God (Father, Son, and Spirit) to defeat the devil's accusations and forgive, cleanse, and save sinners in a way that does not undermine justice and love—the very foundations of God's throne (cf. Ps. 89:14). To this end, Christ's atoning and intercessory ministry demonstrates God's perfect righteousness and love so that he can be both "just and the justifier" of those who have "faith in Jesus" (Rom. 3:25–26 NASB; cf. 5:8).

In this cosmic courtroom drama, the devil stands as "the accuser"—like a malevolent prosecuting attorney, claiming that God cannot save sinners without being unjust (Rev. 12:10; cf. Job 1–2; Zech. 3). On the other hand, Christ stands as our "advocate [*paraklētos*] with the Father" in the heavenly court, presenting himself against the devil's claims and charges as "the atoning sacrifice for our sins" and "also for the sins of the whole world" (1 John 2:1–2)—*the Lamb* who was slain, resurrected, and found worthy to save the world, reclaiming rulership from the devil on behalf of fallen humanity (Rev. 5). Through Christ's victory, the redeemed are victorious over the enemy; in the end they will "have conquered him by the blood of the Lamb and by the word of their testimony" (12:11).

After Christ ascended to minister for us in the heavenly sanctuary, he sent in his place the Holy Spirit "to be with [his people] forever" (John 14:16),

---

42. Lincoln, "God's Name," 176–77. Lincoln notes that Jesus "made known who God is and what God's reputation entails" (164–65).

dwelling in and interceding for all who call on the name of the Lord (see, e.g., Rom. 8:26–27; 1 Cor. 3:16). Indeed, Christ's victory over the powers of darkness through the cross "unleashed" the Holy Spirit to come with special power as another "Advocate" (*paraklētos*) sent by Christ in his place, unleashed to "prove the world wrong about sin and righteousness and judgment" relative to the condemnation of "the ruler of this world"—the devil (John 16:7–11; cf. 7:39; 14:16). In the midst of the cosmic conflict, even as Christ intercedes for us and ministers as our *advocate* (*paraklētos*) in the heavenly court, the Holy Spirit intercedes and ministers as our *advocate* (*paraklētos*) on earth.[43] This intercessory work of the Spirit is crucial. As Bloesch puts it, "Apart from the outpouring of the Holy Spirit there can be no prayer worthy of the name of Christian. . . . It is the Spirit who moves us to pray and who instructs us in the life of prayer."[44]

Jesus identifies the Holy Spirit as the good gift that the Father gives to those who ask (Luke 11:13). One might initially think of good gifts in material terms—blessings of health, wealth, and the like. But, according to Scripture, those who serve God often suffer the most. Thus, just before his high priestly prayer in John 17, Jesus warned, "In the world you will face persecution [or tribulation], but take courage: I have conquered the world!" (John 16:33).

At first, the fact that Christ's followers face great tribulation seems to clash with Christ's proclamation "I have conquered the world." If the Father only gives good gifts to those who ask him (cf. James 1:17), why doesn't God give the full panoply of blessings to his children now? Why are so many faithful Christ followers left to great suffering such that some wonder if they have been abandoned (e.g., John the Baptist)?

Here, we must remember that God grants his people spiritual blessings that far outweigh any temporary, material ones. Further, earlier in John 16, Christ promised that though his followers suffer now, a bright future awaits: "You have pain now, but I will see you again, and your hearts will rejoice, and no one will take your joy from you" (John 16:22; cf. Rom. 8:18). This state of affairs fits with the consistent biblical teaching of the "already, but not yet"—that Christ's kingdom is in some real and significant sense "already" here (Christ has conquered the world) but in other very significant senses

43. Crump adds, "Although Paul never uses the word, his theology comes remarkably close to the Johannine notion of the Spirit as Paraclete, our Advocate with the Father (John 14:16, 26; 15:26; 16:7). In fact, both the Pauline and the Johannine literature link the Spirit with the Son in joint advocacy, for while the Spirit intercedes from within our current human experience, the Son intercedes from the throne of God, continually applying the benefits of his salvation while defeating satanic accusation (Rom. 8:34; 1 John 2:1; also Heb. 7:25)." Crump, *Knocking on Heaven's Door*, 206.

44. Bloesch, *Struggle of Prayer*, 37.

also "not yet" fully established. This "already, but not yet" dynamic suggests that there is more to the story; much more is going on behind the scenes than initially meets the eye.

Strikingly, Jesus does not pray for immediate deliverance for his followers from this world on the whole but instead prays that in the midst of trials they will be protected from the devil. Specifically, Christ prays, "Holy Father, protect them in your *name* that you have given me" (John 17:11). Further, Christ prays for his followers whom "the world has hated . . . because they do not belong to the world" and adds, "I am not asking you to take them out of the world, but I ask you to protect them from the evil one" (17:14–15).

The disciples who were in Christ's presence when he prayed this prayer, however, later faced severe persecution and death for their witness to Christ. Either Christ's prayer on their behalf in John 17:14–15 was not granted, then, or the request was not for their overall protection in this life but rather was aimed at a particular kind of spiritual protection from the evil one such that they would not be lost (fitting with Christ's prayer in 17:11–12). Accordingly, Christ further prays, "Sanctify them in the truth; your word is truth" (17:17; cf. 17:19). Here, the kind of spiritual protection from "the evil one" (the devil) for which Christ prays is closely associated with the truth, over and against the deceptions of the devil—"the father of lies" (8:44).

While we remain in this period of the "already, but not yet" of Christ's kingdom, in the midst of ongoing cosmic conflict, both Christ and the Holy Spirit *continually* intercede for us. Even as we pray, Christ is interceding for us in heaven (cf. Heb. 7:25–26), and "the Spirit helps us in our weakness, for we do not know how to pray as we ought, but that very Spirit intercedes with groanings too deep for words," and "the Spirit intercedes for the saints according to the will of God" (Rom. 8:26–27).

"Even If God Does Not": Trusting in God

King Nebuchadnezzar of Babylon ordered everyone in the kingdom to bow down to his statue of pure gold. Three young Hebrew men refused, enraging Nebuchadnezzar. He demanded that they bow or be thrown into a furnace of blazing fire. Faced with death for their faith in the one true God, they stood firm, replying, "Our God whom we serve is able to rescue us from the furnace of blazing fire; and He will rescue us from your hand, O king. But even if He does not, let it be known to you, O king, that we are not going to serve your gods nor worship the golden statue that you have set up" (Dan. 3:17–18 NASB). Although they knew that God possessed the power to deliver them, they also recognized that he *might not* do so. In the end, God did save them. They were thrown into the fiery furnace, but due to divine protection, they were totally unharmed—even "the hair of their heads was not singed" (3:27).

Deliverance does not always come in this life as it came for those young men. In contrast, James, John the Baptist, and many others—including Jesus himself—were killed for their faithfulness to the living God. Yet, even though deliverance might not come in this life, ultimate deliverance will come *eventually* (in the eschaton) for *all* who call on the name of the Lord.

Never Give Up Hope

In a (less than humane) study conducted many decades ago, a scientist placed wild rats in jars of water, testing how long they would keep swimming. Despite being known for relatively strong swimming skills, the wild rats lasted only a few minutes before giving up and drowning. In a follow-up experiment, the scientist waited until the rats typically gave up, but then rescued them, held them for a little bit, and then placed them back in the water. This time, however, the rescued rats continued to swim not for minutes, or even an hour, but they kept on swimming for tens of hours.[45] This is the power of hope. When the rats believed that rescue would eventually come, they persevered far beyond what previously seemed possible. Whether or not God grants our requests here and now, those who are in Christ by faith can be confident that help is coming. All the help we could ever want will come when Christ returns.

In this regard, it is easy to see that hope and faith are closely connected, for to hope is to believe that deliverance is possible and may be just around the bend. God's promises of eventual deliverance (at least in the eschaton) are sure. Persevering in prayer, even when things *seem* hopeless, serves as a testament to faith in God—a sign of allegiance to the true king even in the midst of this domain of darkness—even when the path ahead is covered in darkness. Although the fulfillment of God's promises might seem to "tarry," "wait for it; it will surely come, it will not delay" (Hab. 2:3). "Weeping may linger for the night, but joy comes with the morning" (Ps. 30:5). Crump comments, "Do not be fooled by the passing of time. Jesus guaranteed that his disciples will be vindicated (Luke 18:8a). Evil will be eradicated. Justice will overflow like a rushing river covering the earth as the waters cover the sea, as the prophets declared (Amos 5:24; Isa. 11:9)."[46]

45. Hallinan, "Remarkable Power of Hope."
46. Crump, *Knocking on Heaven's Door*, 87.

In the meantime, sometimes what God works to bring about for our good hurts in the process, not because God wants to hurt us but because we are entangled in sin and evil in this cosmic conflict. Think of a dog encountering a porcupine, ending up with countless quills in its face. Since a porcupine's quills are filled with backward-facing barbs, pulling them out hurts far more than they hurt going in. To pull them out unavoidably causes *more* pain. We are stuck, as it were, with many quills of the evil one such that painful remedies are sometimes needed to finally deliver us from evil (cf. Rom. 5:3–4; 2 Cor. 12:8–10; 1 Pet. 4:12–14). Likewise, consider a medical professional performing CPR to resuscitate someone whose heart has stopped beating. In many such cases, effective CPR will require breaking the ribs of the patient, but doing so is the only way to save that person's life. In somewhat similar fashion, sometimes the only avenues available to God to save us (in light of all factors) require pain in the short term. This is not because God wants us to suffer but because we live in enemy territory, entangled with evil.

The enemy seeks to steal and destroy your faith and hope, but God stands with you in the midst of every trial. Some might initially think that God is like the scientist in the experiment mentioned above, testing our faith and resolve with hardships, but the cosmic conflict perspective peels back the curtain and shows that it is the enemy, Satan, who claims that our faith is not enough, who tempts, accuses, and slanders God's people day and night in the heavenly court. In contrast, God is our defender, our advocate who (in Christ and the Holy Spirit) intercedes for us and defeats the enemy's allegations. The devil is the "thief" who "comes only to steal and kill and destroy," while Jesus is the "good shepherd" who "came that [we] might have life and have it abundantly" and who "lays down his life for the sheep" (John 10:10–11).

In the midst of profound loss and suffering brought by the enemy, Job maintained hope:

> I know that my Redeemer lives,
> And at the last, He will take His stand on the earth.
> Even after my skin is destroyed,
> Yet from my flesh I will see God. (Job 19:25–26 NASB)

Like Job, you and I might cry out to God with questions, laments, fears, worries, and even doubts, while at the same time maintaining hope for the future and confidence in God's promises, all the while pleading with God, "I believe; help my unbelief!" (Mark 9:24). Whatever you might face, then, do not give up hope. Your requests may not be granted as you would like now, but the sincere prayers of faith, offered in love and hope through Christ, are *always* heard by God, who cares for you with love greater than you can imagine.

Joy Comes in the Morning: The Assurance of Eschatological Deliverance

Hope and gratefulness might persist even in the darkest situations—even in the midst of deep sorrow and lament. Such hope may not manifest itself in good or warm feelings, since the suffering might be too great at times for such feelings. But alongside deep suffering, an underlying confidence in God and an abiding peace might coincide with ongoing pleas and cries to God for deliverance.

This is especially so when one keeps in mind the surety of God's eschatological promises, that God will make all things right in the end for those who love him (cf. Rom. 8:28). With such assurance, we can pray hopeful, thankful, and expectant prayers that look forward to the eventual dawning of the new day when Christ's kingdom will be established in full: "May your kingdom come. May your will be done on earth as it is in heaven" (Matt. 6:10). In this regard, Richard Bauckham points out that prayer for Christ's second coming "encompasses and completes all other prayers. It is, as it were, the most that can be prayed. It asks for everything—for all that God purposes for and promises to his whole creation in the end."[47]

While praying to God in the midst of suffering or distress, remember that the devil "is a liar and the father of lies" (John 8:44)—*the ultimate gaslighter.* He wants you to think that you are a failure, that you cannot win, that your troubles are of your own making, that things would be different if only you prayed harder and worked better to improve your moral character, or if only you were more deserving of God's favor—and so on. These lies are directly countered by the gospel of Jesus Christ. If you are in Christ by faith, you cannot be a failure, whatever befalls you in this life. Christ has already defeated the devil's slanderous allegations at the cross, so if you are in Christ by faith, you cannot lose (see, e.g., Rev. 12:10–11; cf. Col. 1:13–14; 1 John 3:8). You *cannot* in your own power fix your troubles, improve your moral character, or be deserving of God's favor. But, God graciously bestows favor on all willing to receive it and will make all things right in the end. As the saying goes, *Everything will be okay in the end; if it's not okay, it's not the end.* Through the intercession of Christ and the Holy Spirit, God delights to show unmerited favor (grace) to all who call on his name. And God promises

47. Bauckham, "Prayer in the Book of Revelation," 270.

that the day will come when "before [God's people] call I will answer, while they are yet speaking I will hear" (Isa. 65:24).

We now dwell in enemy territory, but the devil "knows that his time is short" (Rev. 12:12) and that Christ's victory is assured. Thus Paul teaches, "I am convinced that neither death, nor life, nor angels, nor rulers, nor things present, nor things to come, nor powers, nor height, nor depth, nor anything else in all creation will be able to separate us from the love of God in Christ Jesus our Lord" (Rom. 8:38–39). Just a few verses earlier, Paul assured those who suffer that "the sufferings of this present time are not worth comparing with the glory about to be revealed to us" (8:18). In the end, God "will wipe away every tear from their eyes; and there will no longer be any death; there will no longer be any mourning, or crying, or pain; the first things have passed away" (Rev. 21:4 NASB).

There is so much more to say about prayer in general, and petitionary prayer specifically. This book has only scratched the surface. But it is my prayer that here readers might find a framework for thinking about and practicing petitionary prayer aimed at calling on God's name in the midst of the cosmic conflict, persevering in fervent prayer until the end. "Weeping may linger for the night, but joy comes with the morning" (Ps. 30:5).

In the meantime, we might pray,

> In you, O LORD, I take refuge;
>   let me never be put to shame.
> In your righteousness deliver me and rescue me;
>   incline your ear to me and save me.
> Be to me a rock of refuge,
>   a strong fortress to save me,
>   for you are my rock and my fortress. (Ps. 71:1–3)

Bibliography

Abraham, William. *Divine Agency and Divine Action*. 4 vols. Oxford: Oxford University Press, 2017–21.

———. "Revelation Reaffirmed." In *Divine Revelation*, edited by Paul Avis, 201–15. Grand Rapids: Eerdmans, 1997.

Acolatse, Esther E. *Powers, Principalities, and the Spirit: Biblical Realism in Africa and the West*. Grand Rapids: Eerdmans, 2018.

Adams, Robert M. "Must God Create the Best?" *Philosophical Review* 81, no. 3 (1972): 317–32.

Alden, Robert L. *Job*. New American Commentary. Nashville: B&H, 1993.

Alston, William. *Divine Nature and Human Language*. Ithaca, NY: Cornell University Press, 1989.

Andersen, Frances. *Job*. Tyndale Old Testament Commentaries. Leicester: InterVarsity, 1976.

Angell, Roger. "Comment." *New Yorker*. February 21, 1970. https://www.newyorker.com/magazine/1970/02/21/comment-5269.

Arcadi, James M. "Prayer in Analytic Theology." In Cocksworth and McDowell, *T&T Clark Handbook of Christian Prayer*, 533–49.

Archer, Gleason L. "Daniel." In *Daniel and the Minor Prophets*, edited by F. E. Gaebelein, 3–160. Expositor's Bible Commentary. Grand Rapids: Zondervan, 1986.

Arnold, Clinton E. *Powers of Darkness: Principalities and Powers in Paul's Letters*. Downers Grove, IL: InterVarsity, 1992.

———. "Principalities and Powers." In *The Anchor Bible Dictionary*, edited by David Noel Freedman, 5:467. New York: Doubleday, 1992.

———. *3 Crucial Questions about Spiritual Warfare*. Grand Rapids: Baker, 1997.

Augustine. *The Confessions and Letters of St. Augustine*. In vol. 1 of *The Nicene and Post-Nicene Fathers*, Series 1. Edited by Philip Schaff. 1886–89. 14 vols. Repr., Grand Rapids: Eerdmans, 1956.

———. *St. Augustin: Sermon on the Mount; Harmony of the Gospels; Homilies on the Gospels*. Vol. 6 of *The Nicene and Post-Nicene Fathers*, Series 1. Edited by Philip Schaff. 1886–89. 14 vols. Repr., Grand Rapids: Eerdmans, 1956.

Aune, David E. "Prayer in the Greco-Roman World." In Longenecker, *Into God's Presence*, 23–42.

Baelz, Peter. *Does God Answer Prayer?* Springfield, IL: Templegate, 1983.

———. *Prayer and Providence*. London: SCM, 1968.

Barth, Karl. *Prayer*. Translated by Sara F. Terrien. Edited by Don E. Saliers. 50th anniversary ed. Louisville: Westminster John Knox, 2002.

Basinger, David. "God Does Not Necessarily Respond to Prayer." In *Contemporary Debates in Philosophy of Religion*, edited by Michael L. Peterson and Raymond J. VanArragon, 255–63. Malden, MA: Blackwell, 2003.

———. "Why Petition an Omnipotent, Omniscient, Wholly Good God?" *Religious Studies* 19, no. 1 (1983): 25–42.

Bauckham, Richard. "Prayer in the Book of Revelation." In Longenecker, *Into God's Presence*, 252–71.

Beale, G. K. *The Book of Revelation: A Commentary on the Greek Text*. New International Greek Testament Commentary. Grand Rapids: Eerdmans, 1999.

———. *A New Testament Biblical Theology: The Unfolding of the Old Testament in the New*. Grand Rapids: Baker Academic, 2011.

Beilby, James K., and Paul Rhodes Eddy, eds. *Understanding Spiritual Warfare: Four Views*. Grand Rapids: Baker Academic, 2012.

Bietenhard, H. "Satan, Beelzebul, Devil, Exorcism." In *New International Dictionary of New Testament Theology*, edited by Colin Brown, 3:468–72. Grand Rapids: Zondervan, 1978.

Block, Daniel I. *Ezekiel: Chapters 1–24*. New International Commentary on the Old Testament. Grand Rapids: Eerdmans, 1997.

———. *The Gods of the Nations: Studies in Ancient Near Eastern National Theology*. 2nd ed. Grand Rapids: Baker Academic, 2000.

Bloesch, Donald. *The Struggle of Prayer*. San Francisco: Harper & Row, 1980.

Blomberg, Craig. *Matthew*. New American Commentary. Nashville: B&H, 1992.

Bonhoeffer, Dietrich. *Selected Writings*. Edited by Edwin Hanton Robertson. London: Fount, 1995.

Botterweck, G. Johannes, and H. Ringgren, eds. *Theological Dictionary of the Old Testament*. Translated by J. T. Willis, G. W. Bromiley, and D. E. Green. 15 vols. Grand Rapids: Eerdmans, 1974–2006.

Boyd, Gregory A. *God at War: The Bible and Spiritual Conflict*. Downers Grove, IL: IVP Academic, 1997.

Brown, Colin, ed. *New International Dictionary of New Testament Theology*. Grand Rapids: Zondervan, 1986.

Brueggemann, Walter. "The Book of Exodus: Introduction, Commentary, and Reflections." In *The New Interpreter's Bible*, edited by Leander E. Keck, 1:675–981. Nashville: Abingdon, 1994.

———. *Praying the Psalms*. 2nd ed. Eugene, OR: Cascade Books, 2007.

Brümmer, Vincent. *What Are We Doing When We Pray? On Prayer and the Nature of Faith*. New York: Routledge, 2016.

Brunner, Emil. *The Christian Doctrine of God*. Vol. 1 of *Dogmatics*. Translated by Olive Wyon. Philadelphia: Westminster, 1950.

Bunyan, John. *The Complete Works of John Bunyan*. Philadelphia: Bradley, Garretson, 1872.

Butterworth, Mike. "רחם." In *New International Dictionary of Old Testament Theology & Exegesis*, edited by Willem A. VanGemeren, 3:1093–95. Grand Rapids: Zondervan, 1997.

Calvin, John. *Institutes of the Christian Religion*. Translated by Ford Lewis Battles. Edited by John T. McNeill. Philadelphia: Westminster, 1960.

Carvalhaes, Claudio. "Praying with the Unwanted People at the End of the World." In Cocksworth and McDowell, *T&T Clark Handbook of Christian Prayer*, 685–704.

CNN. "Dawkins: Evolution Is Not a Controversial Issue." *Light Years* (blog). September 6, 2012. http://web.archive.org/web/20200327010905/https://lightyears.blogs.cnn.com/2012/09/06/dawkins-evolution-is-not-a-controversial-issue/.

Cocksworth, Ashley. *Prayer: A Guide for the Perplexed*. London: T&T Clark, 2018.

Cocksworth, Ashley, and John C. McDowell, eds. *T&T Clark Handbook of Christian Prayer*. London: T&T Clark, 2022.

Cohoe, Caleb Murray. "God, Causality, and Petitionary Prayer." *Faith and Philosophy* 31, no. 1 (2014): 24–45.

———. "How Could Prayer Make a Difference?" *European Journal for Philosophy of Religion* 10, no. 2 (2018): 171–85.

Cole, Graham. *Against the Darkness: The Doctrine of Angels, Satan, and Demons*. Wheaton, IL: Crossway, 2019.

Collins, Adela Yarbro. *The Apocalypse*. New Testament Message. Collegeville, MN: Liturgical Press, 1979.

Collins, John J. *Daniel: A Commentary on the Book of Daniel*. Edited by Frank Moore Cross. Hermeneia. Minneapolis: Fortress, 1993.

Cone, James. *God of the Oppressed*. New York: Seabury, 1975.

Cooper, Lamar Eugene, Sr. *Ezekiel*. New American Commentary. Nashville: B&H, 1994.

Copan, Paul. *Loving Wisdom: A Guide to Philosophy and Christian Faith*. 2nd ed. Grand Rapids: Eerdmans, 2020.

Crisp, Oliver. "Prayer as Complaint." In Crisp, Arcadi, and Wessling, *Analyzing Prayer*, 79–94.

———. *Retrieving Doctrine: Essays in Reformed Theology*. Downers Grove, IL: IVP Academic, 2010.

Crisp, Oliver D., James M. Arcadi, and Jordan Wessling, eds. *Analyzing Prayer: Theological and Philosophical Essays*. Oxford: Oxford University Press, 2022.

Crump, David. *Knocking on Heaven's Door: A New Testament Theology of Petitionary Prayer*. Grand Rapids: Baker Academic, 2006.

Cullmann, Oscar. *Prayer in the New Testament*. Translated by John Bowden. Minneapolis: Fortress, 1995.

———. *Salvation in History*. Translated by Sidney G. Sowers. London: SCM, 1967.

Cyprian. *St. Cyprian on the Lord's Prayer*. Translated by Herbert Bindley. Early Church Classics. London: SPCK, 1914.

Davidson, Richard M. "The Divine Covenant Lawsuit Motif in Canonical Perspective." *Journal of the Adventist Theological Society* 21, nos. 1–2 (2010): 45–84.

———. *A Song for the Sanctuary: Experiencing God's Presence in Shadow and Reality*. Silver Spring, MD: Review and Herald Academic / Biblical Research Institute, 2022.

Davies, W. D., and Dale C. Allison. *A Critical and Exegetical Commentary on the Gospel according to Saint Matthew*. Vol. 2, *Matthew 8–18*. International Critical Commentary. New York: T&T Clark, 1991.

Davis, Stephen T. "Free Will and Evil." In *Encountering Evil: Live Options in Theodicy*, edited by Stephen T. Davis, 73–89. Louisville: Westminster John Knox, 2001.

———. *Logic and the Nature of God*. Grand Rapids: Eerdmans, 1983.

Davison, Scott A. *God and Prayer*. Elements in the Philosophy of Religion. Cambridge: Cambridge University Press, 2022.

———. "Petitionary Prayer." In *The Oxford Handbook of Philosophical Theology*, edited by Thomas P. Flint and Michael C. Rea, 286–305. Oxford: Oxford University Press, 2009.

———. *Petitionary Prayer: A Philosophical Investigation*. Oxford: Oxford University Press, 2017.

Di Muzio, Gianluca. "A Collaborative Model of Petitionary Prayer." *Religious Studies* 54, no. 1 (2018): 37–54.

DiRoberts, Kyle D. *Prayer, Middle Knowledge, and Divine-Human Interaction*. Eugene, OR: Wipf & Stock, 2019.

Dolezal, James E. "Strong Impassibility." In *Divine Impassibility: Four Views*, edited by Robert Matz and A. Chadwick Thornhill, 13–37. Downers Grove, IL: IVP Academic, 2019.

Dougherty, Trent, and Justin P. McBrayer, eds. *Skeptical Theism: New Essays*. Oxford: Oxford University Press, 2014.

Ekstrom, Laura W. "A Christian Theodicy." In *The Blackwell Companion to the Problem of Evil*, edited by Justin P. McBrayer and Daniel Howard-Snyder, 266–80. Malden, MA: Wiley-Blackwell, 2013.

Evagrius Ponticus. *The Praktikos and Chapters on Prayer*. Translated by John Eudes Bamberger. Kalamazoo, MI: Cistercian Press, 1981.

Evans, Tony. *Victory in Spiritual Warfare*. Eugene, OR: Harvest House, 2011.

Faro, Ingrid. *Demystifying Evil: A Biblical and Personal Exploration*. Downers Grove, IL: IVP Academic, 2023.

Farris, Stephen. "The Canticles of Luke's Infancy Narrative." In Longenecker, *Into God's Presence*, 91–112.

Fee, Gordon D. *The First Epistle to the Corinthians*. New International Commentary on the New Testament. Grand Rapids: Eerdmans, 1987.

Feinberg, John S. *No One Like Him: The Doctrine of God*. Wheaton, IL: Crossway, 2001.

Finkel, Asher. "Prayer in Jewish Life of the First Century as Background to Early Christianity." In Longenecker, *Into God's Presence*, 43–65.

Fisher, Fred. *Prayer in the New Testament*. Philadelphia: Westminster, 1964.

Fitzmyer, Joseph. *The Gospel according to Luke I–IX: Introduction, Translation, and Notes*. Anchor Bible 28. Garden City, NY: Doubleday, 1981.

Flint, Thomas P. *Divine Providence: The Molinist Account*. Ithaca, NY: Cornell University Press, 1998.

Fosdick, Harry Emerson. *The Meaning of Prayer*. New York: Association Press, 1916.

France, R. T. *The Gospel of Matthew*. New International Commentary on the New Testament. Grand Rapids: Eerdmans, 2007.

Franks, W. Paul. "Why a Believer Could Believe That God Answers Prayers." *Sophia* 48, no. 3 (2009): 319–24.

Fretheim, Terence E. *Exodus*. Interpretation. Louisville: John Knox, 1991.

Gallusz, Laszlo. *The Seven Prayers of Jesus*. London: Inter-Varsity, 2017.

Garland, David E. *Mark*. NIV Application Commentary. Grand Rapids: Zondervan, 1996.

Gavrilyuk, Paul L. "An Overview of Patristic Theodicies." In *Suffering and Evil in Early Christian Thought*, edited by Nonna Verna Harrison and David G. Hunter, 1–6. Grand Rapids: Baker Academic, 2016.

Goldingay, John. *Daniel*. Word Biblical Commentary 30. Dallas: Word, 1989.

———. *Israel's Faith*. Vol. 2 of *Old Testament Theology*. Downers Grove, IL: IVP Academic, 2006.

Gombis, Timothy G. *The Drama of Ephesians: Participating in the Triumph of God*. Downers Grove, IL: IVP Academic, 2010.

González, Justo L. *Mañana: Christian Theology from a Hispanic Perspective*. Nashville: Abingdon, 1990.

———. *Teach Us to Pray: The Lord's Prayer in the Early Church and Today*. Grand Rapids: Eerdmans, 2020.

Green, Adam, and Eleonore Stump, eds. *Hidden Divinity and Religious Belief: New Perspectives*. New York: Cambridge University Press, 2015.

Green, Joel B. *The Gospel of Luke*. New International Commentary on the New Testament. Grand Rapids: Eerdmans, 1997.

———. "Persevering Together in Prayer: The Significance of Prayer in the Acts of the Apostles." In Longenecker, *Into God's Presence*, 183–202.

Gregg, Brian Han. *What Does the Bible Say about Suffering?* Downers Grove, IL: IVP Academic, 2016.

Griffin, David Ray. *God, Power, and Evil: A Process Theodicy*. Louisville: Westminster John Knox, 2004.

Gupta, Nijay K. *The Lord's Prayer*. Smith & Helwys Bible Commentary. Macon, GA: Smith & Helwys, 2017.

Gutiérrez, Gustavo. *On Job: God-Talk and the Suffering of the Innocent*. Translated by Matthew J. O'Connell. Maryknoll, NY: Orbis Books, 1987.

Hahn, Scott W. *Kinship by Covenant: A Canonical Approach to the Fulfillment of God's Saving Promises*. Anchor Yale Bible Reference Library. New Haven: Yale University Press, 2009.

Hallinan, Joseph T. "The Remarkable Power of Hope." *Psychology Today*. May 7, 2014. https://www.psychologytoday.com/us/blog/kidding-ourselves/201405/the -remarkable-power-hope.

Hamilton, Victor P. "Satan." In *The Anchor Bible Dictionary*, edited by David Noel Freedman, 5:985–89. New York: Doubleday, 1996.

Hammerling, Roy. "An Exegetical History of the Lord's Prayer: The First to the Sixth Century." In Cocksworth and McDowell, *T&T Clark Handbook of Christian Prayer*, 87–102.

Harkness, Georgia. *Prayer and the Common Life*. New York: Abingdon-Cokesbury, 1948.

Hartley, John E. *Job*. New International Commentary on the Old Testament. Grand Rapids: Eerdmans, 1988.

Hartman, Louis F., and Alexander A. Di Lella. *The Book of Daniel: A New Translation with Notes and Commentary*. Anchor Yale Bible. New Haven: Yale University Press, 2008.

Hartshorne, Charles. *Omnipotence and Other Theological Mistakes*. New York: State University of New York Press, 1984.

Heiser, Michael S. "Divine Council." In *The Lexham Bible Dictionary*, edited by John D. Barry et al., 10. Bellingham, WA: Lexham, 2016.

———. *The Unseen Realm: Recovering the Supernatural Worldview of the Bible*. Bellingham, WA: Lexham, 2015.

Hendriksen, William. *Exposition of the Gospel according to Mark*. Moffatt New Testament Commentary. Grand Rapids: Baker, 1975.

Horton, Michael. *The Christian Faith: A Systematic Theology for Pilgrims on the Way*. Grand Rapids: Zondervan, 2011.

———. *Lord and Servant: A Covenant Christology*. Louisville: Westminster John Knox, 2005.

Howard-Snyder, Daniel, and Frances Howard-Snyder. "The Puzzle of Petitionary Prayer." *European Journal for Philosophy of Religion* 2, no. 2 (2010): 43–68.

Hunter, W. Bingham. *The God Who Hears*. Downers Grove, IL: InterVarsity, 1986.

Imes, Carmen Joy. *Bearing God's Name: Why Sinai Still Matters*. Downers Grove, IL: InterVarsity, 2019.

———. "The Ethics of Vengeful Prayer—Psalm 137." *Political Theology Network*. September 30, 2019. https://politicaltheology.com/the-ethics-of-vengeful-prayer -psalm-137/.

Jenni, Ernst, and Claus Westermann. *Theological Lexicon of the Old Testament*. Translated by Mark E. Biddle. 3 vols. Peabody, MA: Hendrickson, 1997.

Jeremias, Joachim. *The Lord's Prayer*. Translated by John Reumann. Philadelphia: Fortress, 1964.

Jerončić, Ante. "The Eye of Charity: Jürgen Moltmann's Practical Theodicy." *Andrews University Seminary Studies* 47, no. 1 (2009): 37–41.

Karris, Mark Gregory. *Divine Echoes: Reconciling Prayer with the Uncontrolling Love of God*. Orange, CA: Quoir, 2018.

Keener, Craig S. *The Mind of the Spirit: Paul's Approach to Transformed Thinking*. Grand Rapids: Baker Academic, 2016.

Keller, Timothy. *Prayer: Experiencing Awe and Intimacy with God*. New York: Dutton, 2014.

Kierkegaard, Søren. *Purity of Heart Is to Will One Thing: Spiritual Preparation for the Office of Confession*. Translated by Douglas V. Steere. Rev. ed. New York: Harper & Row, 1956.

Koehler, Ludwig, Walter Baumgartner, and Johann Jakob Stamm. *The Hebrew and Aramaic Lexicon of the Old Testament*. Translated and edited under the supervision of M. E. J. Richardson. 5 vols. Leiden: Brill, 1994–2000.

Ladd, George Eldon. *The Presence of the Future: The Eschatology of Biblical Realism*. Grand Rapids: Eerdmans, 1974.

Langberg, Diane. *Suffering and the Heart of God: How Trauma Destroys and Christ Restores*. Greensboro, NC: New Growth, 2015.

Laurence, Trevor. *Cursing with God: The Imprecatory Psalms and the Ethics of Christian Prayer*. Waco: Baylor University Press, 2022.

Lewis, C. S. *A Grief Observed*. New York: Bantam, 1976.

———. *Mere Christianity*. New York: HarperOne, 2001.

———. *The Problem of Pain*. New York: HarperOne, 2001.

———. *Reflections on the Psalms*. New York: Harcourt, 1986.

Lincoln, Andrew T. "God's Name, Jesus' Name, and Prayer in the Fourth Gospel." In Longenecker, *Into God's Presence*, 155–80.

Loke, Andrew Ter Ern. *Evil, Sin, and Christian Theism*. New Critical Thinking in Religion, Theology and Biblical Studies. New York: Routledge, 2022.

Longenecker, Richard N., ed. *Into God's Presence: Prayer in the New Testament*. Grand Rapids: Eerdmans, 2001.

———. "Prayer in the Pauline Letters." In Longenecker, *Into God's Presence*, 203–27.

Longman, Tremper, III. *Daniel*. NIV Application Commentary. Grand Rapids: Zondervan, 1999.

Luther, Martin. *The Large Catechism of Dr. Martin Luther, 1529*. Edited by Kirsi I. Stjerna. Minneapolis: Fortress, 2016.

Marshall, I. Howard. *The Epistles of John*. New International Commentary on the New Testament. Grand Rapids: Eerdmans, 1978.

———. *The Gospel of Luke: A Commentary on the Greek Text*. New International Greek Testament Commentary. Exeter: Paternoster, 1978.

———. "Jesus—Example and Teacher of Prayer in the Synoptic Gospels." In Longenecker, *Into God's Presence*, 113–31.

McGrath, Alister E. *The Mystery of the Cross*. Grand Rapids: Zondervan, 1988.

McKirland, Christa. *God's Provision, Humanity's Need: The Gift of Our Dependence*. Grand Rapids: Baker Academic, 2022.

Meister, Chad. "Evil and the Hiddenness of God." In *God and Evil: The Case for God in a World Filled with Pain*, edited by Chad Meister and James K. Dew Jr., 138–51. Downers Grove, IL: InterVarsity, 2013.

Metzger, Bruce M. *The Text of the New Testament*. Oxford: Oxford University Press, 1964.

Michaels, J. Ramsey. "Finding Yourself an Intercessor: New Testament Prayer from Hebrews to Jude." In Longenecker, *Into God's Presence*, 228–51.

Middleton, J. Richard. *Abraham's Silence: The Binding of Isaac, the Suffering of Job, and How to Talk Back to God*. Grand Rapids: Baker Academic, 2021.

Millar, J. Gary. *Calling on the Name of the Lord: A Biblical Theology of Prayer*. New Studies in Biblical Theology. Downers Grove, IL: InterVarsity, 2016.

Miller, Patrick D. *They Cried to the Lord: The Form and Theology of Biblical Prayer*. Minneapolis: Fortress, 1994.

Miller, Stephen R. *Daniel*. New American Commentary. Nashville: B&H, 1994.

Moffitt, David. *Atonement and the Logic of Resurrection in the Epistle to the Hebrews*. Supplements to Novum Testamentum 141. Leiden: Brill, 2011.

Mooney, Edward F. "Becoming What We Pray: Passion's Gentler Resolutions." In *The Phenomenology of Prayer*, edited by Bruce Ellis Benson and Norman Wirzba, 50–62. New York: Fordham University Press, 2005.

Morris, Dolores. *Believing Philosophy: A Guide to Becoming a Christian Philosopher*. Grand Rapids: Zondervan Academic, 2021.

Morris, Thomas V. *Our Idea of God: An Introduction to Philosophical Theology*. Notre Dame, IN: University of Notre Dame Press, 1991.

Mullen, E. T., Jr. "Divine Assembly." In *The Anchor Bible Dictionary*, edited by David Noel Freedman, 2:214–17. New York: Doubleday, 1996.

Mullins, R. T. *The End of the Timeless God*. New York: Oxford University Press, 2016.

———. *God and Emotion*. Cambridge: Cambridge University Press, 2020.

Murray, Michael J., and Kurt Meyers. "Ask and It Will Be Given to You." *Religious Studies* 30, no. 3 (1994): 311–30.

Noll, Stephen F. *Angels of Light, Powers of Darkness: Thinking Biblically about Angels, Satan, and Principalities*. Downers Grove, IL: InterVarsity, 1998.

Nolland, John. *The Gospel of Matthew: A Commentary on the Greek Text*. New International Greek Testament Commentary. Grand Rapids; Eerdmans, 2005.

Oden, Thomas C. *Classic Christianity: A Systematic Theology*. San Francisco: HarperOne, 2009.

Onwuchekwa, John. *Prayer: How Praying Together Shapes the Church*. Wheaton, IL: Crossway, 2018.

Oord, Thomas Jay. *The Uncontrolling Love of God: An Open and Relational Account of Providence*. Downers Grove, IL: IVP Academic, 2015.

Origen. *Homilies on the Psalms*. Translated by Joseph W. Trigg. Fathers of the Church. Washington, DC: Catholic University of America Press, 2020.

———. *Prayer; Exhortation to Christian Martyrdom*. Translated by John J. O'Meara. Ancient Christian Writers 19. Westminster, MD: Newman, 1954.

Ortlund, Eric. *Piercing Leviathan: God's Defeat of Evil in the Book of Job*. Downers Grove, IL: IVP Academic, 2021.

Osborne, Grant R. *Matthew*. Zondervan Exegetical Commentary on the New Testament. Grand Rapids: Zondervan, 2010.

Oswalt, John N. *Isaiah 1–39*. New International Commentary on the Old Testament. Grand Rapids: Eerdmans, 1986.

Padgett, Alan. "Eternity as Relative Timelessness." In *God and Time: Four Views*, edited by Gregory Ganssle, 92–110. Downers Grove, IL: InterVarsity, 2001.

Page, Sydney H. T. *Powers of Evil: A Biblical Study of Satan and Demons*. Grand Rapids: Baker, 1995.

Parker, Ryan M., and Bradley Rettler. "A Possible-Worlds Solution to the Puzzle of Petitionary Prayer." *European Journal for Philosophy of Religion* 9, no. 1 (2017): 179–86.

Pascal, Blaise. *Pensées*. Translated by W. F. Trotter. New York: Dover, 2003.

Peckham, John C. *Divine Attributes: Knowing the Covenantal God of Scripture*. Grand Rapids: Baker Academic, 2021.

———. "The Influence Aim Problem of Petitionary Prayer." *Journal of Analytic Theology* 8 (2020): 412–32.

———. *The Love of God: A Canonical Model*. Downers Grove, IL: IVP Academic, 2015.

———. "Show Me Your Glory: A Narrative Theology of Exodus 33:12–34:10." In *Meeting with God on the Mountains: Essays in Honor of Richard M. Davidson*, edited by Jiří Moskala, 583–603. Berrien Springs, MI: Andrews University Press, 2016.

———. *Theodicy of Love: Cosmic Conflict and the Problem of Evil*. Grand Rapids: Baker Academic, 2018.

Pickup, Martin. "Answer to Our Prayers: The Unsolved but Solvable Problem of Petitionary Prayer." *Faith and Philosophy* 35, no. 1 (2018): 84–104.

Plantinga, Alvin. *God, Freedom, and Evil*. Grand Rapids: Eerdmans, 1977.

———. *The Nature of Necessity*. Oxford: Clarendon, 1974.

———. "Self-Profile." In *Alvin Plantinga*, edited by James E. Tomberlin and Peter van Inwagen, 3–97. Profiles. Dordrecht: D. Riedel, 1985.

———. *Warranted Christian Belief*. New York: Oxford University Press, 2000.

———. *Where the Conflict Really Lies: Science, Religion, and Naturalism*. Oxford: Oxford University Press, 2011.

Post, Stephen G. *A Theory of Agape: On the Meaning of Christian Love*. Lewisburg, PA: Bucknell University Press, 1990.

Rah, Soong-Chan. *Prophetic Lament: A Call for Justice in Troubled Times*. Downers Grove, IL: InterVarsity, 2015.

Rasmussen, Joshua. "The Great Story Theodicy." In *Is God the Best Explanation of Things? A Dialogue*, edited by Joshua Rasmussen and Felipe Leon, 223–42. Cham, Switzerland: Palgrave Macmillan, 2019.

Rea, Michael. "Divine Hiddenness, Divine Silence." In Rea, *Evil and the Hiddenness of God*, 156–65.

———, ed. *Evil and the Hiddenness of God*. Stamford, CT: Cengage, 2015.

———. "Hiddenness and Transcendence." In Green and Stump, *Hidden Divinity and Religious Belief*, 210–25.

Reibsamen, Jonathan. "Divine Goodness and the Efficacy of Petitionary Prayer." *Religious Studies* 55, no. 1 (2019): 131–44.

Richter, Sandra L. *The Epic of Eden: A Christian Entry into the Old Testament*. Downers Grove, IL: IVP Academic, 2008.

Ritz, H.-J. "βουλή." In *Exegetical Dictionary of the New Testament*, edited by Horst Balz and Gerhard Schneider, 1:224–25. Grand Rapids: Eerdmans, 1978.

Roberts, Alexander, and James Donaldson, eds. *The Ante-Nicene Fathers*. 10 vols. Buffalo: Christian Literature Company, 1885–87.

Rogers, Katherin A. *Perfect Being Theology*. Reason and Religion. Edinburgh: Edinburgh University Press, 2000.

Schellenberg, J. L. "Divine Hiddenness Justifies Atheism." In Rea, *Evil and the Hiddenness of God*, 61–70.

———. *The Hiddenness Argument: Philosophy's New Challenge to Belief in God.* New York: Oxford University Press, 2015.

Seitz, Christopher R. "Prayer in the Old Testament or Hebrew Bible." In Longenecker, *Into God's Presence*, 3–22.

Simundson, Daniel. *Where Is God in My Praying? Biblical Responses to Eight Searching Questions.* Minneapolis: Augsburg, 1986.

Smith, Nicholas D., and Andrew C. Yip. "Partnership with God: A Partial Solution to the Problem of Petitionary Prayer." *Religious Studies* 46, no. 3 (2010): 395–410.

Smith-Christopher, Daniel L. "Daniel." In *The New Interpreter's Bible*, edited by Leander E. Keck, 7:17–152. Nashville: Abingdon, 1996.

Sonderegger, Katherine. "The Act of Prayer and the Doctrine of God." In Cocksworth and McDowell, *T&T Clark Handbook of Christian Prayer*, 139–53.

———. "Does God Pray?" In Crisp, Arcadi, and Wessling, *Analyzing Prayer*, 136–48.

Spiegel, James S. *The Making of an Atheist: How Immorality Leads to Unbelief.* Chicago: Moody, 2010.

Stefanovic, Ranko. *Revelation of Jesus Christ: Commentary on the Book of Revelation.* 2nd ed. Berrien Springs, MI: Andrews University Press, 2009.

Stevenson, Kenneth, and Michael Glerup eds. *Ezekiel, Daniel.* Ancient Christian Commentary on Scripture 13. Downers Grove, IL: IVP Academic, 2008.

Stoebe, H. J. "רחם." In *Theological Lexicon of the Old Testament*, edited by Ernst Jenni and Claus Westermann, translated by Mark E. Biddle, 3:1225–30. Peabody, MA: Hendrickson, 1997.

Strobel, Kyle, and John Coe. *Where Prayer Becomes Real: How Honesty with God Transforms Your Soul.* Grand Rapids: Baker Books, 2021.

Stuart, Douglas K. *Exodus.* New American Commentary. Nashville: B&H, 2006.

Stump, Eleonore. *The Image of God: The Problem of Evil and the Problem of Mourning.* Oxford: Oxford University Press, 2022.

———. "Petitionary Prayer." *American Philosophical Quarterly* 16, no. 2 (1979): 81–91.

———. *Wandering in the Darkness: Narrative and the Problem of Suffering.* Oxford: Oxford University Press, 2012.

Suchocki, Marjorie Hewitt. *In God's Presence: Theological Reflections on Prayer.* St. Louis: Chalice, 1996.

Swinburne, Richard. *The Coherence of Theism.* Rev. ed. Oxford: Clarendon, 1993.

———. *Providence and the Problem of Evil.* Oxford: Clarendon, 1998.

Thomas, Gabrielle. "The Cappadocians on the Beauty and Efficacy of Prayer." In Cocksworth and McDowell, *T&T Clark Handbook of Christian Prayer*, 287–301.

Thomas Aquinas. *Summa Theologiae.* Translated by the English Dominican Fathers. London: Burns, Oates & Washbourne, 1920.

Thornhill, A. Chadwick. *The Chosen People: Election, Paul and Second Temple Judaism*. Downers Grove, IL: InterVarsity, 2015.

Tiessen, Terrance. *Providence and Prayer: How Does God Work in the World?* Downers Grove, IL: InterVarsity, 2000.

Timpe, Kevin. "Toward an Account of Lamenting Well." In Crisp, Arcadi, and Wessling, *Analyzing Prayer*, 95–115.

Trible, Phyllis. *God and the Rhetoric of Sexuality*. Overtures to Biblical Theology. Philadelphia: Fortress, 1978.

Tsumura, David Toshio. *The First Book of Samuel*. New International Commentary on the Old Textament. Grand Rapids: Eerdmans, 2007.

VanGemeren, Willem A., ed. *New International Dictionary of Old Testament Theology & Exegesis*. 4 vols. Grand Rapids: Zondervan, 1997.

Vanhoozer, Kevin J. *Faith Speaking Understanding: Performing the Drama of Doctrine*. Louisville: Westminster John Knox, 2014.

Waltke, Bruce K., James M. Houston, and Erika Moore. *The Psalms as Christian Lament: A Historical Commentary*. Grand Rapids: Eerdmans, 2014.

Walton, John. "Job 1: Book of." In *Dictionary of the Old Testament: Wisdom, Poetry and Writings*, edited by Tremper Longman III and Peter Enns, 333–46. Downers Grove, IL: IVP Academic, 2008.

Warren, Tish Harrison. *Prayer in the Night: For Those Who Work or Watch or Weep*. Downers Grove, IL: InterVarsity, 2021.

Weil, Simone. *Waiting for God*. Translated by Emma Craufurd. New York: Harper & Row, 1973.

Weinfeld, Moshe. "כָּבוֹד." In *Theological Dictionary of the Old Testament*, edited by G. Johannes Botterweck, Helmer Ringgren, and Heinz-Josef Fabry, translated by David E. Green, 7:22–38. Grand Rapids: Eerdmans, 1995.

Wesley, John. *How to Pray: The Best of John Wesley on Prayer*. Uhrichsville, OH: Barbour, 2007.

———. *Wesley's Standard Sermons*. Vol. 1. London: Epworth, 1966.

Wessling, Jordan. "Interceding for the Lost: On the Effectiveness of Petitioning God for Human Salvation." In Crisp, Arcadi, and Wessling, *Analyzing Prayer*, 20–37.

Westphal, Merold. "Prayer as the Posture of the Decentered Self." In *The Phenomenology of Prayer*, edited by Bruce Ellis Benson and Norman Wirzba, 11–31. New York: Fordham University Press, 2005.

Wicker, Christine. "Do Atheists Pray? You Better Believe It." *Psychology Today*. September 25, 2013. https://www.psychologytoday.com/us/blog/pray-me/201309/do-atheists-pray.

Williamson, Dorena. "Botham Jean's Brother's Offer of Forgiveness Went Viral. His Mother's Calls for Justice Should Too." *Christianity Today*. October 4, 2019. https://www.christianitytoday.com/ct/2019/october-web-only/botham-jean-forgiveness-amber-guyger.html.

Wilson, Lindsay. *Job*. Two Horizons Old Testament Commentary. Grand Rapids: Eerdmans, 2015.

Wink, Walter. *Walter Wink: Collected Readings*. Edited by Henry French. Minneapolis: Fortress, 2013.

Wolterstorff, Nicholas. *Inquiring about God*. Vol. 1 of *Selected Essays*. Edited by Terence Cuneo. Cambridge: Cambridge University Press, 2010.

———. *Lament for a Son*. Grand Rapids: Eerdmans, 1987.

Woznicki, Christopher. "Is Prayer Redundant? Calvin and the Early Reformers on the Problem of Petitionary Prayer." *Journal of the Evangelical Theological Society* 60, no. 2 (2017): 333–48.

———. "What Are We Doing When We Pray? Rekindling a Reformation Theology of Petitionary Prayer." *Calvin Theological Journal* 53, no. 2 (2018): 319–43.

Wright, N. T. *The Lord and His Prayer*. Grand Rapids: Eerdmans, 1996.

———. "The Lord's Prayer as a Paradigm of Christian Prayer." In Longenecker, *Into God's Presence*, 132–54.

Wykstra, Stephen J. "Rowe's Noseeum Arguments from Evil." In *The Evidential Argument from Evil*, edited by Daniel Howard-Snyder, 126–50. Bloomington: Indiana University Press, 1996.

Yancey, Philip. *Prayer: Does It Make Any Difference?* Grand Rapids: Zondervan, 2006.

Yong, Amos. *Spirit of Love: A Trinitarian Theology of Grace*. Waco: Baylor University Press, 2012.

Zagzebski, Linda. "Omnisubjectivity." In *Oxford Studies in Philosophy of Religion*, edited by Jonathan Kvanvig, 1:231–47. Oxford: Oxford University Press.

Scripture Index

Subject Index